Searching for Japan

Twentieth-century Italy's Fascination with Japanese Culture

Transnational Italian Cultures 3

Transnational Italian Cultures

Series editors:
Dr Emma Bond, University of St Andrews
Professor Derek Duncan, University of St Andrews

Transnational Italian Cultures will publish the best research in the expanding field of postcolonial, global and transnational Italian studies and aim to set a new agenda for academic research on what constitutes Italian culture today. As such, it will move beyond the physical borders of the peninsula as well as identifying existing or evolving transnational presences within the nation in order to reflect the vibrant and complex make-up of today's global Italy. Privileging a cultural studies perspective with an emphasis on the analysis of textual production, the series focuses primarily on the contemporary context but will also include work on earlier periods informed by current postcolonial/transnational methodology.

Searching for Japan

*Twentieth-century Italy's
Fascination with Japanese Culture*

Michele Monserrati

LIVERPOOL UNIVERSITY PRESS

First published 2020 by
Liverpool University Press
4 Cambridge Street
Liverpool
L69 7ZU

Copyright © 2020 Michele Monserrati

The right of Michele Monserrati to be identified as the author of this book has been asserted by him in accordance with the Copyright, Designs and Patents Act 1988.

All rights reserved. No part of this book may be reproduced, stored in a retrieval system, or transmitted, in any form or by any means, electronic, mechanical, photocopying, recording, or otherwise, without the prior written permission of the publisher.

British Library Cataloguing-in-Publication data
A British Library CIP record is available

ISBN 978-1-78962-107-5 cased

Typeset by Carnegie Book Production, Lancaster
Printed and bound by CPI Group (UK) Ltd, Croydon CR0 4YY

For Nicole and Livia

Contents

List of illustrations	viii
Acknowledgments	ix
Introduction: Searching for Japan	1
1. Cosmopolitan Possibilities in Translation: Views from the Russo-Japanese War	37
2. Mussolini in Japan: Japanese Representations in the Age of Fascism	85
3. Little Italy, Big Japan: Patterns of Continuity and Displacement among Italian Writers in Japan	137
4. *Madama Butterfly* Revised	193
Postscript	233
Index	239

List of illustrations

Fig. 1   Daniele Pecorini and his lover Fuji
(photo property of the Manzoni-Pecorini family)   45

Fig. 2   Cover of a propaganda brochure circulated in Italy at the end of 1944
(Image by courtesy of the Department of Special Collections, Memorial Library, University of Wisconsin-Madison)   121

Fig. 3   Interior of the Japan exhibition in Rome
(*L'Illustrazione Italiana* VII, 18 (May 4, 1930), 767)   134

Acknowledgments

The idea for this book evolved over many years. It was first conceived nearly two decades ago while I was an undergraduate at the University of Florence, where I attended a lecture by Fosco Maraini that prompted me to read his books, and thereby become engrossed in Japanese culture. From this initial encounter, the project took more definitive shape during my years as a graduate student at Rutgers University, where I was fortunate to benefit from the immense knowledge and intellectual curiosity of Paola Gambarota, an invaluable mentor. Her incisive comments and constructive criticism, and our many extensive conversations, were of immense help. I am also beholden to Silvia Ross of University College, Cork, both for her thoughtful observations and for drawing my attention to research on the connections between travel and translation, particularly that done in the United Kingdom.

Since arriving at Williams College in 2017, I have benefited from numerous intellectual exchanges with many colleagues. In particular I would like to thank Christopher Bolton, Christopher Nugent, Gail Newman, Amal Eqeiq, Brahim El Guabli, Janneke van de Stadt, Edan Dekel and Jennifer French. I am also grateful to Brian Martin for allowing me to present a section of the book at the Research Colloquium, where I received much constructive commentary from colleagues at the Center for Foreign Languages & Cultures. For their insightful ideas about the project, I thank Azade Seyhan and Nathalie Hester, who also offered valuable comments on the first chapter, and I am equally appreciative to Ishii Motoaki for reading a section of the manuscript. I am specifically indebted to the Oakley Center for Humanities and Social Sciences at Williams College, in particular to Krista Birch, Administrative Director, and Jana Sawicki, former Director, for organizing a manuscript review session that served to further refine my arguments. The stimulating conversations that transpired with the participants – Williams faculty members Leyla Rouhi and Katarzyna Pieprzak, Derek Duncan of the University of St Andrews and Rebecca Suter of the

University of Sydney – provided me with new insights, while also broadening the interdisciplinary scope of this work.

Other institutions provided crucial support in the form of fellowships and grants, and it is a pleasure for me to acknowledge them here. The second and third chapters particularly benefited from the numerous unpublished documents and other critical sources that I was able to consult thanks to a Resident Fellowship at the National Library of Australia in Canberra. I am very much obliged to Robyn Holmes and Marie-Louise Ayres for their great generosity as my hosts while working at the National Library. I owe particular thanks to three colleagues in Canberra – especially to Paul Diamond for acting as a liaison with the National Library of New Zealand for my research on Arundel Del Re, as well as to Masafumi Monden and Ayhan Turhan Aktar for being supportive interlocutors. I would also like to thank the Friends of the University of Wisconsin-Madison Libraries for providing me with a grant to conduct research on Fascist propaganda, during which time I also had the opportunity to meet and discuss my project with Emiko Ohnuki-Tierney, an inspiring and generous scholar, whose encouragement was most welcome. In the early stages of my writing, during a seminar organized by the University of Notre Dame in Rome, I was fortunate to exchange ideas with Theodore Cachey Jr., Roberto Dainotto, Stiliana Milkova and Gaoheng Zhang, who inspired me to reflect on the intersection of local and global networks in Italian history. I am grateful to Bryn Mawr College for a faculty research award to conduct research in Italy, and to two of my colleagues there, Roberta Ricci and David Cast. I would like to extend special thanks to the Maraini family, who kindly granted me access to Fosco Maraini's manuscript archive at the Archivio Contemporaneo A. Bonsanti in Florence and to the staff of the Special Collections Unit of the Library of the University of St Andrews for providing me with scans and offering helpful guidance during my research. I extend warm thanks to Luisa Adorno for sharing information about her uncle, Daniele Pecorini, including the photographs that document the existence of his Japanese love affair.

At Liverpool University Press, I have been exceptionally fortunate to work with editors Derek Duncan and Emma Bond, whose enthusiasm for this book has never wavered over the long period of its gestation. I could not have asked for a more sympathetic home for this manuscript, whose editors share my interest in pursuing the trajectories of the Italian presence outside the peninsula. I would also like to thank commissioning editor Chloé Johnson for her steady guidance and kindness through the long process of preparing this manuscript for publication.

An earlier version of Chapter 3 appeared in *Italian Studies in Southern Africa*, 25(1) (2012): 9–18, and a portion of Chapter 1 appeared, in different form, in the volume of proceedings of the 2017 international conference *Italia e Giappone a confronto: cultura, psicologia, arti* (Florence: December 13–14, 2016), (Florence: Pontecorboli): 129–49.

No one has supported me more than my wife, Nicole Brown. Over the last ten years Nicole has been a loving partner, a true advocate, a relentless, though patient, editor and the person whose wisdom and selfless spirit I've admired most in life. This book is dedicated to her, and to our daughter, Livia, whose high-spirited enthusiasm brings endless joy to our lives.

Introduction: Searching for Japan

> Is it lack of imagination that makes us come to
> imagined places, not just stay at home?
>
> (Elizabeth Bishop, "Questions of Travel")

1. A "Relational Orientalism"

Walking the streets of Florence the sociologist Georg Simmel marveled at the beauty of the city where the Western traveler could experience the rare comfort of being at home in the modern world. Florence, in his view, represented the culmination of a humanistic project of unity and harmony between mind and nature – or appearance and essence – obtained by eliminating any contradictory or spurious element that could taint its unmistakable classical spirit.[1] In this ideal map of cultural and aesthetic homogeneity that downtown Florence represents, the *Biblioteca orientale* located in the quintessentially Renaissance Strozzi Palace features today as a disruptive act of displacement. This symbol of noncompliance with the designs of the humanistic planners is the result of a life-long commitment of the Florentine ethnologist and photographer, Fosco Maraini (1912–2004), to his native city. The almost 9,000 volumes shelved on the top floor of the building have traveled to Florence from around the world, following the trajectories of Maraini's own interests in Asia, in particular, Japan.

---

1 Georg Simmel, 2007, "Florence," *Theory, Culture & Society*, December, 24(7–8): 38–41. See also Efraim Podoksik, 2012, "In Search of Unity: Georg Simmel on Italian Cities as Works of Art," *Theory, Culture & Society*, 29(7/8): 101–23. Literature that extols the value of the Florentine Renaissance includes Jacob Burckhardt's *Civilization of the Renaissance in Italy* (1860), Bernard Berenson's *The Italian Painters of the Renaissance* (1930), Mary McCarthy's *The Stones of Florence* (1959).

In contrast with the Orientalist vision of a "library of *idees reçues*" (Said, 1978: 94) that informed Napoleon's campaigns in Egypt, this library was built on a different premise, one that sought to challenge Western-conceived views about the East, in order to pose Japan as a leading world nation for years to come. Maraini's library defeats the "discourse of Orientalism" by breaking what Said terms as the "relation between Western writing [...] and Oriental silence" (Said, 1978: 94–95). The library includes texts in both Western and Asian languages (as well as Asian books in translation), in a way that limits the Western monolog on the Orient, and suggests the idea of an intercultural dialog. The overall project of the Asian library in Florence, established in 1997, is an allusion to the existence of "contemporary alternatives to Orientalism," which Said himself acknowledged in response to the criticism directed to his theory asserting Western hegemony over a fictionalized Orient. It posits the possibility of approaching other cultures from a "nonrepressive and nonmanipulative perspective" (Said, 1995 [1978]: 24).

Indeed, the present study privileges such alternative narratives by eschewing Said's readings of Anglo-French imperialist texts to focus instead on Italian "accidental" Orientalists[2] that complicate the idea of an Oriental "Other," which served as a mirror to enable the subject formation of the Western "Self." Rather than revisiting grand narratives to define the East–West relationships, *Searching for Japan* pursues the specific case of Italian travel narratives in the Far East, through a focus on the experience of Japan in works by Italian writers who visited the Land of the Rising Sun beginning in the Meiji period (1868–1912) and during the concomitant opening of Japan's relations with the West. By adopting a methodological lens that integrates Travel Literature Studies with the recent transnational turn in Italian Studies, *Searching for Japan* shows how Italian travelogs to Japan collaborated in both building an imagined national community and in exposing the Italian public to alternative and complementary ways of life, even at great distances.

While travel writings remains a privileged genre for postcolonial analysis, aimed at exposing the "asymmetrical relations of domination and

---

2   The adjective "accidental" is borrowed from Barbara Spackman's *Accidental Orientalists: Modern Italian Travelers in Ottoman Lands* (Liverpool: Liverpool University Press, 2017). The adjective refers to the fortuitous circumstances that brought the Italian authors of Spackman's book to travel across the Ottoman Empire (political exile, desertion, opportunism, happenstance). But it also indicates the fact that these authors were neither colonizers, nor colonized, as they wrote from the margin of the European metropole, which positioned them as subjects bearing a labile national identity, therefore more inclined to be permeated by foreign influence.

subordination" between subjects (Pratt, 2008: 8), this study wants to broaden the scope of possible interpretations that the multifarious travel narratives make available to readers.[3] The close readings of texts presented in this study will grant space to an interpretation of travel that is transnational in the way that travelers establish social bonds with locals to encompass multiple national affiliations. Unlike migrant or diasporic writers, the authors that I consider do not belong to more than one nation. Regardless of their multiple birthplaces, I am interested less in their biographies and more in the cultural mobilities and concrete mediations between identities that are set in place by what James Clifford defines as the experience of "dwelling-in-travel" (Clifford, 1992: 102).

However, what makes these texts useful for this study is their exploration of a central question: what does it mean to imagine Japanese culture as contributing to Italian culture? To answer this question, I depart from an exclusive focus on the "contact zone" of travel literature, to take a closer look at the "reception zone" of the national public. This is a space where the cross-cultural representations that take place in travel writing are eventually received, contributing to the national perception of the foreign country visited. This perspective suggests a specific Italian version of Orientalism(s) toward Japan as a background that informs the specific responses by the individual travel authors.

I argue that the variety of Orientalist discourses in the Italian peninsula stems from the historical period of post-unification, during which the process

---

3 In his recent essay, entitled *Avant-garde Orientalism: The Eastern "Other" in Twentieth-Century Travel Narrative and Poetry*, David LeHardy Sweet makes a similar point when he invites a reading of twentieth-century avant-garde works without necessarily reasserting the post-colonial suspect of a "cultural conspiracy between literature and empire" (Sweet, 2017: 7). Thus he proposes a reading of these texts as expressing "standard deviation from the norms of Orientalist procedure – in other words, a willingness either to celebrate the Orient's reputed 'difference' in mockery of Western values or to regard it with an alternative critical lens" (8–9). For readings of travel literature that propose alternatives to the Eurocentric paradigm see Inderpal Grewal, 1996, *Home and Harem: Nation, Gender, Empire, and the Cultures of Travel* (London: Leicester University Press). Travel writings, he says, can unsettle the "consolidation of stable unitary identities of nation, class, sexuality or gender, and suggest forms of Selfhood that evade such consolidations" (3). For an interpretation of travel writings as a genre that accounts for transnational movements of people, goods and ideas see Janet L. Abu-Lughod, 1989, *Before European Hegemony: the World System A.D. 1250–1350* (New York: Oxford University Press), and Avtar Brah, 1996, *Cartographies of Diaspora: Contesting Identities* (London and New York, NJ: Routledge).

of forming the Italian nation-state overlapped with the creation of transnational imagined communities.[4] When these contrastive yet concurrent dynamics of identity formation are examined in relation to Japan, multiple Orientalist perspectives emerge and, occasionally, intersect, sometimes in the same author (as in the cases of Pecorini and Barzini discussed in ch. 1), or in the same historical period (see the analysis of the Fascist period in ch. 2). Such a variety of representations of Japan ranges between two extreme poles of identity theory discourse. On one hand, a "'territorial either/or' theory of identity" (Beck, 2006: 5) operates on the premise that stressing differences in regard to foreign cultures is an effective way to build a solid and homogeneous national identity (or any type of identity). On the other hand, forms of "co-national" types of identities, which unsettle national borders and offset cultural demarcations between the "native" and the "foreigner," are also possible. In fact, these latter are more likely to manifest during the period of an emerging global market place, which ushered in an era of increased mobility for people, goods and ideas around the world.

Therefore Italian representations of Japan, from their outset until at least the end of World War II, are caught in between the construction of a nationalist Italian identity, in reaction to the perceived Japanese "yellow peril," and the construction of a transnational Italo-Japanese identity, in response to the opening of Japan to the West. While the first type of identity formation falls into Said's theory of Orientalism, for its systematic emphasis on differences[5] and demarcations between "familiar West" and "foreign East," I propose the notion of a "relational orientalism" to indicate an opposite approach that builds on commonalities and integration by claiming what is "Oriental" as one's own.

---

4   For this point I am building on Ulrich Beck's idea that "behind the façade of enduring nationality, processes of transnationalization are everywhere taking place": Ulrich Beck, 2006, *The Cosmopolitan Vision*, translated by Ciaran Cronin (Cambridge, UK and Malden, MA: Polity Press): 64. Of course, different forms of Orientalism stem also from different locations in the Italian peninsula. Roberto Dainotto, for instance, calls attention to the identity of the Southern Italian region comprising Eastern and Western roots, therefore undoing the binary structure of the European Orientalist discourse: Roberto Dainotto, 2007, *Europe (in Theory)* (Durham, NC: Duke University Press): 172–217.

5   See, for instance, when Said says: "For Orientalism was ultimately a political vision of reality whose structure promoted the difference between the familiar (Europe, the West, 'us') and the strange (the Orient, the East, 'them'). This vision in a sense created and then served the two worlds thus conceived. Orientals lived in their world, 'we' lived in ours": Edward W. Said, 1978, *Orientalism* (New York: Pantheon Books): 43–44.

This latter approach should not be confused, I hope, with a flat sentiment of "togetherness," or an unproblematic sense of brotherhood, for most of the authors I include in the following chapters are not elusive about cultural differences, yet they repeatedly try to disrupt ideas about dichotomies and unbalanced power relationships between East and West.

This type of "relational Orientalism" is enabled by Orientalist practices that many Japanese authors have accepted as constitutive of their self-identification. Indeed, as Toshio Miyake noticed (Miyake, 2010: 57–94), the anomaly of Japan is to be the first non-Western country to accept Western modernity while remaining a sovereign, non-colonized country. In fact, during the Meiji period, Japan responded to the violent pressure from the United States to establish commercial relationships by becoming a Western-like imperialistic power.

The alternative Japan had to face was either to surrender and be colonized, or to imitate the colonizers by adopting a similar strategy. However, Japan's appropriation of Western knowledge implied the acceptance of an imposed marginal role as recipient of a European-made modernity, in fact enabling the analogy between the assigned geographical location of a country in the "Far East" and its relegation to the status of a subordinate civilization.

While Italian Orientalism certainly did not lack representation of the Japanese as passive imitators of Western modernity, it also drew from this Orientalist view a set of similarities with the Italian position in the Western world that resulted in an increasing sense of proximity with the Japanese "Other." Indeed, as Italy shared with Japan the perception of being an outcast within the geopolitical map of the more developed European nations, by virtue of being located in the "backward" and "decrepit" Mediterranean region, it also shared an ambition to become an imperialistic power, spreading the seeds of a superior Western civilization to countries deemed as inferior. In other words, the "relational Orientalism" that Italy developed in relation to Japan depended largely on the perception of sharing a similar fate: an "Orientalized" nation determined to become an "Orientalist" one, by virtue of the Italian participation in the "scramble for Africa," or the Japanese expansionist campaigns in China and Korea.

This is not to say that the Italian Orientalism toward Japan should be regarded as "pure" and untainted by external influences: the national outlook should be commeasured against a transnational background of intersecting European discourses – in particular, the *fin-de-siècle* Italian Japanophilia aligned with British representations of Japan during the two decade-long Anglo-Japanese military alliance, from 1902 to 1922. Britain at the beginning of the twentieth century was entering a period of industrial decline, having exhausted the forward impetus of two industrial revolutions. The alliance with an energized Japan inevitably suggested both a disenchanted self-perception of national stagnation and a positive view of the allied nation. British Socialists lauded Japanese society for what they perceived as a set of collective ethics, in contrast to the damaging individualistic values that allegedly undermined Western societies. In *A Modern Utopia* (1905) H.G. Wells, for instance, evoked the figure of the "samurai" to describe the ethical principle that should inspire his ideal ruling elite, while Beatrice Webb, visiting Asia in 1911, appreciated the "innovating collectivism" in Japan to the point of foreseeing the dawning of a "benevolent bureaucracy of the future socialist state" (Cumings, 1993: 99).

Furthermore, some Orientalist positions that are discussed (see ch. 3) were influenced by French thinkers such as Lévi-Strauss and Roland Barthes. The desire to be displaced in Japan in order to escape the pervasive Western logocentrism is an experience that Maraini, Moravia and Parise share with Barthes as a visitor to Japan and the writer of *L'Empire des signes* (1970). This search for literary references that would embed Italian representations of Japan within a recognizable European tradition would continue, but it would largely overlook the historical background that framed relations between these two countries throughout the modern period.

The complexity of Italian Orientalist discourses in Japan is reflected also in the way the exotic experience is conceptualized. Again, the reduction of the term "exoticism" to a monolithic interpretation aimed at supporting a Western colonialist policy fails to account for the range of possible uses of the term seen in the authors treated here. Chris Bongie indeed has already noted a common denominator to the different interpretations of the word "exotic," consisting of "a discursive practice intent on recovering 'elsewhere' values 'lost' with the modernization of European society" (Bongie, 1991: 5). The nineteenth-century perception of a loss of heterogenous and distinguished cultures at the expense of the progressively global reach of European modernity posited the creation of "elsewhere" spaces where supposedly traditional values were still preserved and an encounter with cultural diversity still deemed possible. From this common feeling of entropic fear as a prelude to the imaginary recreation of safe havens, Bongie derived two opposing nineteenth-century expressions of exoticism: on the one hand, an "imperialist exoticism," predominant at the beginning of the colonialist period, used a dehumanizing characterization of the "Other" to validate the invasion as a "civilizing mission." On the other, an "exoticizing exoticism" describes the attitude of those who traveled to territories that modernity had not yet reached. The historical conflation between the coming into being of the Italian State and the African exploit brought Italian Studies scholars to focus especially on the first type of exoticism. The Italian production of a colonialist discourse aimed at legitimatizing violence and territorial conquest hinged on the opposition between the present time of European modernity and the prehistorical, archaic time of colonial space. While examples of this type are present in the authors discussed here, including Bongies' "exoticizing exoticism," my readings of Italian exotic representations of Japan also showcase a different expression of exoticism, one that contemplates an alternative geotemporal relation. In fact, Italian narratives from the perspective of a country with no serious colonial interests in East Asia and projected toward a country, like Japan, that was gradually becoming a Western-like colonialist and economic power, contribute to disrupting the asymmetrical power relation between the present time of the colonizer and the prehistorical time of the colonized. Indeed, they focus on a perception of exoticism that is not threatened by modernity's tendency to reduce individual cultures to forms of sameness; or, in other words, they bring to the fore a perception of diversity that share the present time of the European observer and contribute to enriching, or at times even to critiquing, the Western project of modernity in comparison. In this sense, I will refer to "coeval exoticism" to describe this representation of a diverse culture coexisting with the reductionist forces of modernity. The analysis of Daniele Pecorini's *Japanese Maple* (see ch. 1) will explore the multiple meanings of exoticism that I have here presented as they interact within the same text. Thus an imperialist exoticism is at stake in the section of the plot whereby the protagonist Paolo, pervaded with italocentric sentiment, seduces and abandons a traditional Japanese geisha, portrayed as a woman from a different time than the modern present, in her traditional role as a poetic creature and subservient lover, even to the point of death. An "exoticizing exoticism" is present in the choice to set up the love story between Paolo and Fuji outside a main city, in the less industrialized areas between Shimonoseki and Kobe. Finally, a "coeval exoticism" aimed at celebrating cultural diversity without being necessarily reductionist or assimilationist informs other sections of the book that pose Italian culture *vis-à-vis* Japanese tradition and language.

Another chapter (ch. 3) discusses the case of an Italian neo-exoticist, or *tiers-mondiste*, like Alberto Moravia, in his quest for areas of the world not yet contaminated by neocapitalist forces. The contrast between his views of Africa and Japan highlights the type of "coeval exoticism" that a destination like Japan enables, in contrast with other non-Western areas. While his journeys to Africa lead him to conclude that he was experiencing "a continent as yet poised between prehistory and history" (Bongie, 1993: 210), in Japan Moravia saw a country eroded by the invasion of American neocapitalism, yet still capable of infiltrating the West with its own culture and spirituality. For Moravia, Japanese culture is able to cohabit with Western-sponsored modernity to the point of extending its area of influence in Western countries, as well as by acting upon the spiritual void that affects an increasingly secularized West. Like Moravia, his traveling companion in Africa and India, Pier Paolo Pasolini, can also be framed within this binary alternative between a primitive exoticism in Africa and a "coeval exoticism" in Japan.

Bongie observed that Pasolini evoked the myth of a prehistorical Africa in order to inscribe himself into the privileged status of the "last eyewitness" of a disappearing world – a common rhetorical feature of exotic discourse, always in deferral of the end of the "unknown." Although Pasolini did not travel to Japan himself, he was nonetheless responding to the growing popularity of Japanese literature and film in 1960s Italy, which gained momentum especially after the writer Yasunari Kawabata was awarded the Nobel prize for literature in 1968.[6] Furthermore, the 1960s is the decade of the Italian discovery of Tanizaki in translation[7] and Pasolini reacted to this discovery by writing a review of Tanizaki's *Sasameyuki* ("The Makioka Sisters" in English translation and "Neve sottile" in Italian), which he read in

---

6 In the 1960s Italian readers could access several works of Mishima Yukio (*La voce delle onde*; *Dopo il banchetto*; *Il padiglione d'oro*; *Il sapore della gloria*; *Confessioni di una maschera*), Kawabata (*Mille gru*; *Koto*; *Il suono della montagna*), Akutagawa Ryūnosuke (*Kappa e altri racconti*), Fukazawa Shichirō (*Le canzoni di Narayama*) and Inoue Yasushi (*La montagna Hira*). The most important publication of this period is the anthology *Narratori giapponesi moderni*, edited by Atsuko Ricca Suga, who presented writers such as Hayashi Fumiko, Higuchi Ichiyō, Ibuse Masuji, among others, in Italy for the first time.

7 In Italy the popularity of Tanizaki benefited of the work of translators such as Mario Teti and Suga Atsuko. Up to the year 1997, Italy was the country with the highest number of Tanizaki's translations in Western languages. The situation in the year 2000 was as follows: fifty-four French translations; and forty-six Italian translations; thirty-five English translations: see Adriana Boscaro and Maria Roberta Novelli, 2000, *Tanizaki in Western Languages: A Bibliography of Translations and Studies* (Ann Arbor: Center of Japanese Studies, University of Michigan).

the 1962 Italian translation.[8] Pasolini does not read the progressive decline of the Makioka family as an elegy of pre-war Japanese life written in the midst of the war. Instead of a rupture, he perceived in the novel a sort of "coexistence" (*convivenza*) between an "intact antiquity" (*antico intatto*) and an "antiquated modernity" (*moderno antichizzato*), in the sense that, in his view, the traditional mores of Japanese society were able to absorb the new wave of modernity, represented in the plot by life in an industrialized Osaka (Pasolini, 1999, vol. 2: 2010).[9]

The concept of transnationalism at stake in this study is an alternative to the one that Homi Bhabha put forth in his essay, "The Postcolonial and the Postmodern," specifically when he writes that, "Culture as a strategy of survival is [...] transnational because contemporary postcolonial discourses are rooted in specific histories of cultural displacement" (Bhabha, 2004 [1994]: 247). While Bhabha considers transnational cultures as "rooted in specific histories of cultural displacement," *Searching for Japan* steers away from the literature generated by, or related to, former Italian colonies, to concentrate on a transnational relationship that is not systematically based on discourses of power imbalances, center and periphery, and hybrid identities. Instead, the meaning of transnationalism in the present study draws on the one presented by Wilson and Dissanayake that builds on Benedict Anderson's groundbreaking concept of "imagined communities":

> What we would variously track as the "transnational imaginary" comprises the *as-yet-unfigured* horizon of contemporary cultural production by which national spaces/identities of political allegiance and economic regulation are being undone and imagined communities of modernity are being reshaped at the macro political (global) and micro political (cultural) levels of everyday experience. (Wilson and Dissanayake, 1996: 6, original emphasis)

---

8   Junichirō Tanizaki, 1961, *Neve sottile*, translated by Olga Ceretti Borsini and Kizu Hasegawa (Milan: Martello). Pasolini read the 1973 reprint of the same translation by the publisher Longanesi. Ceretti Borsini's translation is probably a translation of the 1957 English translation by Edward G. Seidensticker, although in disguise. In fact, Olga Ceretti Borsini was an Italian translator of mainly English and French texts. Furthermore, the unknown identity of Kizu Hasegawa and the fact that such a name would not be used in the following reprints leads one to conclude that such Japanese name is used as device to sell the book as a translation from the original.

9   Pasolini's review was published on the periodical *Tempo*, on March 15, 1974 with the title "Un'antica storia di dame trapiantata nel Giappone moderno."

The "imagined communities" that are the object of the present work feature Italian authors describing experiences and situations in which national boundaries are renegotiated, and affiliations between Japan and Italy established. The progressive form of the verb included in the title *Searching* alludes to the fact that these transnational narratives are aspirational and subject to contradiction in the same book, or by the same author's fictional persona. In fact, they are undermined by contrapuntal narratives that stress the divisive nature of national identities and reinstate the unequal condition of the traveler's superior gaze, which exoticizes the local inhabitant by creating and mastering a space of absolute difference.

Travel writings from abroad are, in part, forms of cultural translation in which the author introduces the foreign culture to the home audience by eliding, or simplifying, linguistic and unfamiliar cultural differences. Loredana Polezzi has warned about the hegemonic power of travel books to reshape the representation of the "Other" for the use and consumption of the public at home. Indeed, she writes:

> by denying the presence of translation, the voice of the other can be denied altogether: instead of reproducing the powerful voice of author, as translation does, travel writing posits itself as an authoritative representation of places and peoples, in which the Other does not necessarily have any voice (let alone, any authority) and, if required, can even be introduced to the state of nature – simply as an object of description rather than as an interlocutor. (Polezzi, 2001: 93)

Even if Western travel accounts often deceive the reader by presenting an allegedly unmediated personal encounter with the "Other," all the while rehearsing the catalog of Orientalist clichés, alternative, less imperialistic readings are also available,[10] showing the benefits of travel writings in

---

10   Dennis Porter, for instance, in response to Said's use of the Foucauldian theory of "discourse" to explain the preconceived body of knowledge around which Europeans converged to describe the "Orient," calls attention to the individual agency of the writer/traveler as a decisive factor in the ideological outcome of travel books. Indeed, he notices that "at best that heterogeneous corpus of works I am calling European travel writing has been an effort to overcome cultural distance through a protracted act of understanding. At worst it has been the vehicle for the expression of Eurocentric conceit or racist intolerance": Dennis Porter, 1991, *Haunted Journeys: Desire and Transgression in European Travel Writing* (Princeton: Princeton University Press): 3. More recently Susan Bassnett has invited readers to "reapprais[e] translation", including travel writing, as cultural translation. In

expanding the geographical and cultural horizons of the home audience, as well as in enhancing a sense of empathy for people of other cultures. In this sense travel writings share the potentially positive effect that translations exercise on the receiving readership by virtue of bringing the "Other" into focus.[11] In Michael Cronin's words: "The potential contribution of translation to society is to arrest the murderous process of *dehumanisation*. It is the imaginative empathy of the act of translation that restores humanity to the other, not the espousal of absolutist cultural separatism" (Cronin, 2000: 91).

The importance of context (that is, the relation between the author and the target readership in a specific historical timeframe) in appraising a travel account is also relevant. In the case of the Italian travelogs to Japan presented here, the point of view of the traveler is not necessarily oriented toward increasing the prestige of the home culture in contrast with the culture of the country traveled. For instance, the journalistic reports of Luigi Barzini

---

fact, she begins with an example of Gabriel García Márquez commenting on the diary of the Florentine navigator Antonio Pigafetta, who traveled together with Magellan in the first world circumnavigation. While Márquez describes the fantastic stories that Pigafetta includes in his account of South America, Bassnett points out that Pigagetta's fantastic descriptions of creatures were not pure invention, but rather an attempt to write "about penguins, spoonbills and llamas, seeking a way of recording his impressions for readers back in Europe [who had never seen these species of animals before]; in other words, he was trying to translate his experience into a frame of reference that his fellow Florentines would understand. [...] What Pigafetta was doing was translating, and through translation he was able to include his compatriots in his discoveries of an expanded world": Susan Bassnett, 2014, *Translation* (New York: Routledge): 169. This example suggests three points that Bassnett makes about how to appraise a translation (either linguistic or cultural): first, each translation must be put into context, that is, in the case of representing a culture from the perspective and for the consumption of another culture, is necessary to consider the reader's expectation of a given culture in a particular moment (in the case of Pigafetta, the target culture is an Italian readership that must visualize animals that they have never seen). She then reminds us that each translation bears the footprint of the individual translator, or the point of view of the single traveler. Finally, skepticism around the operation of translating seems to suggest the problematic existence of a pure original, or, in the case of travel as translation, the idea that the gaze of the local inhabitants is original and uncontaminated by other "traveling" cultures.

11   The link between travel and translation that I am suggesting here becomes evident when considering the etymology of the two terms. Indeed, the Latin roots of both *translatio* and *traductio* (*trado, tradere* "to hand over, or to give") convey a sense of movement, of transporting a material, or abstract, object from one place to another. Therefore, travel literature shares with translation the potential benefit to introduce a new, provisional level of understanding of a foreign country.

from the Russo-Japanese war showcase the narrator's struggle to convey the humanity of the Japanese, at a time when all over Europe and America Japanese militaries were regarded as terrifyingly efficient machines of war. In the same constructive tone is the pedagogical approach of the polyglot Pietro Silvio Rivetta, aimed at bridging the knowledge gap about Japan among the Italian public – by providing simple introductions to the language and the culture – during a time in which the World War II alliance between Italy and Japan demanded that both countries become more acquainted with each other. The *penchant* to increase the prestige of contemporary Japan in Italy is more radical in Fosco Maraini, who is adamant in asserting the superiority of Japanese civilization in contrast to the Western world, which he conceives as decadent and unfit for future human challenges. Finally, the experience of Antonietta Pastore in Japan debunks many of the most die-hard Orientalist tropes to haunt Western perceptions of Japanese women, by showing their humanity and demonstrating the possibility of building strong bonds of friendship with them. Overall, these examples support a notion of transnationalism in travel writings that is predicated upon the desire to reshape the social imaginary[12] of the receiving country by importing the cultural contribution of the country traveled.[13] By broadening the national imaginary,

---

12   I use the key-term "social imaginary" in the way the philosopher Charles Taylor described it, as the "ways people imagine their social existence, how they fit together with others, how things go on between them and their fellows, the expectations that are normally met, and the deeper normative notions and images that underlie these expectations": Charles Taylor, 2004, *Modern Social Imaginaries* (Durham, NC and London: Duke University Press): 23. These travelogs in Japan contribute to modifying the Italian social imaginary by including the presence of Japanese individuals and cultures, lessening the perception of an impenetrable exotic distance between the two countries.
13   It is not the intention of this book to deny the validity of post-colonial readings of travelogs. As mentioned earlier in the Introduction, the aspirational nature of this transnational literature, as well as the importance of context (who speaks to whom? From which socio-historical circumstances? Under what constraints? etc.), creates the condition for these narratives to be counteracted by Orientalist examples that are documented in this study. For instance, in chapter 1, Daniele Pecorini's *Japanese Maple* can be seen as a typical Orientalist narrative *à la* Loti. The second chapter, on the Fascist period, shows both animal-like descriptions of Japanese people, as well as preposterous manipulations of their supposed love for Mussolini and Italian Fascism, as part of the war propaganda. In chapter 3, the novel *L'eleganza è frigida* presents a highly exoticized Japan as a dreamy escape from the political nightmare that 1970s Italy represents, in the eyes of the author Goffredo Parise. In chapter 4 Angela Terzani Staude echoes stereotypes about Japan, writing from within the circle of Western journalists in the Far East.

Italian travelers do not necessarily intend to replicate the monolog of Western universalism, instead they often introduce Japan as a challenge posed to Western civilization. The perspective that is adopted here echoes the position of French geographer and Orientalist Augustin Berque, who concentrates on manifestations of Orientalism that have introduced a critical perspective against the Modern Western Paradigm, rather than substantiations of it: in fact, he asks: "d'où viennent, en effet, sinon d'Orient, les défis les plus explicites qui soient portés à la civilisation occidentale, à ses fondements métaphysiques aussi bien qu'à l'expression matérielle de sa puissance?" (Berque, 1993: 217) [From where, if not the East, have the most explicit challenges to Western civilization come – both to its metaphysical foundations and the material expression of its power?].

As the concept of transnationalism in use in this study puts an emphasis on crossing boundaries and finding intercultural affinities at a long distance from home, cosmopolitanism(s) represent the culmination of this ethical practice with respect to strangers. The use of this term is connected to the most recent debate on cosmopolitan ethics, which can be dated back to the events of September 11, 2001. It is a discussion generated in response to the reality of cultural, religious and political clashes on a global scale, in an attempt to counteract the wave of nationalism, populism and xenophobia that is compromising the world order. This is to say that the conversation has moved beyond the univocal interpretation of "cosmopolitanism," whose modern genealogy traces back to Kant and his universalistic vision of a single world community, where humans peacefully coexist.[14] In this older version the term has been repeatedly criticized and even mocked for its Eurocentric prerogatives, which inevitably fall short when tested in real life situations, such as the eponymous protagonist of Voltaire's *Candide* encountering a slave from the "New World."[15]

---

14   It must be said that neo-Kantian transcendental theories enjoy wide currency, especially in relation to the political project of the European Union. Some major actors in these debates are: Jürgen Habermas and his concept of "cosmopolitan democracy", Ulrich Beck's "Cosmopolitan Europe," and David Held's "moral cosmopolitanism": these are key concepts that must inspire global governance.

15   However, attempts to redefine the cosmopolitan tradition involve even the more elitist and Eurocentric eighteenth-century period. See Eugenia Zuroski Jenkins, 2012, "Introduction: Exoticism, Cosmopolitanism, and Fiction's Aesthetics of Diversity," *Eighteenth-Century Fiction*, 25(1): 1–7. For an in-depth analysis of the new formulations of cosmopolitan ethics, see Rosi Braidotti, Patrick Hanafin and Bolette Blaagaard (editors), 2012, *After Cosmopolitanism* (New York: Routledge). On the critical discussion related to

In its pluralistic and renovated form, the term has perhaps lost its normative force to become a descriptive and empirical concept, almost ubiquitous in the way it is associated across social, economic and geopolitical domains (such as the "cosmopolitan of the poor," "Afropolitanism," "economic cosmopolitanism," etc.). Given the broad and inclusive understanding of cosmopolitanism, Bruce Robbins and Paulo Lemos Horta have recently defined the concept as "any one of many possible modes of life, thought, and sensibility that are produced when commitments and loyalties are multiple and overlapping, no one of them necessarily trumping the others" (Robbins and Lemos Horta, 2017: 3). This interpretation has the advantage of grounding the discussion of cosmopolitanism in travel writings in observable manifestations of cosmopolitan ethics, detected through close readings of travel narratives, instead of assuming from the start the existence of a cosmopolitan identity that the subsequent close reading is meant to confirm and validate. I thus use the term "cosmopolitan aspirations" both to single out examples of the writers'/travelers' multiple "commitments and loyalties" to more than one country, as well as to express the fragile, utopic nature of these affinities that expose them to contradictions and, sometimes, to failure.[16] A particularly telling example in this study of such a complex dynamic (discussed in ch. 2) is the multicultural journey of Arundel Del Re, across the numerous

---

"cosmopolitanism," see Pheng Cheah and Bruce Robbins (editors), 1998, *Cosmopolitics: Thinking and Feeling beyond the Nation*, (Minneapolis: University of Minnesota Press); Steven Vertovec and Robin Cohen (editors), 2002, *Conceiving Cosmopolitanism: Theory, Context and Practice* (New York: Oxford University Press); Kwame Anthony Appiah, 2006, *Cosmopolitanism: Ethics in a World of Strangers* (New York: W.W. Norton); Nina Glick Schiller and Andrew Irving (editors), 2015, *Whose Cosmopolitanism? Critical Perspectives, Relationalities and Discontents* (New York: Berghahn Books).

16 This approach to cosmopolitanism moves in the same direction of Tariq Ramadan's notion of "critical cosmopolitanism" premised on the rejection of the universalist tradition of the concept, in order to situate the discussion on the ground of human behavior in action, with its typical openness toward the desire for sharing humanity with other people and, simultaneously, its awareness of its own self-denial and inconsistency: see Ramadan, 2015, "Cosmopolitan Theory and the Daily Pluralism of Life," in Nina Glick Schiller and Andrew Irving (editors), *Whose Cosmopolitanism?: Critical Perspectives, Relationalities and Discontents* (New York: Berghahn Books): 57–64. The idea of a "critical cosmopolitanism" was first expressed by Walter Mignolo, who argued for the importance of considering "hegemonic imagery from the perspective of people in subaltern positions": Mignolo, 2002, "The many faces of Cosmo-Polis: border thinking and critical cosmopolitanism," in Carol A. Breckenridge et al. (editors), *Cosmopolitanism* (Durham, NC: Duke University Press): 174.

homelands among which he divided his life and career: Italy, England, Japan, New Zealand and Australia. Born of an Irish mother and an Italian father in Florence in 1892, his nomadic life made him particularly skilled and versatile in building human relationships with locals and promoting the cultural heritage of each of those countries and their intercultural dialog. Yet his desire to feel at "home" fell short in Japan where he perceived an impenetrable cultural and linguistic barrier that ultimately prompted his decision to relocate, after twenty-seven years, to an Anglophone country. Despite this setback, his commitment to Japan continued in different forms, as he found in New Zealand and Australia a midway point between East and West. His affiliation with Japan continued from these countries; he became a founding member and secretary of the Oriental Society of Australia (1955–57) and a member of the Japanese Society in Wellington, while serving the post of English Lecturer at Victoria University and being an active member of the Circolo Italiano.

In the case of Antonietta Pastore's most recent book (2016), focused on the life of her former relative and Hiroshima survivor (see ch. 4), the cosmopolitan aspiration goes beyond the Italy–Japan cross-cultural framework, in order to recast Japan from a global cultural standpoint. The reference to her relative suffering the consequences of the atomic blast in Hiroshima projects Japan into the iconic image of the mushroom cloud, tapping into the visual archive of global violence and human civilization under threat of extinction. The particular national perspective and personal experience are subsumed within the context of international human rights, as the specific story of a relative being affected by radiation touches a critical point of twentieth-century global human history.

While Pastore's book brings back to life residual memories of the Italian–Japanese alliance that lay buried beneath the geopolitical map of the new post-World War II order, it also highlights one of the most recent manifestations of cosmopolitan solidarity and empathy across national borders. The visual nature of these global threats and the extensive use of traditional and social media to spread these images worldwide play a key role in this new form of cosmopolitanism. Pastore links the stories of Hiroshima survivors having to cope with the consequences of nuclear radiation with similar stories of Japanese affected by the Fukushima nuclear fallout (in 2011). The link between the two events is not only represented by the physical source of energy at the origin of the disasters, but is also provided by the visual realities of the irradiated bodies that news media outlets have made available and familiar, for anyone, on a global scale. If Rey Chow considered the dropping of the atomic bomb as the event after which the "world becomes virtual" (Chow, 2006: 33) – with its outpouring of violent images making their way into the daily life of average people through the contemporary rise of mass media technologies – the Fukushima fallout partakes of the same virtual reality – although on a lower scale of relevance, given the non-bellicose nature of the event. Pastore's *Mia amata Yuriko* is thus a response to the nuclear fear that the images of the Fukushima Daiichi powerplant have reawakened. It belongs to the wave of transnational solidarity that individuals across the world have generated in reaction to the virtual reality that TV and social media have brought within domestic walls.[17] From this cosmopolitan perspective, in which the global and the local are not in opposition, the use of media outlets represents another distinct aspect of this transnational space, in its being determined by the speed and far-reaching circulation of the global media. The transnational experience of Antonietta Pastore in her most recent semi-fictional book represents therefore a point of departure from that of other authors examined here, for it is no longer solely inscribed in the physical experience of travel and cross-cultural encounter, but, instead, is located in the virtual space of a globalized media, which is able to generate and mobilize transnational public communities.

***

Cosmopolitanism in relation to travel writings is manifested particularly in the traveler's perception of where "home" is. The feelings of being "at home" correspond to an experience of belonging and affective engagement that does not necessarily (or exclusively) indicate birthplace. When the Greek Cynic philosopher Diogenes (412–323 BC) was asked the question "where are you from?" his answer, "I am a citizen of the World" (*kosmopolitês*), became the first formulation of this elusive concept. The definition of cosmopolitan as "citizen of the world" can be interpreted in a dual sense of being "at home" both everywhere and nowhere, indicating in the first case the utopian dream of the "globetrotter," and in the second case a nomadic idea of roaming from place to place, where temporary "homes" are elected and supplanted. If in the first sense cosmopolitanism is connected to a

---

17 See Pedro Iacobelli, Danton Leary and Shinnosuke Takahashi (editors), 2016, *Transnational Japan as History: Empire, Migration, and Social Movements* (Houndmills, Basingstoke, Hampshire: Palgrave Macmillan).

dimension of universality and transcendence, in the second the dimension of temporality and impermanence prevails. This latter interpretation has become the predominant way to describe the worker's mobility in an increasingly globalized labor market, representing a category of visitor to Japan that is shared by several authors in this book. The most significant example of this category of cosmopolitan is perhaps Antonietta Pastore (ch. 4), who migrated to Japan in the late 1970s to take up a teaching position in French and Italian at Osaka University. For a long time, Japan represented for Pastore the place she called "home," thanks to a special relationship with her Japanese in-laws, who created for her a safe and nourishing space, in contrast with the rigid and inhospitable family environment of her upbringing in Italy. Yet after sixteen years of life in Japan the perception of "home" shifted again and a feeling of nostalgia for her native country prompted her to return to Italy.

A second aspect that cosmopolitan travelers share in this study is a sense of moral obligation and empathy to strangers encountered along their journeys. This is to say that such travelers do not become cosmopolitan by virtue of simply sharing cultural aspects of the local country, such as sleeping on a tatami-mat or attending a Noh performance at the theater. It is also a level of engagement with locals far deeper than the multicultural forms of tolerance for the diversity of the "Other" that is often considered as a cosmopolitan marker. Beyond the goal of respecting different values and cultures, the cosmopolitan travelers in this study are frequently willing to engage with the "Other," in situations of constructing comparison and opening dialog. In general, they share a position of curiosity for the diversity of the "Other," whether the outcome of this exchange is an acknowledgment of differences, or a discovery of commonalities. An example of this attitude can be detected in Fosco Maraini's appreciation for what he considers secular Japanese ethics (Confucianism), which do not pose any sort of prejudice toward scientific progress – quite the reverse of the skeptical approach taken by Christianity in the West over many centuries. Another more nuanced example is offered by Daniele Pecorini's *Japanese Maple*, which, in many aspects, represents a Eurocentric text written by an elitist white male European who wears the badge of cosmopolitanism to disguise an underlying patronizing attitude. Yet occasionally the ideological bias of this travelog leaves room for attempts at comprehension and a willingness to be captivated by the differences between the two cultures. For instance, if *seppuku* remains an exotic ritual in the eyes of this Italian protagonist, he does not dismiss the practice as irrational and barbaric; instead, he resorts to an attempt at explanation in laying out for his readers the Buddhist indifference toward death. Finally, his sympathetic position toward Japanese culture even suggests to him a comparison between the notion of *seppuku*, intended as an heroic gesture, and the sacrificial death of Italian patriots during the *Risorgimento*.

Examples such as these, indicating a sympathy for Japanese culture and values, are recurrent in most texts examined in this book. The travel writings presented here reveal, in combination, an historical perspective on Italian "Japanophilia" that has been otherwise overlooked or mostly ignored. This attraction for Japan was possible largely as a result of the historical pattern of similarities that brought Italians to regard Japan as a country from which they could learn and that they could even possibly imitate. Japan represented to Italians a model of how a late imperialist nation, whose territory was on the same scale as Italy's, could seek to assert a leading role on the global stage. An historical overview of Italian's encounters with Japan will help support this view.

2. Catching up with Superpowers

After Marco Polo described "Zipangu" (Japan) as a legendary island, where apparently "they have gold in the greatest abundance" (Polo, 2008: 237), it was only in the climate of sixteenth-century geographical exploration that Italians chronicled their arrival in the East Indies as missionaries at the service of the Portuguese crown, among whom Alessandro Valignano (1539–1606) was the major protagonist of the Christian Jesuit mission in the Far East. He was appointed as "visitor" of China and Japan in 1595 and continued to serve in this role until his death in Macau. In contrast with the evangelizing practices of his predecessor Francisco Cabral, Valignano reorganized the mission by stressing the principles of respect and dialog with locals (the so-called accommodation method, or *accomodatio*), beginning with mastery of the language, translations of Buddhist texts, adoption of a Japanese lifestyle by the Jesuits (including adoption of the Japanese diet) and the decision to make clergy-hood available to Japanese men. He promoted the establishment of a school in Funai in which the traditional Western curriculum (namely, Latin and Greek texts) was integrated with readings of texts in Japanese and Chinese.

In brief, "Alessandro Valignano's method of accommodation [...] points to a formula of globalization that rejects unidirectional Westernization and opens itself to multicultural encounters and reciprocal learning processes"

(Casanova, 2016: 270).[18] In the same time period the lesser known Jesuit missionary Organtino Gnecchi-Soldo from Brescia (1530–1609) further explored the possible implications of Valignano's inclusive approach by embracing Japanese life and culture, to the point of inviting his superiors to reconsider their biases toward the locals. His deferential tone does not subtract from his bold statement, in a letter dated October 15, 1577, clearly inviting his superior in Rome to change his mind about the way Japanese should be regarded, writing: "I advise Your Excellency to beware of thinking that these people are Barbarians, because apart from faith [...] in fact compared to them we are extremely uncivilized, and in truth I must confess that every day I learn from them" (Suter, 2015: 15). Organtino's self-perception of being more Japanese than Italian helped the Jesuit mission, by allowing him to operate as a credible mediator when the time came to discuss the construction of a *seminario* in Azuchi, or to represent the Jesuit cause during the difficult period leading up to the Christian ban of 1587. While Organtino's name plays a minor role in the context of the Jesuit mission, he enjoyed a larger popularity among Japanese scholars of foreign religions in Japan, as well as among modern Japanese authors, who used the character of Padre Organtino in several fictional works (Suter, 2015: 39–71).

While at the end of the sixteenth century Totoyomi Hideyoshi (1536–98) began the persecutions that would end the Christian missions in Japan, the Florentine merchant Francesco Carletti (1573?–1636), with his father Antonio, set out from Spain on slave trade business (1594) based on the scheme of acquiring slaves in the Cape Verde Islands to sell in the New World. They eventually revisited and expanded their initial plan and, after reaching the West Indies (Panama, Peru and Mexico), they continued toward the East Indies to visit the Spanish Philippine Islands, Japan (in 1597), Macau (where his father Antonio died), Malacca and Goa. Carletti eventually came back to Florence penniless (in 1606, after the failure of his trading scheme), but with a rich baggage of stories to tell to the Grand Duke of Tuscany that were later published (1701) under the title of *Ragionamenti di Francesco Carletti fiorentino sopra le cose da lui vedute ne' suoi viaggi* ["Discourses of the Florentine Francesco Carletti on the things he saw in his journeys"]. Here,

---

18   On Alessandro Valignano, see also Andrew C. Ross 1999, "Alessandro Valignano: The Jesuits and Culture in the East," in John W. O'Malley... et al. (editors), *The Jesuits: Cultures, Sciences, and The Arts, 1540–1773* (Toronto and Buffalo: University of Toronto Press): 336–51; Joseph Francis Moran, 1993, *The Japanese and the Jesuits: Alessandro Valignano in Sixteenth-century Japan* (London and New York: Routledge).

he describes how, upon his arrival in Japan Carletti had declared to the local authorities that he was a member of "la natione italiana" [the Italian nation], in order to position himself as neutral observer, uncommitted either to the Spanish or Portuguese Crown, thus describing his national identity in terms of an unthreatening cultural and linguistic affiliation. Although there are occasions in which Carletti seems to desire a colonialist presence for Italy in Asia, he self-proclaims as a stateless citizen and a globetrotter. In Nathalie Hester's words: "A 'tourist' despite his original intentions, the Florentine traveler creates a narrative that is identifiably Italian in its references to literary culture and in its construction of a point of view that is authoritative because it is removed from expansionist impulses" (Hester, 2008: 49).[19]

During the eighteenth century the anti-Christian policies of the Edo period (based on martyrdom and enforced apostasy) brought the Christian missions in Japan to an end. The only example of a Catholic priest landing on Japanese soil before the mid-nineteenth century was Giovanni Battista Sidotti (1668–1714), born in Palermo to an upper-class family and educated in Rome. He was ordained a priest at a very young age, yet he refused the comfort of a prestigious ecclesiastic career by convincing his superiors to send him to Japan after the last Portuguese embassy closed in 1639, resulting in a bloodbath. In 1708 Sidotti arrived in the Yakushima Island (in present-day Kagoshima Prefecture), to the curiosity of the locals. He was soon taken to Edo (Tokyo) where the Confucian philosopher, historian, geographer, bureaucrat and poet Arai Hakuseki interrogated him. The Japanese scholar was fascinated by Sidotti, during a series of conversations whose topics ranged from spirituality to history, geography, science and law. In spite of the radical differences between the two of them and the restricting context in which the dialogs took place, Hakuseki and Sidotti developed a mutual respect, to the point that Hakuseki advised the official authorities that Sidotti be deported rather than receiving the capital sentence that was normally reserved for entering the country illegally. He was detained in a *Kirishitan-yashiki* [Christian mansion], under the mild surveillance of an elderly Japanese couple. However, the discovery that Sidotti converted and baptized his custodians caused him to be moved to an underground cell in the mansion, where he died in 1714.[20] Arai Hakuseki used the precious

---

19 See also Elisabetta Colla, 2008, "16th century Japan and Macau described by Francesco Carletti (1573?–1636)," *Bulletin of Portuguese-Japanese Studies*, 17: 113–44.
20 In April 2014 during excavation work for the construction of a new condominium complex on the site of the old *Kirishitan Yashiki*, human remains were discovered. A DNA

knowledge that he learned during his conversations with Sidotti as the source for three books: the first one, titled *Seiyō kibun* ["Record of things heard from the West"], helped to introduce Western knowledge about technology, politics, astronomy, geography and religion to Japan.[21] Hakuseki was not particularly impressed by theological matters, indeed, he wrote that "When he [Sidotti] came to speak about his religion, it appeared to me to be not in the slightest respect like the true way [...] At first I thought him very intelligent, but when he began to explain his doctrine he became like a fool" (Arai Hakuseki, *Seiyō kibun*, cited in Farge and Doak, 2016: 219–20).[22] But Hakuseki did emerge from his conversations with Sidotti with a deep understanding that the strength of the West lay in its scientific and technological progress. In sum, "Hakuseki acquired a degree of knowledge about these things unmatched by anyone [in Japan] of his time" (De Bary et al., 2001: 1271).

The names of the Italian travelers and missionaries mentioned up to this point belong to the "prehistory" of the relationship between the two countries, that is, when foreigners were limited from entering Japan (with exceptions made for Dutch and Chinese ships in the area of Nagasaki), while Italy had not yet achieved unity and independence. The situation changed drastically for both countries in a time span that was almost identical. In 1854 the American Commodore Matthew Perry forced the Tokugawa government to sign a trade agreement with the United States under threat of military action, paving the way for other Western nations to follow suit. Japan was quick to realize that a necessary measure to counteract aggressive Western policies,

---

test in 2016 confirmed that the skeleton is that of Giovanni Battista Sidotti. "Based on the skull and recorded descriptions of Sidotti, the National Museum of Nature and Science in Tokyo proceeded to create a replica of his head, and put it on display. Now it is part of the Kirishitan exhibition which goes on display at least once a year at the Tokyo National Museum": Stutler, 2018: ""Kirishitan Sites in Tokyo," available at www.stutler.cc/russ/kirishitan.html (accessed June 24, 2018).

21 The second book, entitled *Yohan Bacchisuta Monogatari* ("The story of Giovanni Battista"), tells the story of Sidotti in Japan. The third *Sairan Igen* ("Collection of strange things") contains, among other things, geographical notions about the West.

22 Of course, it should not be discounted the fact that Hakusei was seeking government approval, therefore his views on religious matters were necessarily influenced by the Japanese anti-Christian policy. His disapproval of Sidotti's Christian doctrine was not enough for the *bakufu* (shogun's office) to approve the book for publication, in fact *Seiyō kibun* was published only in 1882. On Sidotti see also Fosco Maraini, 1992, *Italia e Giappone: incontri e reincontri attraverso i secoli*. Prolusione per il conferimento della Laurea Honoris Causa (University of Siena), May 23.

which had already caused China to lose its independence, was to build a strong army. Indeed, following the arrival of the American fleet, an increasing flow of Western people, goods and ideas arrived in a country that had until then observed a strict policy aimed at limiting foreign influence. As a result, the Tokugawa government appeared politically undermined both inland and abroad, and in fact the enemies of the Shogunate seized the opportunity to initiate the civil war that brought the end of the Tokugawa regime and the restoration of the imperial system, with supreme power returning to new emperor Meiji in 1868.

Italy entered a new chapter of its history as well. Having obtained national unification only in 1861, reversing its long-standing status as territory available for foreign conquest, it faced an uncertain role within the existing system of power relationships among the European States. Externally, states like Britain, France, Germany and Hungary challenged Italy with the potential loss of its political independence, while internally, the authority of the ruling House of Savoy was severely weakened by opposition from the Catholic Church, the country's southern regions and members of the Republican political coalition. Nonetheless, the country's rulers were determined to pursue the ambition of making Italy "the last of the great powers" (Samuels, 2003: 12), overcoming its previous Mediterranean isolation, and therefore competing with other European nations in asserting an influential role on the global stage. Within this grandiose scheme for international legitimacy, Italian officials decided to organize a commercial and diplomatic maritime mission aimed at signing a commercial treaty with China and Japan. The delegation, led by the Commander Vittorio Arminjon, arrived at the Yokohama port on July 4, 1866 aboard the Pirocorvette *Magenta*.[23] Less than two months later

---

23   Vittorio Arminjon is the author of his own travelog about his Japanese journey: *Il Giappone e il viaggio della corvetta Magenta nel 1866: Coll'aggiunta dei trattati del Giappone e della China e relative tariffe*. Genova: Co tipi del R.I. dei sordo-muti, 1869. Arminjon describes Japan right before the technological, scientific, political and cultural revolution of the Meiji period. Therefore, he insists on depicting the backwardness, immobility and stagnation of the Japanese society, without suspecting the imminent radical change. Arminjon also visited the country during the period of violent demonstrations against the Meiji politic after they opened the country to the presence of foreigners, leading him to deem the Japanese immoral and decadent: "L'apertura del Giappone non avrà dunque per noi altra importanza utile ed immediata fuorché lo scambio dei prodotti del suolo e dell'industria. Non abbiamo nulla da acquistare moralmente al contatto di quella società asiatica, il cui decadimento è vicino se non già principiato" (1869: 22).

the two countries declared their first institutional agreement, which included the installation of an Italian diplomat in Tokyo and a commercial *attaché* in Yokohama. The beginning of the Meiji era and the Unification of the Italian Kingdom thus set up the comparative framework for an historical outlook of these two emerging countries. Richard J. Samuels in *Machiavelli's Children: Leaders and their Legacies in Italy & Japan* (2003) argues convincingly for the utility and significance of comparing Italy and Japan, positioning them among the models of countries that were "late-comers," to the global stage, and therefore including Japan in a larger international context. Parallel views of these two "late-developers" (Samuels, 2003: 87) reveal a strikingly similar set of problems: both Italy and Japan grappled with issues related to late industrialization and democratization, fragile liberalism, nationalism and corruption, among others. Massimo D'Azeglio's well-worn aphorism after the mission of Italian unification had been accomplished, "L'Italia è fatta, ora bisogna fare gli italiani" [Italy has been made; now we need to make the Italians], is echoed in the words of the Meiji intellectual Fukuzawa Yukichi in 1875: "Japan has never been a single country [...] In Japan there is government but not nation" (quoted in Samuels, 2003: 34). As Samuels goes on to comment, "Like the Italians, the Japanese also had to be made; like the Japanese, the Italians also found deep reservoirs of common past and future purpose" (Samuels, 2003: 32). For both countries, domestic problems related to a fluid definition of common identity were paired with a similar foreign agenda aimed at catching up with imperialist nations: "As in the Italian case, much of this challenge was animated by Japanese's pursuit of parity with the Western powers" (34).

While the two countries struggled to achieve international prestige, their relationship became ever closer as a result of an increasing mutual exchange of artists and intellectuals traveling between East Asia and Europe. In the process of westernizing Japanese society, the young Meiji state chose Italy as the country most suitable for providing introduction to the established fields of the fine arts. Artists such as the painter Antonio Fontanesi (1818–82), the sculptor Vincenzo Ragusa (1841–1927) and the interior architect Vincenzo Cappelletti (1843–1905) were appointed to Tokyo University of the Arts (Tokyo Geijutsu Daigaku) to introduce Japanese students to Western art. It was Edoardo Chiossone (1833–98), an Italian engraver living in Tokyo, who received the highest honor of being commissioned to create a portrait of the emperor.

At the same time, the diffusion of Japanese culture into Italy was also proceeding at a fast pace. At first the reception of Japan was objectified in the international aesthetic movement called *japonisme*. A few Japanese considered Italy as a travel destination. Still, a wave of objects and images began to proliferate in the private collections and drawing rooms of distinguished and affluent Italians, not directly from Japan but primarily through the cultural mediation of France and England. In fact, Italian intellectuals and artists were – once again – trying to catch the wave of a movement conceived in the northern provinces of Europe. The first exhibition of Japanese art was at the Universal Exposition of London (1862), while Japanese painters arrived in the *Bel Paese* only much later, at the Venice Biennale in 1897. Similarly, Vittorio Pica's *L'arte dell'estremo Oriente* (1894) ["The art of the Far East"] was hugely indebted to Edmond de Goncourt's *Outamaro: Le Peintre des Maisons Vertes* (1891) ["Utamaro, the painter of green houses"],[24] while the plot of Giacomo Puccini's opera *Madama Butterfly* (1904) relied heavily on the novel *Madame Chrysanthème* (1887) by Pierre Loti.

In line with the Parisian interest in *japonisme*, the opening in 1905 of the Edoardo Chiossone Museum of Oriental Art in Genoa contributed to the Italian wave of fascination with the Japanese aesthetic. On the political front, news at the turn of the century about Japanese imperialist ambitions was welcomed in Italian nationalistic discourse and used to spur on the young nation's foreign policy. The military victories against first China (1894–95), then Russia (1904–05) were admired and considered ideal examples for possible Italian imitation. An unusually belligerent Giovanni Pascoli (1855–1912) called on Italy to follow the example of Japan where day laborers became "formidable little soldiers" (*soldatini formidabili*), defeated Russia and conquered territory for settlers. The futurist and nationalist intellectual Marinetti celebrated the efficiency and state-of-the-art equipment of the invincible Japanese army in a poem asserting the aesthetic beauty of the machine ("Automobile ebbrrra di spazio, / che scalpiti e frrremi d'angoscia / rodendo il morso con striduli denti [...] / formidabile mostro giapponese" [Automobile thirsting for space / shuffling and trembling in anguish, / pulling at the bit with strident teeth! / O formidable Japanese monster]).[25]

---

24 For this aspect see Ishii Motoaki, 1998, "Vittorio Pica e la critica dell'arte giapponese in Italia," *Annali dell'Università degli Studi di Napoli "L'Orientale": Rivista del Dipartimento di Studi Asiatici e del Dipartimento di Studi e Ricerche su Africa e Paesi Arabi*, 58(3–4): 495–518.
25 The quote by Giovanni Pascoli is from his infamous speech "La grande proletaria si è mossa" (November 26, 1911) in celebration of the Italian military invasion of Libya. Marinetti's quote is from "A mon Pégase," in *La Ville charnelle* (Paris: E. Sansot and Co., 1908), also "À l'automobile," in *Poesia* (Milan, 1905). The English translation is from *Futurism: An Anthology*, edited by Lawrence Rainey, Christine Poggi and Laura Wittman, 2009 (New Haven and London: Yale University Press): 425.

The perception of Japan as a young, imperialistic nation, capable of inspiring a rising Italian nationalistic front, was further ignited by the presence in Italy, for almost two decades (1915–33), of the right-wing Japanese scholar Shimoi Harukichi (1883–1954). Little known in Japan at the time, Shimoi became a popular figure shortly after he arrived in Naples in 1915 to take up a position as lecturer in Japanese at the Regio Istituto Orientale [Royal Oriental Institute]. The presence of a native Japanese intellectual attracted the attention of a group of modernist artists, loosely connected to the literary journal *La Diana* (1915–17) and its idea of pursuing a renovation of national culture. For the Neapolitan group Shimoi represented an opportunity to have direct access to contemporary Japanese art and literature, without passing through French or English mediation. Translations of Japanese poets, such as Yosano Akiko and Yosano Tekkan, made regular appearances in *La Diana*, generating an interest that suggested the publication of the volume *Poesie giapponesi* ["Japanese poems"], in March 1917. The fortune of this collection of Japanese poetry in translation relied largely on the enthusiastic reception by the modernist milieu of the seventeen-syllable poetic form known as *haiku*. To Italian poets, such as Giuseppe Ungaretti, the *haiku* form appealed to their modernist fascination with fragmented and concise forms, essential expressions and lightness.

As World War I broke out, Shimoi moved closer to the front in the north of Italy to experience directly the reality of the combat zone, gathering impressions and ideas that became part of a memoir titled *La guerra italiana* (1919) ["The Italian War"]. The book represents a first significant step in the direction of Shimoi's nationalistic politic by embracing the Futurist enthusiasm for the war, viewed as a privileged vehicle to foster the patriotic sentiment of the masses. Shimoi meshes Japanese patriotism with the enthusiasm of the Italian crowd for the successful conclusion of the conflict: "La popolazione felice della liberazione, corse incontro a me ed alle truppe che passavano. Tutti ci lanciavano i gridi di gioia e ci salutavano come pazzi. Anch'io gridavo appassionatamente '*Viva l'Italia! Viva l'Italia!*' Mi sentivo come se mi fossi trovato nella mia patria" (Shimoi, 1919: 43) [The crowd happy for the liberation ran to meet me and the troops that passed by. Everyone shouted for joy and greeted us like madmen. I too shouted passionately "Hurray for Italy! Hurray for Italy!" I felt like I was in my homeland]. The post-war years saw Shimoi joining Gabriele D'Annunzio in the expedition to Fiume for military conquest of the territories that Italy was supposed to receive during the peace negotiations, leading to the myth of the so-called "mutilated victory." Later, with the affirmation of Mussolini and Fascism,

Shimoi designed for himself a role of *trait d'union* between Italy and Japan, trying to convince government officials that Italian Fascism presented a set of solutions to solve the crisis of parliamentary democracy in Japan, which was troubled by corruptions and suspected of promoting the interest of social elites instead of serving the masses.[26]

In this comparative history between these two late-developing powers, the political and military alliance of the Anti-Comintern (1937) and Tripartite Pact (1940) represent the culmination of their diplomatic relationships, and the possibility of intersecting imperialistic designs. As we shall see in chapter 2, this political rapprochement promoted a discourse of propaganda predicated on the assumption that Italians and Japanese had more in common than they had ever thought before.

This model of cross-cultural closeness and mutuality that became popular during Italy's Fascist period would be completely overthrown during the post-World War II recovery years. The historical context that produced this change of perspectives was the debate about the war and the necessity for rebuilding a national identity in both countries. In Italy, the fall of Fascism came with the demise of a national dream for historical glorification, built on the rhetorical image of the ancient Roman Empire. The perception of a majestic past inherited by the Italian Kingdom became recognized as an enormous delusion, being called by Gaetano Salvemini "il cancro romano-imperiale" [the Roman-Imperial cancer] filled with "sogni di primati impossibili" [dreams of impossible primacies] (quoted in Samuels, 2003: 181).

Many Italians shared Salvemini's negative image of the nation, and resulting inferiority complex. The Japanese also had to come to terms with the humiliation of defeat and being forced to accept a constitution imposed by the US, however unlike the Italians they were able to rebuild a national identity as a strong and unique family of citizens based on the *Yamato-damashii* [Japanese spirit]. Similarities continued during the Cold War years, as both countries operated within the geopolitical control of the US's sphere of influence: each pursued the goal of becoming a "normal" functioning democracy by accepting a subaltern role in an American established order. Also, both registered a quick and unexpected (albeit proportionally different) "economic miracle": "Italy was the sixth largest manufacturing economy in the world by 1975 and surpassed Great Britain

---

26 For an in-depth reconstruction of the relations between Italy and Japan that Shimoi Harukichi was able to build and control, see Reto Hofmann, 2015, *The Fascist Effect: Japan and Italy, 1915–1952* (Ithaca, NY: Cornell University Press): 8–37.

as number five in the early 1980s. Japan was by then the second largest economy in the world and challenging the dominance of the United States" (Samuels, 2003: 190). Yet as chapter 3 will demonstrate – while Japanophilia became an international phenomenon that again increased Italy's interest in Japan as well – Italians perceived a new sense of exotic distance from Japan after the artificial rapprochement of the war years. Paradoxically, in spite of the growing opportunity to travel offered by mass tourism, the larger editorial market for translations of Japanese authors, the success of Japanese cinema and pop culture, the perception of distance only increased. The model of parallel growth by these two late developers came to be replaced by a polarized model in which Italy held a backward status in opposition to an attractive image of Japan.

Within this historical landscape, briefly sketched here, *Searching for Japan* offers numerous examples of how the formation process of the Italian nation state overlapped with a contemporaneous creation of transnational imagined communities, which impacted the everyday life of Italians. Specifically, this volume engages with the *fin de siècle* attempts to expand the horizons of Italian culture, while also looking at the political alliance of the 1930s and 1940s to explore how the Fascist regime imported knowledge related to Japan into Italy, as part of a strategy aimed at bridging the differences between the two allied nations. It will bring to the fore the Italian thirst for Japanese culture and literature of the 1960s–1980s to explain why Italians saw in the Far East country a superior model compared to the Italian Republic. Finally, in the last chapter, the focus turns to the experience of Italian women traveling to Japan to challenge established gender clichés while seeking, in the case of Antonietta Pastore, the possibility of a female cosmopolitanism, based on solidarity and action.

3. Meetings between Italy and Japan

The four chapters that follow demonstrate how images of Japan are refashioned through time, oscillating between fascination and, occasionally, abjection.

In chapter 1, I look at three texts revolving around the events of the Russo-Japanese war of 1904–05, first examining the diary/novel of Italian-born Daniele Pecorini, who traveled in Korea and Japan as British Commissioner of the Imperial Maritime Customs Service, before turning to a compilation of Luigi Barzini Sr.'s dispatches from Manchuria and Tokyo written for *Corriere della Sera*, Italy's premier newspaper. Finally, the travel account by the "Baronessa di Villaurea," who visited Japan after the end of the hostilities, will introduce the perspective of gender and social class to the chapter. If Barzini was arguably one of the top war correspondents of the early twentieth century, Pecorini was a relatively unknown figure, a cosmopolitan adventurer who became a writer only at the end of his life. The result of his adventures are narrated in *Japanese Maple*, which was written in Italian but, oddly enough, first published in London in 1935 in English translation, with the original version coming out only posthumously in 1937. Despite their different profiles, both authors shared the difficult task of narrating their experiences of the Russo-Japanese war within a frame of reference that their Italian readers would be able to recognize.

In response to the lively debate on the notion of cosmopolitanism (James Clifford, Anthony K. Appiah, Bruce Robbins, Srinivas Aravamudan), it is argued in this chapter that both Pecorini and Barzini articulate a specific version of cosmopolitanism because, for different reasons, they were in need of establishing empathetic boundaries between Europe and Japan, especially in a moment when the East Asian country was proving itself capable of defeating a European superpower. In fact, despite the trauma of being spectators of a cruel war, the absence of cross-cultural shock is what defines the positive journey of discovery of these two European adventurers in the face of the inevitable cultural differences presented by the host country. While both tend to shy away from what they deem truly incomprehensible, they often dignify the Japanese, even to the extent of showing respect and empathy for their very diversity. In the first part of this chapter, on Pecorini's *Japanese Maple*, the focus is on the interplay of different ideological elements in the plot, including exoticism, nationalism and cosmopolitanism. But the conclusion is that, by stressing the protagonist's effort to learn the language of the visited country, to engage in personal conversations with locals and to introduce his readers to Japanese words in translation, Pecorini creates a cosmopolitan fictional character aimed at correcting Western propaganda against the "yellow peril," which the Japanese military victory against Russia had helped generate. The second section of the chapter turns to Luigi Barzini's war reports from Manchuria and Tokyo. In contrast with readings of Barzini's articles that present him as an Orientalist, it is argued here that Barzini's interviews with Japanese soldiers in translation were a cosmopolitan strategy aimed at moving the Italian public beyond the *fin de siècle* wave of aesthetic *japonisme*. Through this strategy, Barzini was attempting to pave the way for an aesthetic of diversity, which extended beyond racial and cultural biases (despite his own limitations in this regard).

In chapter 2, the focus is on travel literature on Japan during the Fascist period, with specific attention to the shift in the mode of representing Japan before and after the Anti-Comintern Pact between Italy, Germany and Japan of November 6, 1937. This historical event is the watershed moment that serves to separate the chapter in two sections. Before the ratification of the anti-communist pact, a nationalistic approach informed by a sense of Italian cultural supremacy defined the attitude of Italians writers who landed in the East Asian country. Thus, in this first section, I focus first on journalistic reports by Clemente Ferraris (*Al di là del Paese di Butterfly*, 1928) and Arnaldo Cipolla (*Per la Siberia in Cina e Giappone: racconto di viaggio*, 1924; *Nel Giappone dei grattacieli, viaggio da Tokio a Dehli*, 1931), then on two authors, Giovanni Comisso and Ercole Patti, who were both fiction writers working as special correspondents in Asia for the national papers *Gazzetta del Popolo* and *Corriere della Sera*. They both revisited their articles in order to republish them as books, whose titles stress the sexist image of Japan as an erotic Disneyland: Patti's *Ragazze di Tokio* (1934) and Comisso's *Donne gentili* (1958). The two authors were not aligned with the ideas of the regime, and their fictional stories were inspired by their journalistic production in Japan. Comisso published his journalistic writings as a novel, *Amori d'Oriente*, for the first time in 1949, in order to elude the Fascist censors. Despite all the evidence regarding their non-affiliation with the dictatorship and the use of fiction as a way to evade the propaganda authorities, a close reading emphasizes how images of Japan circulating during the *Ventennio* had a deep impact on their writings. Accordingly, in the chapter's second half I trace Mussolini's attempts to reshape the image of Japan in Italian public opinion. When the moment came for justifying the ideological basis for the Axis alliance, the Fascist regime also stressed cultural similarities, common political goals and long-standing historical relations.

Although propaganda and racial biases, both for and against the Japanese, are the dominant tone of these narratives, this chapter offers alternative perspectives that complicate the earlier Italian views of Japan. Despite his affiliation with the Fascist regime, Pietro Silvio Rivetta (1886–1952) seized the opportunity presented by the military alliance to reinforce his long-standing cultural project of introducing Japanese culture to Italy. Through widely accessible publications, Rivetta celebrated Japanese culture and explained its differences, not as intrinsically irrational, but as offering insights into the language, history and the people's customs. Finally, a call for a more nuanced assessment of this literary production is suggested by the case of Arundel Del Re (1892–1974), whose life spent across countries and continents exposed him to the pitfalls of his cosmopolitan identity (causing him to leave Japan), but also to an awareness of being part of a cultural network of connections and sense of belonging, from East to West, that transcend the limits posed by national borders.

Chapter 3 fast-forwards to the post-war years and the period of reconstruction, which featured rapid economic growth in both Italy and Japan. I look at the writings of Fosco Maraini, Goffredo Parise, Alberto Moravia and Italo Calvino through the ideological framework of continuity and change that was widely debated in Japan at the time of its rapid modernization. Anthropologists, sociologist and philosophers (Chie Nakane, Robert N. Bellah, Maruyama Masao, among others) in the 1960s debated the nature of the intensive Japanese recovery by highlighting the paradox of a society that was rapidly embracing modernization, democracy and a capitalist economy, while by the same token maintaining unaffected the major features of its traditional structure. The paradox of pursuing radical change and preserving continuity with the past was of particular interest to Italian observers because their society embraced a similar set of problems at the dawn of the foundation of the Italian Republic (1946). I contend that the Japanese model of societal evolution played a central role in the writing of Italians traveling to Japan in this period by virtue of generating a contrast with the Italian model of evolution, which was predicated upon rupture and displacement. During the 1950s and 1960s, Italy experienced similar economic development followed by an intense phenomenon of migration from the south to the cities driving the "economic miracle" in the north. The consequence of this rapid growth was unprecedented social and cultural transformations that engendered a perceived discontinuity with the past and a change in the national identity. I analyze this sense of disappointment among Italian intellectuals by referring to the thesis of Emilio Gentile in his essay *La Grande Italia: The Myth of the Nation in the 20th century* (1997). According to Gentile, at the outset of the new Republican government, leading Italian intellectuals suffered from an inferiority complex despite the fact that the democratic process was leading the country toward unexpected economic growth. As Fascism brought the nationalistic project of building "La grande Italia" to a tragic end, Italians came to terms with the fallacy of the nationalistic myth of continuity between the ancient Roman Empire and the modern colonialist project. In fact, I argue that the waning of the political dream that Mussolini's propaganda stirred up ultimately informed the social imaginary of Italians traveling to Japan.

The chapter begins by highlighting how this inferiority complex is played out in Fosco Maraini's *Japan: Patterns of Continuity* (1971), Alberto Moravia's journalistic reports from Japan and Goffredo Parise's novel *L'eleganza è frigida* (1982). Next, the framework of continuity and change is considered from the perspective of race and culture by comparing Parise's racial views with Italo Calvino's antithetical observations from his Japanese trip included in the volume *Collezione di sabbia* (1984). I focus on racial assumptions, as they emerge in Parise and Calvino's accounts of their separate journeys to Japan, to illustrate the ongoing process of redefining the concept of race in Italian society. The conclusion of the chapter advances the hypothesis of a neo-exotic wave of interest in Japan, predicated upon post-Marxist intellectuals' quest for areas of the world that (unlike Europe) had not yet fallen under the ideological and cultural dominion of the Cold War's bipolar order.

The book ends with a view of the journey in Japan from a female perspective. The few examples of Italian women writers in Japan are concentrated in the second half of the twentieth century, in particular the 1980s, with the increasing transformation of women's roles in both societies. As travel was traditionally conceived of as a male privilege and dominated by a male mode of narration, the chapter argues that the women's travelogs to Japan bring (although not always) a fresh perspective and an alternative look at Japanese society, with particular regard to the image of women.

For Japan and Italy the 1980s represented a decade of increasing prosperity and rapid modernization. This economic success implied rapid changes in societies in which traditional values and, above all, gender relations were reconsidered as the result of ongoing improvements in education and unprecedented material wealth. This chapter builds on the reactions that Italian women travelers experienced when observing a similar process of change in gender power relations in Japan. By contrasting Eurocentric views (Angela Staude) with cosmopolitan approaches (Antonietta Pastore), I show the shortcomings of a gender theory that poses essentializing differences between men and women's travel narratives, while at the same time recognizes in the woman traveler a "potential" ability to detect and, therefore, sanction inequalities and discrimination. The case of Antonietta Pastore is a demonstration of this last point, as her perspectives contradict traditional male fabricated tropes about Japanese women. Her books on her life in Japan are not only outspoken about gender inequalities, or differences, but they also reveal a sense of empathy and solidarity toward marginalized individuals (such as the *hibakusha*) that is unique among the authors examined here.

4. On Travel Writings

This study considers a wide array of sources: classical travelogs, novels, journalistic reports, propaganda pamphlets, cultural essays and so on. The authors of these texts travel to Japan for various reasons: some of them are simple tourists, others are journalists, academics, government officials, temporary workers, writers, etc. Because they all refer to, or imply, a physical journey through space, including a return home, they all belong to the genre of travel writing, which is, as Jonathan Raban famously puts it, "a notoriously raffish open house where different genres are likely to end up in the same bed" (Raban, 1987: 253). In this sense, "travel writing" is both a misleading and a valuable all-encompassing label. It is misleading because the physical journey from home to the final destination is a significant part of the genre's picaresque aspect. While mobility is not so much at stake in this study, the comparative cross-cultural framework that travel engenders is more so. On the other hand, traveling and living in Japan offer these writers the possibility to consider a different relationality, one not necessarily dominated by colonialist discourses. As Carl Thompson suggests, "Travel writing may enlighten and challenge readers, by revealing cultural and historical perspectives which have otherwise been overlooked or suppressed" (Thompson, 2011: 166). The following readings of Italian travelogs will bring to the fore perspectives that do not fit the binary logic of representing the "Other" in negative, or traditionally exotic terms, while by the same token acknowledging that contradictions and inconsistencies are likely to occur, given the inorganic nature of the genre itself. In spite of these shortcomings, this study will give priority to disruptive narratives that sidestep (rather than suppressing) physical distance, linguistic barriers and cultural differences to pose the creation of imagined communities, where Italians feel connected and in relation with the Japanese. This search for a Japan that is attractive to the Italian public does not apply simply to the realm of pure fantasy, but in fact generates new reconfigurations of both "nation" and "identity," drawing on sources that span far beyond the Mediterranean borders. In fact, the transnational networks situating Italy within the southern European region should not lead us to neglect an alternative Euro-Asian axis, which operated across Italian history.

Works Cited

Appiah, Kwame Anthony. 2006. *Cosmopolitanism: Ethics in a World of Strangers*. New York: W.W. Norton.

Arminjon, Vittorio. 1869. *Il Giappone e il viaggio della corvetta Magenta nel 1866: Coll'aggiunta dei trattati del Giappone e della China e relative tariffe*. Genova: Co tipi del R.I. dei sordo-muti.

Barthes, Roland. 1970. *L'empire des signes*. Genève, Switzerland: Albert Skira.

Bassnett, Susan. 2014. *Translation*. New York: Routledge.

Beck, Ulrich. 2006. *The Cosmopolitan Vision*, translated by Ciaran Cronin. Cambridge, UK and Malden, MA: Polity Press.

Berque, Augustin. 1993. *Du geste à la cité: formes urbaines et lien social au Japon*. Paris: Gallimard.

Bhabha, Homi. 2004 [1994]. *The Location of Culture*. Abingdon and New York: Routledge.

Bongie, Chris. 1991. *Exotic Memories: Literature, Colonialism and the Fin de Siècle*. Stanford: Stanford University Press.

Casanova, José. 2016. "The Jesuits through the prism of Globalization, Globalization through a Jesuit prism." In *The Jesuits and Globalization: Historical Legacies and Contemporary Challenges*, edited by Thomas Banchoff and José Casanova, 261–86. Washington, DC: Georgetown University Press.

Chow, Rey. 2006. *The Age of the World Target: Self-Referentiality in War, Theory, and Comparative Work*. Durham, NC: Duke University Press.

Clifford, James. 1992. "Traveling Cultures." In *Cultural Studies*, edited by Lawrence Grossberg, Cary Nelson and Paula A. Treichler, 96–116. New York and London: Routledge.

—. 1997. *Routes: Travel and Translation in the Late Twentieth Century*. Cambridge, MA: Harvard University Press.

Cronin, Michael. 2000. *Across the Lines: Travel, Language, Translation*. Cork, Ireland: Cork University Press.

Cumings, Bruce. 1993. "Archaeology, Descent, Emergence: Japan in British/American Hegemony, 1900–1950." In *Japan in the World*, edited by Masao Miyoshi and Harry Harootunian, 79–111. Durham, NC: Duke University Press.

Dainotto, Roberto M. 2007. *Europe (in Theory)*. Durham, NC: Duke University Press.

De Bary, William Theodore, Gluck, Carol and Tiedemann, Arthur E. 2001. *Sources of Japanese Tradition: Vol. 2. 1600–2000*. New York: Columbia University Press.

Farge, William J. and Doak, Kevin M. 2016. *A Christian Samurai*. Washington, DC: Catholic University of America Press.

Grewal, Inderpal. 1996. *Home and Harem: Nation, Gender, Empire, and the Cultures of Travel.* London: Leicester University Press.
Hester, Nathalie. 2008. *Literature and Identity in Italian Baroque Travel Writing.* Aldershot, UK; Burlington, VT: Ashgate.
Mignolo, Walter. 2002. "The many faces of Cosmo-Polis: border thinking and critical cosmopolitanism." In *Cosmopolitanism*, edited by Carol A. Breckenridge et al., 157–88. Durham, NC: Duke University Press.
Miyake, Toshio. 2010. *Occidentalismi: la narrativa storica giapponese.* Venice, Italy: Cafoscarina.
Pasolini, Pier Paolo. 1999. *Saggi sulla letteratura e sull'arte*, edited by Walter Siti and Silvia De Laude. Milan: Mondadori, 2 vols.
Polezzi, Loredana. 2001. *Translating Travel: Contemporary Italian Travel Writing in English Translation.* Burlington: Ashgate.
Polo, Marco. 2008. *The Travels of Marco Polo, the Venetian*, translated by William Marsden and revised by Thomas Wright; newly revised and edited by Peter Harris with an introduction by Colin Thubron. New York: Alfred A. Knopf.
Porter, Dennis. 1991. *Haunted Journeys: Desire and Transgression in European Travel Writing.* Princeton: Princeton University Press.
Pratt, Mary Louise. 2008 [1992]. *Imperial Eyes: Travel Writing and Transculturation.* New York: Routledge.
Raban, Jonathan. 1987. *For Love & Money: Writing, Reading, Travelling, 1969–1987.* London: Collins Harvill.
Ramadan, Tariq. 2015. "Cosmopolitan Theory and the Daily Pluralism of Life." In *Whose Cosmopolitanism?: Critical Perspectives, Relationalities and Discontents*, edited by Nina Glick Schiller and Andrew Irving, 57–64. New York: Berghahn Books.
Robbins, Bruce and Lemos Horta, Paulo. 2017. "Introduction." In *Cosmopolitanisms*, edited by Bruce Robbins and Paulo Lemos Horta; with an afterword by Kwame Anthony Appiah. New York: New York University Press.
Said, Edward W. 1995 [1978]. *Orientalism.* New York: Pantheon Books.
Samuels, Richard, J. 2003. *Machiavelli's Children: Leaders and their Legacies in Italy & Japan.* Cornell: Cornell University.
Simmel, Georg. 2007. "Florence." *Theory, Culture & Society*, 24(7–8): 38–41.
Shimoi, Harukichi. 1919. *La guerra italiana.* Naples: Libreria della Diana.
Spackman, Barbara. 2017. *Accidental Orientalists: Modern Italian Travelers in Ottoman Lands.* Liverpool: Liverpool University Press.
Stutler, Ross. 2012. "Kirishitan Sites in Tokyo." Available at www.stutler.cc/russ/kirishitan.html (accessed on June 24, 2018).

Suter, Rebecca. 2015. *Holy Ghosts: The Christian Century in Modern Japanese Fiction*. Honolulu: University of Hawaii Press.

Sweet, David LeHardy. 2017. *Avant-garde Orientalism: The Eastern "Other" in Twentieth-Century Travel Narrative and Poetry*. Cham, Switzerland: Palgrave Macmillan.

Taylor, Charles. 2004. *Modern Social Imaginaries*. Durham, NC; London: Duke University Press.

Thompson, Carl. 2011. *Travel Writing*. London and New York: Routledge.

Wells, Herbert George. 1905. *A Modern Utopia*, with illustrations by E.J. Sullivan. New York: Charles Scribner's Sons.

Wilson, Rob and Dissanayake, Wimal. 1996. "Introduction." In *Global/Local: Cultural Production and the Transnational Imaginary*, edited by Rob Wilson and Wimal Dissanayake, 1–18. Durham, NC: Duke University Press.

CHAPTER ONE

Cosmopolitan Possibilities in Translation: Views from the Russo-Japanese War

> Supériorité? Infériorité? Pourquoi tout simplement ne pas essayer de toucher l'autre, de sentir l'autre, de me révéler l'autre? Ma liberté ne m'est-elle donc pas donnée pour édifier le monde du Toi?
>
> (Frantz Fanon, *Peau noire, masques blancs*)

1. Introduction

In this chapter I turn to three texts revolving around the events of the Russo-Japanese war of 1904–05. Two of them are set at the time of the military confrontation: on the one hand the diary/novel of Daniele Pecorini, who traveled in Korea and Japan as British Commissioner of the Imperial Maritime Customs Service, and on the other hand, Luigi Barzini's dispatches from Manchuria and Tokyo written for *Corriere della Sera*, Italy's most important newspaper. The third text chronicles the journey of the Baronessa di Villaurea, a Sicilian woman who independently traveled to Japan in 1908 and published an account of her adventures after returning home.

If Luigi Barzini was arguably the most popular Italian journalist at the time and one of the top war correspondents of the early twentieth century, Daniele Pecorini was a relatively unknown figure, a cosmopolitan adventurer who turned himself into a writer at the end of his life. Despite their different profiles, both authors shared the difficult task of narrating their experiences of the Russo-Japanese war within a frame of references that their Italian readers would be able to recognize. Even when the difficulties of linguistic translation are sidestepped by presenting texts that seem to ignore the burden of interlingual communication, the problem of finding a coping strategy to elude the sense of displacement, or the cultural gaps that are untranslatable in the process of "writing cultures," is relevant for both authors. Here it is useful to remind what Clifford Geertz says about the fact that "we can never apprehend another people's or another period's imagination neatly, as though it were our own," since each culture exists within the limits of a signifying system that includes language. However, Geertz continues, we can achieve a great deal of knowledge about another culture "not by looking behind the interfering glosses that connect us to it but through them" (Geertz, 1993: 44). This analysis concerns the "interfering glosses" that make the cultural translation intelligible to the target audience. Both authors are proponents of individual cosmopolitan ethics in an effort to describe the humanity of the Japanese to Italian readers, as a way to defuse the global syndrome of "yellow peril" that emerged in the aftermath of the Russo-Japanese war. In fact, cultural differences are not perceived as irrational behavior, as the authors are open to negotiating their respective diversity. Even though occasionally they pay lip service to popular representations of Japan in the West, they are determined to undermine essentializing differences between East Asia and Europe.

With this military victory, Japan sent waves around the world that prompted Western tourists to visit the new rising power. From a small town in Sicily the Baronessa di Villaurea set out to explore Japan in 1908. Her narrative calls the reader to compare her journey to the exotic views of Pierre Loti's *Madame Chrysanthème*, or Giacomo Puccini's *Madama Butterfly*, which was at that time becoming a global success. While she warns her readership of the possible decline of Puccini's traditional Japan, where doll-like Japanese girls play the role of faithful lovers to the point of death, she also resorts to a coeval exotic narrative (see the Introduction) to reassure her public about the survival of the old Japan in the present. In this case, her "interfering glosses" are directed toward representatives of her social class, who are eager to read stories about old social privileges outliving current historical transformations.

2. Daniele Pecorini's *Japanese Maple*

Japanese Maple is a semi-fictional account of Daniele Pecorini's experience in Korea and Japan during the Russo-Japanese war. The plot is divided into two distinct sections: the beginning and the end of the book chronicle Japan's secret preparations leading up to the conflict, followed by the eyewitness narration of the crucial naval battle of Tsushima. The central part is dedicated to a love story between the protagonist and a local geisha, which comprehends a love journey through the southern regions of Japan, between Shimonoseki and Kobe, aboard a ship named *The Lotus Blossom*. The first section paints a personal perspective of macro-historical events, showing the cunning strategy and hatred of the "white race" (195) that supposedly inspired the Japanese decision to wage a war against Russia. The second section is an account of a personal love story that is based on real events (Figure 1) and narrates the protagonist's happy encounters with locals and his love for Japanese culture.

About the life of Daniele Pecorini (1872–1936) and the circumstances related to the late publication of his book *Japanese Maple* (1935), very little is known. He was born in Padua to the noble family Pecorini-Manzoni and in his hometown he studied law. Instead of pursuing a forensic career, Pecorini decided to give an adventurous spin to his life by embarking on a bike tour around Europe. Eventually he landed in London where he successfully applied for the position of Officer of the British Commissioner of Customs in China. In 1897 he was sent to Shanghai, then moved to Beijing to study Chinese and to discover with great pleasure the beauty of China's art, until he reluctantly had to accept his superior's decision to appoint him to a post in Korea. At the beginning of *Japanese Maple*, Pecorini's autobiographical character explains that as an employee of the British Empire in East Asia, he unwillingly had to be complicit with the Anglo-Japanese plan to destroy the Russian fleet in order to establish the supremacy of the Korean peninsula. At the end of the war in 1905 Pecorini returned to Shanghai where he spent five more years of service until he eventually made his way back to Italy. Based in Rome, Pecorini became the ambassador for China while pursuing the goal of forming a collection of Asian art. In Rome he lived with his wife, the American painter Margaret Bucknell (1879–1963), daughter of the tycoon William Bucknell. In this later part if his life Daniele Pecorini lived between Italy and the United States, becoming an international fine art dealer with a special focus on Chinese art. In 1929 he co-authored the English edition of *The Game of Wei-Chi*, which is still considered today the most accurate description of the ancient Chinese game for English readers. He spent the last years of his life in his hometown Bassano del Grappa, near Padua, until his death in 1936.

It was only at the end of his life that Pecorini thought again about the time spent in Korea and Japan by writing the autobiographical novel. *Japanese Maple* was published first in London in 1935 in English translation, then in the original Italian in 1937. Certainly, by publishing his manuscript abroad, Pecorini addressed the Italian Fascist community in England,[1] while at the same time he appealed to English readers by selling his book in a country where the genre of "travel literature" was significantly more popular than it was in Italy. Arguably the publication in the UK of *Japanese Maple* was meant to follow the same path of commercial success inaugurated by Isabella Bird's *Unbeaten Tracks in Japan* (1880), whose popularity is reflected in the large number of new editions that have continued to be printed in the UK until today. The narrative plots of the two travelogs take into account the allure for exotic stories set in East Asia for a British audience. In fact, they both attempt to introduce the reader to an exotic region of Japan not yet contaminated by the quick process of modernization and opening to Western influence that is characteristic of the Meiji period. Isabella Bird travels to the lesser known northern regions where the native population of the Ainu live, seeking a meeting with a supposedly untainted Japanese culture and ethnicity. Pecorini, on the other hand, at the core of his novel moves away from the war zone, where the Japanese navy is overpowering the Russian fleet, and sets the love story between the main character Paolo and his local lover Fuji in the primitive space of an inland Japanese lake. Rapture with the exotic is only one element in common between the two books; the other is the growing sense of the threat that Japanese imperialistic ambitions represent to Western powers and a subsequent desire to warn the British audience of this danger. In a study on Bird's revisions of *Unbeaten Tracks in Japan* (1880; 1885; 1900), Steve Clark has demonstrated that the Victorian writer gradually becomes more alert to the Japanese plan of belligerent expansion with each succeeding draft (Clark, 2015: 17–34). Similarly, Pecorini offers a retroactive – having published the novel in 1935 – and even more explicit interpretation of the Russo-Japanese war as a single episode of Japan's broader strategy of building an Asian empire.

Besides the reasons determining his choice, the English translation of a work of travel literature written for an Italian audience invites a reflection at large on the effect of the book on the target audience. In fact, the relation between travel writing and translation is by no means a simple matter of expanding access to the book to a wider group of readers, but it implies a renegotiation of the relation between the narrator and the readers. As

---

1   The Fascist intellectual Camillo Pellizzi was founder and member of the Italian *Fasci* in London (1925–38), where he held a position of lecturer in Italian at University College London (1920–38).

Loredana Polezzi has pointed out, "travel writing is essentially directed to the home audience and posited on the identification between the point of view of the reader and the one of the traveler/narrator" (Polezzi, 2001: 92). While "traveling" to a different language, the translated text must adapt to an alternative cultural system and meet a different set of expectations that are generated by the new audience. Indeed, a cultural identity is not a stable and invariable image, but it takes place in the hybrid space of what Mary Louise Pratt calls "contact zones," that is, an area of encounter where individuals and groups attempt to describe themselves to one another, resulting in the creation of new discourses. The point of view of the traveler/narrator is contingent on his own cultural and political identity. As James Clifford observes: "in most cases, what matters politically is who deploys nationality or transnationality, authenticity or hybridity, against whom" (Clifford, 1997: 10). Clifford's ethnographic theory is predicated upon the idea that travel is the ground on which cultural encounters and mutual representations are carried out, conferring on translation the function of representing cultures. In this respect, the work of the translator as mediator between cultures plays a crucial role.

However, the case of *Japanese Maple* complicates the scenario by presenting an author whose choice is to publish his original manuscript in English translation, in fact avoiding reaching out to the Italian audience that is often indirectly addressed by the narrator. The name of the Italian protagonist, Paolo, seems to be inspired by a Gabriele D'Annunzio's novel (for example, "Paolo Tarsis" in *Forse che sì Forse che no* [1910]), and his love affair at the beginning of the novel with the wife of an American missionary in Korea is consistent with the hedonistic characters of Dannunzian narrative. Even though he is in the service of the English Crown, Paolo refuses to pass as British by marking very clearly his Italian national identity. The English translation presents a text that is overtly critical of British imperialism abroad and does not indulge in any sympathy for the target audience. At the beginning Paolo makes no mystery of his frustration with the British decision to send him to Korea: "He felt insignificant, discontented, humiliated to have to play the Englishman's game" (1935: 6). More than just a personal issue, Paolo blames the British monarchy for the short-sighted alliance with the Japanese against Russia as he foresees a future racial conflict between the "yellow race" and the "white race":

> After living for many years in the Far East he had come to see that the yellow instinctively despise and hate the white races.

Only a few years earlier, the Boxer rising of 1900 should have opened European eyes and made them realize that the yellow peril was truer and greater than the short-sighted English diplomats could see. The hatred of the yellow for the white was a fact bound to have terrible consequences sooner or later. (1935: 195)

By publishing the novel in 1935, as Japanese imperialistic aspirations materialized in the invasion of Manchuria (1931) and the creation of the puppet state Manchukuo in 1932, Pecorini projects a shadow back on to the origin of Japanese imperialism in which he finds Britain accountable for having favored the rising of such a nationalistic superpower. From the same retroactive perspective, it is clear that the reason of such anti-British sentiment in the above-quoted passage lies in the tensions between Anglo-American powers and Italy in the 1930s as Mussolini was facing the opposition of the League of Nations (led by Britain) in his attempt to legitimatize his colonial aspirations. While it is dubious that Pecorini had any sympathy for the military campaign in Ethiopia, it is undeniable that a strong nationalistic and Fascist spirit nourishes his anti-British sentiment.[2] The root of such nationalism is highlighted in the plot of the novel by the contrast between Paolo and the Irish-British Imperial Commissioner Patrick O'Connor. While the former is adamant in stressing his Italian nationality and marking his uncompromising diversity from the British, O'Connor on the contrary chooses a radical disavowal of his Irish identity seeking to "pass" as British. The contrasting points of view come to the fore in a snapping dialog, in which O'Connor claims his allegiance to the English Crown and mocks the Italian Paolo:

> I should hate to belong to an unimportant country like Holland or Belgium or Italy [...] You Italians would do better if you attached yourself to us. If you could say that you were under our protection no one would dare to touch you. If you don't, the French cock, one of these fine days, will have a peck at the Italian hen. (78)

---

2   In a letter of 1932 to the Scottish business man and philanthropist Sir David Russell (1872–1956), Pecorini expresses his enthusiasm for the Fascist government: "I wish you were coming to Italy soon. You would see wonders in Rome, a 'novus ordo,' new broad roads all over Italy, and schools and hospitals every where [sic]. With a powerful grasp Mussolini has shaken Italy from the dead waters, and put it on firm ground to work and to hope for" (Daniele Pecorini, letter to David Russell, Rome, November 7, 1932. Courtesy of the University of St Andrews Library, Scotland (UK), Box 5, folder 4 ms. 3815-3, Papers of Sir David Russell).

Paolo's answer is peppered with nationalistic discourse, reviving the myth of Italy as the heir of the Roman Empire, on one hand, and stressing the virility of the *identità italica* on the other:

Ever since manhood counted in the struggle between man and man the Italian hen has pecked at plenty of other cocks and torn out their feathers, and even your own island bears marks of the Roman hen. (79)

From this and from other passages we can definitively infer that the book was geared toward the Italian target audience, therefore the English translation must be seen as anti-British, especially at a time when England was opposing, through the League of the Nations, both Italy and Japan in their decisions to invade respectively Ethiopia (1935) and Manchuria (1931). Paolo's nationalistic tone – his insistence on embodying the "ardent Italian temperament" (10) and being a "true Italian" (11) – lays the foundation for the exotic representation of Japan.

On first impressions, exoticism seems to contradict nationalism, in fact exoticism underlines what is foreign and diverse, while nationalism reaches out to readers of the author's home country by stressing what is intelligible and familiar. However, since at least the publication of Said's *Orientalism*, exoticism has been typically associated with colonialism and has become a popular term in postcolonial studies for explaining the fetish and the commodification of the Oriental "Other" in Western fictional travel accounts. In this sense, Paolo's trip in one of the most remote parts of Japan, after he seduces a local beauty, is no exception. As the plot shifts from the Russo-Japanese war to this romantic story, exoticism and nationalism are tightly intertwined.

This section begins when Paolo leaves Fusan in Korea for a month's vacation in Japan. One night, while in Nagasaki, he manages to seduce a geisha named Fuji and, having instantly fallen in love with her, he decides to pay the price for her freedom. Subsequently, the two lovers decide to set out on a journey to a remote and dreamlike area of the inland lakes of Japan, going from one island to another, aiming to arrive at Kobe, where Fuji's mother lives. By exoticism I intend a kind of containment strategy, whereby the shock, mixed with desire, for the discovery of the vastness and diversity of the world is contained by reference to a catalog of images and objects made or imported in the West, aimed at representing the Orient. Exotic representations focus on whatever is pleasing and amusing in the eyes of the beholder, while ignoring everything else. Even though in Pecorini's case the exotic discourse is not instrumental to national colonial expansion – as it is considered in Said's *Orientalism* – Eurocentric stereotypes and European perspectives still substantially inform its syntax. First of all, the choice of setting for the exotic plot is indicative of the Western fear for the decline of the exotic itself, as a result of rising global capitalism and mass tourism, as well as colonial enterprises. These entropic fears of losing the experience of anthropological diversity drive Pecorini away from the already "Westernized" Japan to the inner regions of the country between Shimonoseki and Kobe. In such a primeval setting, Pecorini relies on the pan-European aesthetic movement of infatuation with Japanese art, known as *japonisme*, to narrate the love story between Paolo and Fuji. The romantic plot features first the two lovers in tender discovery of their mutual passion; then, at the apex of the romantic plot, Paolo begins to feel homesick and it soon becomes clear that he does not want to live the rest of his life in Japan with Fuji or to live with her in Europe. At this point Fuji, in order to avoid Paolo's heartbreaking dilemma between staying with her in Japan and going back to his country, decides to end her life, facilitating his choice to return home.

The ingredients of this love story are unmistakably connected to the literary paradigm of Oriental travel and adventure that Pierre Loti helped create with many of his novels. In these Japonist *fin de siècle* fictions, normally "a Western male meets exotic females, possesses her, and abandons her; Western male departs (usually unscathed by his experience) whilst foreign female, irreparably altered, is left to languish and die" (Forsdick, 2000: 52). When confronted with radical diversity, Pecorini plunges into a Western (mainly French) Japonist aesthetic to represent his journey with Fuji, in order to relate better with his audience.

The well-known phenomenon called *japonisme* first arose in the second half of the nineteenth century in the field of fine arts, in response to the wave of Japanese woodblock prints arriving in Europe. Especially popular was Hokusai's *Manga*, a small instructional book whose pages were decorated with drawings of animals, birds and plants. Therefore, the first manifestation of interest in the Japanese world in Europe was directed toward its woodblock prints, not to its culture and literature (the latter being latent because few works of translation were available until the 1920s).[3]

---

3   Appreciation of Japanese art in France in particular followed a reverse chronological order, because "British and German scholars, and Japanese government officials, countered that the woodblock was a vulgar art form, having originated only recently in the late eighteenth century, and that it should be considered at best a minor form": Walsh J. Hokenson, 2004, *Japan, France, and East–West Aesthetics: French Literature, 1867–2000* (Madison, NJ: Fairleigh Dickinson University Press): 121.

Fig. 1   Daniele Pecorini and his lover Fuji
(photo property of the Manzoni-Pecorini family)

Nevertheless, in literature, as well as in painting, French Naturalists, Impressionists and post-Impressionists, introduced a minor and vulgar Japanese art to generate modern aesthetics. In Pierre Loti's Oriental tales, the description of an artwork is often instrumental in creating the exotic atmosphere. Loti thus inverts the usual way of considering representation as a function of the real by noticing how the "real" is similar to its remembered aesthetic image. This Orientalist attitude of privileging Japanese representations and elevating them to the level of the *tableaux vivants* of Japanese society, while ignoring the cultural context behind the artistic production, is strikingly present in Pecorini's account of his love escapade. Thus, the experience of being one of the first Europeans to visit a lesser known Japanese region is translated through the reference to *Manga*'s sketches: "Paolo was seeing now the *Manga* in actuality. Villagers, fishermen, farm workers, woodcutters, priests, geishas – all looked to him like the living embodiment of these drawings" (112). The conflation of reality and aesthetic representation generates pleasure that consists in arousing Paolo's expectations, as well as the expectations of the reader. The point of view of the traveler/translator is here identified with that of the reader, resulting in an effacement of the presence of the "Other." In this regard Jonathan Culler has pointed out that the experience of meeting the traveler's expectations is one of the secrets of the travel industry, in so far as it transforms the common traveler into a semiotician seeking to inscribe images into signs: "All over the world the unsung armies of semioticians, the tourists, are fanning out in search of the signs of Frenchness, typical Italian behavior, exemplary Oriental scenes, typical American thruways, traditional English pubs" (Culler, 1981: 127). Commenting on this passage Michael Cronin notices how "Culler's semioticians are looking for visual not linguistic presence of otherness" (Cronin, 2000: 83). In fact, in *Japanese Maple* the language of the "Other" is offered in translation, as the narrator's voice is endowed with the authority of translating Fuji's voice. The presence of linguistic difference, as well as the uncertainties and gaps that the traveler/translator must face, are eliminated by virtue of an "invisible" translator who operates on behalf and for the sake of the reader at home.[4] In the case of Paolo, the traveler-narrator himself carries out the task of the translation, without recurring to any interpreter. Paolo, in the relationship with Fuji, is in the position of "linguistic transcendence," as he is the one who is able to learn the language of the visited country. It is the voice of the narrator that informs the reader that Paolo "knew enough Japanese to understand her poetic thoughts" (103).

3. Beyond Exoticism

Paolo's effort to deepen his knowledge of the visited country to the extent of mastering the language allows an alternative interpretation of this exotic plot, leading to a different conclusion from the consideration we have been outlining so far. In *Japanese Maple*, exoticism should not invite a monolithic analysis that necessarily associates it with a superficial absorption of the Oriental "Other," from a Eurocentric and colonial perspective. The opposite movement is also possible, featuring a notion of exoticism in which it is the central, Western translator/traveler subject who is "absorbed into the periphery" (Forsdick, 2000: 38) of the foreign culture. According to

---

4 "The critical literature on travel writing has, over the decades, strangely neglected the question of language in travel writing (Cronin, 2000). The omission is all the more curious in that even the most unreflective experience of foreign travel leads to the traveler having to find a coping strategy for dealing with the foreign language": Michael Cronin, 2003, *Translation and Globalization* (New York: Routledge): 153.

this xenophilic notion of exoticism, the unknown, alien culture is exalted in opposition to the known and familiar national culture. Paolo's exotic adventure with Fuji is located somewhere in between these two opposite poles. On the one hand Paolo continues to be aware of his *italianità*; on the other, he is willing to yield his selfhood to intercultural hybridity. In contrast with Paolo's previous attitude of refusal toward any form of contamination with British culture, the exotic setting and the love story help achieve the extraordinary result of Paolo's passing as non-Italian, almost as Japanese:

> There was nothing to remind him that he was a European. Ever since leaving Shimonoseki he had worn the kimono, had dressed, spoken and lived like a Japanese. A whole age seemed to separate him from his earlier life. A volume of Dante – an inseparable companion – was his only memento of that former existence. (127)

While the traditional notion of exoticism emphasizes anything that is foreign and irreconcilable with the home culture, here the narration builds a comparative framework in which differences are molded and the evidence of an unexpected common ground gradually emerges. If Paolo is at ease speaking Japanese and wearing a kimono, on the other hand Fuji identifies Paolo's gentle manners with Shintoist virtues that are familiar to her: "Fuji adored him. She saw and admired in him all the Shintoist virtues; gentleness towards her and everyone else, and even towards animals" (109). As the love story unfolds, Pecorini is less concerned with replicating Pierre Loti's Orientalist stereotypes as a way of making sense of an otherwise incomprehensible reality; instead in his effort to explain the unknown experience he resorts to the artifice of connecting the two distinct cultural spheres. For instance, while he is explaining to readers the traditional Japanese notion of *seppuku*, that is, the practice of committing suicide as the ultimate way to preserve a samurai's honor, Pecorini tries to make the concept less unfamiliar for the Italian reader by mentioning a similar example of heroic death in Italian history, that of Pietro Micca, who – as Pecorini reminds us – "threw himself into the midst of the enemy with bombs tied to his shoulders" (125). This Italian hero was a Piedmontese soldier who in 1706 prevented a plot by French troops to assault the city of Turin by detonating two barrels of gunpowder into a mine gallery, after first rescuing his comrades. Needless to say how inappropriate this single example is in explaining the practice of *seppuku*, but what it is relevant here is the interfering cultural gloss that stresses commonality over diversity, affinity over difference.

The strategy of translating a foreign term by means of a supposedly similar term in the target language represents a case of what Lawrence Venuti calls the "domesticating method" of translation, which consists of "an ethnocentric reduction of the foreign text to target-language cultural values, bringing the author back home." On the opposite pole, the "foreignizing" approach represents an "ethnodeviant pressure on those values to register the linguistic and cultural difference of the foreign text, sending the reader abroad" (Venuti, 1995: 20). Loredana Polezzi has adapted terms such as "foreignization" and "domestication," used to describe the work of translation, to the textual practices of travel writing. She argues against the bias of deeming positive in themselves translating solutions that aim to show the complexity and partiality of the intralingual communicative process, at the expense of the fluency of the translation. Using foreign words in the travel account, as well as in a work of translation, does not necessarily result in an effect of displacement and estrangement for the reader; in fact can produce the opposite reaction of fostering the trend of repeating a few well-known words from the visited country, so as to reproduce the atmosphere of the exotic Oriental tale. Pecorini does not represent an exception in this regard, as words such as *geisha*, *maiko* or *mousmee* are scattered throughout the text. However, while in these examples Pecorini opts for a smooth and domesticating strategy of translation, sometimes he also uses a foreignizing strategy, choosing not to translate words, thus breaking the illusion of the pure cultural translation. For instance, when the narrator attempts to explain the fundamental characteristics of the Japanese personality, he dedicates an entire paragraph to the Japanese word *omoshiroi*. After having translated the word *omoshiroi* as "funny" and "interesting," he eventually admits that no Italian word can offer a valid translation of the term. Accepting Polezzi's argument that the decision not to translate words must not always be deemed positive, in this case the choice of exposing the reader to the complexity of the work of the translator retains the ethical value of representing the diversity of the foreign culture in a positive fashion. In fact, *omoshiroi* does not belong to the Orientalist vocabulary of Pierre Loti's erotic *japonisme*; on the contrary, this term discloses what Pecorini considers the secret of the Japanese zest for life. Anthony Appiah has defined the notion of "cosmopolitanism" as an "ethic in a world of strangers"; in this respect Pecorini's ethical move consists of crossing the cultural boundaries to highlight the diversity of the "Other," while retaining the possibility of learning from such experiences.

4. Truths, Lies and the Cosmopolitan Possibilities

To conclude, *Japanese Maple* narrates the extraordinary experience of an Italian adventurer in Korea and Japan during the 1904–05 Russo-Japanese war; however, the love story between Paolo and Fuji represents the core of the novel. The division of the plot into two distinct parts reflects a contrasting order of representation of the Japanese. When the plot focuses on the war, Pecorini resorts to a racist portrait of the Japanese "Other," using the formula of the "yellow peril," or describing the Japanese as cunning and untrustworthy. When the narration moves to the love story, Pecorini resorts to outlining an exotic plot that cannot be dismissed as patronizing and Eurocentric, because it displays an attempt to spark an interest in a foreign culture and to represent the visited country in a comparative framework, rather than in a binary contrast. Traditional exotic novels focus on a fictionalized "Other," that is the result of projecting Western aesthetics and phantasies onto the unknown country visited. Pecorini's exoticism highlights a fictionalized "Self" traveler/translator who explores the possibilities of Western culture's encountering the East Asian world. Paolo is the name of the character that Pecorini invents in order to perform a self-representation, while at the same times blurring the boundaries between the real account of the voyage and the imaginary travel narrative. In other words, the appeal of the novel does not consist in the degree of truthfulness of the story, but in the cosmopolitan possibilities that are represented.

The ambiguity of the relation between Paolo/traveler and Pecorini/narrator brings to the fore the cogent issue of subjectivity in the genre of travel literature. Susan Bassnett has pointed out that "authenticity" is a basic requirement for a successful travel narrative:

> Authenticity, the truthful account by a traveler of what he or she sees, is presented as a fundamental element of travel writing. Readers are invited to share an experience that has actually happened. When we read a travel account, we do not expect to read a novel; rather we assume that the author will be documenting his/her experience in another culture. But the dialogues are so often patently invented that authenticity begins to dissolve. We could say that one of the bases upon which travel writing rests, is the collusion of writer and reader in a notion of authenticity, that is the reader agrees to suspend disbelief and go along with the writer's pretence. (Bassnett and Lefevere, 1998: 35)

The claim of "authenticity" is a fundamental premise of Pecorini's travelog as he makes it clear in a private letter, announcing to his friend the imminent publication of *Japanese Maple*:

> You will read in it of a rather strange life in a strange world, but it is a real picture of what was happening in those hey-days of my life which was after all more or less the life of many others in the Far-East. You, that will read in short pages a compendium of that wild life, which I passed through in my juvenile days, when quite a different one from what I am now, please give my story that fair and kind consideration and do not weigh with the scruple balance, which was given away by the ton.[5]

While the author remarks on the truthfulness of his story, he also admits that his account is based on a selection of episodes (a "compendium") chosen with the intention to inscribe his narration within the genre of Oriental tales ("the life of many others in the Far-East"). The result is so distant from Pecorini's current persona and life that he feels the need to justify the claim of authenticity by evoking the existence of a "juvenile" "Self." At the core of *Japanese Maple* lies an ambiguity between fiction and non-fiction, or between plot and story; in this regard, Susan Bassnett's concept of "collusion" between author and reader helps explain why the author does not need to provide historical evidence of his account. In fact, the invention of the persona "Paolo" is a narrative device that grants the author a fictional "Self," who is free to craft the plot in order to meet the reader's requests for an exotic story. Ironically, the more the plot responds to the expectations of the target culture, the less readers will question the authenticity of the account.

In this partial and domestic representation of the other culture, travel literature and translation studies share a common feature of being mediators of cultures. Again, in Susan Bassnett's words, travel literature "is the genre

---

5   Pecorini, Daniele. Letter to David Russell. Rome, July 27, 1935. Courtesy of the University of St Andrews Library, Scotland (UK), Box 5, folder 4 ms. 3815-3, Papers of Sir David Russell. In the preface of the Italian edition of *Japanese Maple* we read a similar statement about the authenticity of Pecorini's account: "Questo libro è soprattutto (sebbene in terza persona) l'ampio e fedele diario di un italiano che osservò e ricorda lucidamente queste vicende. Non solo; ma questo libro è un raro e prezioso contributo storico, in quanto sostiene notizie inedite di capitale importanza sulla guerra russo-giapponese, dall'osservatore italiano, vissute in un ambiente dove, per la particolare ed elevata sua posizione, egli aveva il privilegio di conoscere ed ebbe la fortuna di poter narrare" (Pecorini, 1937: viii).

in which individual strategies employed by writers deliberately to construct images of other cultures for consumption by readers can be most clearly seen" (Bassnett and Lefevere, 1998: 138). On the other hand, Lawrence Venuti has pointed out that "translations never simply communicate foreign texts because they make possible only a domesticated understanding, however much defamiliarized, however much subversive or supportive of the domestic" (Venuti, 2009: 360). As travel literature and translation studies share the limits of their cultural practice, they are also similar in pursuing "the Utopian dream of a common understanding between foreign and domestic cultures" (Venuti, 2009: 371). The word "cosmopolitan" best describes the idea that this chapter illustrates. In fact, as a word of Greek origin, cosmopolitan means "citizen of the world," thus carrying in itself the utopia of a nomadic individual living in a homogeneous world. Both translation and travel literature show their own being "situated" in a specific cultural area, yet they purport the notion that people from different parts of the world can share knowledge of each other, speaking from their situated points of view.

In Daniele Pecorini's *Japanese Maple* there is at least one example of this idea of cosmopolitanism that is less a universalistic ideology and more an impulse, in Bruce Robbins' words, to "transcend partiality that is in itself partial" (Robbins, 2009: 323) among diverse people in a mutual and reciprocal fashion. In a Shintoist temple on Oshima Island, Paolo and Fuji have an encounter with a Buddhist monk, whose kind attitude and friendly manners turn into excitement upon learning that an Italian guest is visiting him:

> When Fuji said that Paolo was an Italian the priest expressed his pleasure, adding that Italy was the most cultured country in the West and that the capital, Rome, was the mistress of the world. Paolo was surprised and asked him if he knew anything of Italian literature, whereupon the priest replied that Dante was the greatest poet there had ever been. It was with lively emotion that Paolo heard that shaven head speak with so much love of Italy and Dante. He asked the priest if he had ever seen an edition of Dante, and when he replied "No," Paolo invited him on board to show him his copy. The priest accepted the invitation, and Paolo showed him the small leather-bound volume. The priest looked at it carefully, observed the smallness of the print, and then with his closed eyes lifted it above his head in an attitude of the greatest respect and reverence. "Today I have been vouchsafed a special grace," he remarked when taking his leave, "and if you will come to the temple tomorrow I shall be very pleased to see you." He departed, bowing, much pleased with his adventure. (128)

The cosmopolitan possibility that takes place in the temple is what triggers Paolo's surprised reaction. In fact, the experience of having a conversation with a Japanese monk who knows Dante and has familiarity with Italian culture counteracts Pecorini's interest in Japanese culture, resulting in a mutual attraction. This cross-cultural encounter is an uncanny experience for Paolo because it breaks the binary division of traveler/native by posing the latter as someone whose culture is already contaminated and connected on a global scale. Conversely, by traveling through Japan the Italian Paolo discovers that his own culture has preceded him, therefore he comes to realize that Italian culture has gone global, by virtue of an increasingly far-reaching network of international press and publishing houses. This reciprocal cultural encounter complicates the traditional notion of cosmopolitanism predicated upon the universal values of humanity, by pointing in the direction of what James Clifford defines as a "discrepant cosmopolitanism." While traditional cosmopolitanism features a Western elite class of travelers engaging with local cultures, this different approach to the subject is concerned with the multiple expressions of cosmopolitanism that involve travelers and non-travelers, as cultures also "travel" around the globe, resulting in an unpredictable map of connections. In Clifford's words, "The notion that certain classes of people are cosmopolitan (travelers) while the rest are locals (natives) appears as the ideology of one (very powerful) traveling culture" (Clifford, 1997: 36). Nevertheless, the limit of this interaction is located in the voice of the narrator who translates the dialog. As the characters are lacking their own voices, it is inevitable that the narrator interpreting the scene is setting the stage for a domesticated representation, in which the monk's appreciation for Dante is meant to imply a paean of the homeland.

While it is true that even the most scientific ethnographic account – let alone a travelog – is based on a selection of episodes, and therefore a principle of exclusion is operating to satisfy the partial view of a community of readers, the creation of a fictional character suggests that the author is conscious of the mixture of truths and lies deployed in his narrative. It must be said that the corresponding cosmopolitan identity that is generated carries the stain of being unstable and full of contradictions. In fact, the hybrid relationship between Paolo and Fuji ends up unraveling all of the perfect mosaic of East–West integration on which it was premised at the outset. Eventually Paolo begins to feel homesick and, upon planning his return home, he dismisses the idea of bringing Fuji along, on the ground that she may not be able to adapt living in a foreign country.

Nevertheless, *Japanese Maple* succeeds in its attempt of moving beyond exoticism and nationalism by transcending the bounds of Italian cultural particularity. The cosmopolitan character that Pecorini creates for his exotic plot represents a counterfactual fiction aimed at correcting the cultural bashing that the Russo-Japanese war was about to generate. If concerns for the rise of the Japanese empire are at the root of Western propaganda against the "yellow peril," the creation of an exotic plot aims at breaking through those divisions through the creation of a fictional "Self" that explores the possibility of global citizenship.

5. Luigi Barzini, War Correspondent

While Pecorini observed the unfolding of military operations from a safe distance, a closer view of the events of the Russo-Japanese war was offered by the Italian journalist Luigi Barzini Sr. (1874–1947). As a reporter for the *Corriere della Sera*, Barzini was sent onto the battlefield with the task of narrating the day-to-day operations of the Japanese army in Manchuria and from Tokyo. At the time of the conflict Luigi Barzini was a thirty-year old journalist with an already well-established career. He was born in Orvieto in 1874 and, after a few years as cartoonist, he joined *Corriere della Sera* in 1898. The young new director Luigi Albertini (only a few years older than Barzini) was undertaking an ambitious project of creating a newspaper that could live up to the professional standards of quality and breadth of the best British press. With this idea in mind, Albertini sent his inexperienced employee to London to learn about the English style of journalism. Barzini worked as a correspondent from London until 1900, when Albertini decided to invest in his talent by sending him to the Far East to cover the Boxer rebellion. His dispatches from China helped him to build a reputation as one of the most influential journalists in Europe (Knightley, 2004: 62). According to Phillip Knightley, "Italian journalism had never known such immediacy and veracity" (63). He became famous in 1908 for accompanying Prince Scipione Borgese on a motor race from Peking to Paris. After a two-month journey across China and Siberia, he published a memoir of this experience that became an international best-seller.[6]

---

6 See Luigi Barzini, Sr., 1908, *La metà del mondo vista da un'automobile da Pechino a Parigi in sessanta giorni* (Milan: Hoepli).

Notwithstanding Barzini's European origins, he was adamant in criticizing the violence used by the European powers in suppressing the local insurgence, as well as openly denouncing the Italian government for poorly providing the necessary equipment for the Italian troops participating in the international coalition. But his polemical arguments did not exacerbate his mocking style; in fact he proved to have absorbed the British journalistic style of defusing the drama by deploying a witty and, at times, wry humor in order to expose the distortions and the contradictions involved in the war (except when he witnessed a massacre in a battle, when he could obviously only resort to an anguished narration).

While his articles on the Boxer rebellion made his name popular in Italy, his dispatches from the Russo-Japanese war gave him international fame. Indeed the conflict between the two nations was widely broadcast all over the Western world, with reporting of such writers as the novelist Jack London and the Australian George Ernest Morrison, working for the British newspaper *The Times*. However, all the journalists soon came to realize that Japanese-imposed censorship would force them to narrate the war in Manchuria either from a Tokyo hotel or from designated locations far from the combat zone. While most reporters expressed frustration but eventually resigned themselves to their marginal role, Barzini patiently worked to gain the trust of the army and, as a result, he became the only Western journalist to report the crucial battle of Mukden, in which the Japanese army defeated its numerically superior Russian opponent at the end of a bloody confrontation in February 1905. The subsequent series of articles published in the *Corriere* were collected in the book *Guerra russo-giapponese: La battaglia di Mukden narrata da Luigi Barzini* (1907), which offers a detailed account of the battle that, even today, according to Knightley, is "still studied in Japanese staff schools" (65).

Phillip Knightley emphasizes the role played by Barzini in the history of war correspondents by locating him historically at the apex of the so-called "golden age" of war correspondence, roughly a period that began with the American Civil war through the First World War, which featured the rapid growth of the newspaper industry due to the increase of literacy on the one hand, and the emerging of *grand reportage* on the other. It was a time when the readership marveled at press reports, by war correspondents writing from the most remote locations, delivered only a very short time after events actually took place, thanks to the invention of the telegraph. While nineteenth-century war accounts offered romantic descriptions of battles "treating combat as an invigorating and character-building experience" (Sweeney, 2015: 45), early twentieth-century war was based on eyewitness accounts, indulging in the details both of battle strategy and individual episodes of violence.

As a witness and writer of a war between two superpowers both speaking languages that were foreign and unknown to him, Barzini had to rely heavily on the work of translators. It is characteristic of Barzini's narration to alternate his description of the conflict with interviews with both Japanese soldiers and Russian prisoners of war, in which the presence of official translators must have played a crucial role. Yet the work of such linguistic and cultural mediators is mostly obliterated from the final report, leaving the Italian reader with the illusion that the language exchange did not present any challenge in terms of communication and comprehension. Reflecting on the (often neglected) importance of language in travel writing Michael Cronin traced an interesting parallel between Lawrence Venuti's well-known theory of the "translator invisibility" and the apparent facility of verbal communication in travel literature:

> Just as translators and their achievement are often ignored in critical commentary and book reviews, as if texts were magically and unproblematically transparent, the experience of travel can be presented as if the traveler enjoyed unmediated access to the foreign reality through an enigmatic process of simultaneous translation, rarely if ever described. The traces of the translation's signature are carefully erased. (Cronin, 2003: 153)

What it is kept hidden from the reader is a liminal space of mutual representation and recognition that Emily Apter famously defined using the term "translation zone" in which Mary Louise Pratt's notion of "contact zone" is adapted to the field of translation studies. In this transnational region of linguistic exchange "that is neither the property of a single nation" (Apter, 2006: 5), different groups represent themselves to one another through language. Barzini inhabits this space where the Russian, Japanese and Chinese languages converge and clash in attempting to inscribe one another into their own language. By understating the role of interpreters who work as proxies for him to report the oral testimonies from the battlefield, Barzini obscures from the reader the inevitable glitches of a translation that must journey over the interpreter's English or French translation from the original Japanese or Russian to land finally in Barzini's Italian version.

Nevertheless, in the rest of the chapter, I will argue first that Barzini's strategy of offering Japanese voices in translation responded to a specific quest of the Italian public to move beyond the exotic wave of *japonisme* and establish closer contact with the Far Eastern world. By moving from an aesthetic perception to a political and sociological awareness of the "Land of the Rising Sun," this strategy aimed at expanding the international horizons of the recently born Kingdom of Italy. Second, I will compare Barzini's reports from the "translation zone" with the unpredictable effects (and probably unwanted by the author himself) generated in the "reception zone," whereby the complex process of cultural translation must come to terms with the historical expectations and simplifications of the readership in the author's home country. Finally, in response to the distorted reception of Barzini's dispatches from Manchuria I will reflect on the agency of individual narratives in both affecting and being affected by collective narratives.

6. Beyond *Japonisme*: Face-to-Face with the Japanese

The Russo-Japanese war was perhaps the first conflict that generated a wave of interest on a global scale before the outbreak of World War I ten years later. Reasons may vary, stemming from the Euro-Asian system of alliance (Japan and England on one hand opposing Russia and France on the other), to the technological innovation of the telegraph. Although Italy maintained a position of neutrality in the face of the conflict, nevertheless it played the role of an interested observer, watching from a distance the unraveling of a geopolitical reshaping of the Asian continent. The Italian Kingdom was looking to expand its geopolitical interests beyond the Mediterranean, in an attempt to enter the colonial race in East Asia together with France, Russia, England, Germany and the United States. As Alfredo Oriani wrote in an article written in the midst of the Russo-Japanese conflict:

> La storia dovrà ricominciare il proprio lavoro: quella che noi chiamavamo storia universale, non era fatta che di echi mondiali nel Mediterraneo: tutte le nostre storie fin qui furono parziali, e quindi false: in una storia davvero universale ogni nazione potrà soltanto e finalmente scoprire il proprio segreto. (Oriani, 1915: 319)

> [History will have to restart its work: what we called universal history was nothing but global echoes in the Mediterranean: all our histories so far were partial, and therefore false: in a truly universal story every nation can only and finally discover its own secret.]

As Italy was trying to find its "own place in the sun," the presence on the battlefield of a professional group of native Italian-speaking journalists was part of an ambitious program to reduce the geographical distance from these Eastern countries, while encouraging readers to perceive Italian interests on a global scale. Barzini was hardly the only Italian reporter in Manchuria. *La Stampa* sent Guido Pardo to follow the conflict on the side of the Russian army, while *Il Mattino* published reports from Alberto Troise. However, none of these names was able to challenge the authority and effectiveness of Barzini's work. In fact, Pardo concluded his mission prematurely as soon as he was dismissed by the Russian authorities on allegations of being too intrusive, while Troise resigned himself to the Japanese restrictions on the press and followed events remotely from a Tokyo hotel.

The magnitude of Barzini's goal to expose Italian readers to the voice of the Japanese must be measured against the contemporary status of knowledge of Japan in Italy, in which the Western aesthetic movement of *japonisme* was still the main source of reception of the Japanese culture. In 1898, the playwright Luigi Illica and the composer Pietro Mascagni debuted the opera *Iris*, which narrates the tragic story of a stereotypical geisha in the traditional Japan. The libretto adopts a metaphoric reading of Japanese culture popular among decadent and symbolist writers of the time which tended to "put into Japanese trappings a story that was more European than Japanese" (Tarling, 2015: 270). On February 17, 1904, right at the outset of the Russo-Japanese war, Giacomo Puccini presented the opera *Madama Butterfly* at La Scala in Milan, drawing from the analogous play of the American playwriter David Belasco (premiered in 1898). Against this backdrop of an aestheticized and Westernized image of the Japanese, Barzini introduced the Italian public to the voice in translation of authentic soldiers caught in the midst of a war.[7]

---

7 In parallel with the aesthetic phenomenon of *japonisme*, Italy also pursued an academic interest in Japanese language and culture. In 1871 the first "Società Italiana per gli Studi Orientali" was created in Florence. In 1876 a "Bollettino Italiano degli Studii Orientali" was established. In the same period publication of the first works of Japanese literature in translation began. In 1872 Antelmo Severini translated a novel by Ryūtei Tanehiko with the title *Uomini e paraventi*. As for the news from Japan, before Barzini's correspondence and translation Italy relied extensively on articles from French and British journalists: "Spesso, però, e per alcuni anni ancora, vedremo che sui nostri giornali molte notizie non appartengono alla penna dei nostri giornalisti, ma sono traduzioni di articoli presi da giornali francesi e inglesi" (Cuomo, 2003: 257).

While Illica and Puccini captivated their audiences by staging the backwardness and weakness of a society supposedly so inferior, and yet attractive, to the Western world, on the contrary Barzini brought to the fore aspects of Japanese society that, although different, are akin to the political scenario of the Italian Kingdom. In other words, Barzini, while underplaying the ancient image of Japanese society (before its opening to the West), made the case for the potential paradigm of contemporary Japan as a model for Italy's imperialistic ambitions. Indeed, he discounted the image of medieval Japan to concentrate on the dignity and attractiveness of the contemporary Japanese people.

7. Patriotic Cosmopolitanism

One aspect of this adaptation of the Japanese to the Italian reader is to debunk the myth of the Asian people as inherently violent and unnecessarily ruthless[8] in pursuing social justice. In this regard, Barzini offers examples of military behavior that specifically challenge this notion. For instance, at the end of a fierce battle near the city of Liaoyang, Barzini is allowed to approach the Japanese commanding official and his troops as they were taking Russian soldiers into custody. The soldiers have been charged with breaking the military rule by not ceasing fire after the end of a hostile engagement.

Surrounded by enemies, they eventually resign their weapons, hoping to have their lives spared. Barzini asks the captain what Japanese soldiers would do in an equivalent situation and, when he hears that they would commit suicide rather than accept the humiliation of being captured, he observes aloud that it is for this reason that the Japanese are considered barbarous people according to European standards of human dignity. To this objection the captain replies, questioning the coherence and logic of those who hold such a view: "Uccidere gli altri non è considerato barbarie e uccidere se stessi sì?" [Killing others is not considered barbarism and killing oneself is?] (Barzini, 1959: 281). The reaction of the captain challenges the stereotypical indictment of Japanese moral inferiority, on the grounds that participation in a war (especially if its goal is territorial expansionism) is an immoral act per se and one in which the European nations are fully implicated. Moreover, the

---

8   For an analysis of the trope of inherent violence and ruthlessness associated with Asian people see Rana Kabbani, 1986, *Imperial Fictions: Europe's Myths of Orient* (Bloomington: Indiana University Press).

captain, who by addressing Barzini perhaps also wants to make an impression on the Italian readers, communicates to the Russian soldiers that they will not be killed provided that they completely surrender and, later, he delivers this message to Barzini:

> Il capitano che mi era vicino dopo avere osservato i prigionieri da presso, mi abborda di nuovo. I suoi occhi sfavillavano di collera repressa e mi dice:
> "Vedete che nemici combattiamo? Ecco degli uomini del corpo sanitario armati di fucile, che ci ammazzano gli ufficiali e i soldati a tradimento! Sono fuori d'ogni diritto, fuori della legge delle genti; in una guerra contro altro esercito che non il nostro verrebbero massacrati senza pietà. Chi potrebbe trattenere gli uomini e impedire una giustizia sommaria? E invece, avete visto i nostri soldati? [...] E poi" ha aggiunto dopo una breve pausa come ripensando a quello che gli avevo detto poco prima "e poi ci dicono barbari." (Barzini, 1959: 285)

> [The captain, who was close to me after observing the prisoners from nearby, again approaches me. His eyes sparkled with repressed anger and he told me:
> "Do you see what kind of enemies we fight? Here are some men of the sanitary body armed with rifles, who kill our officers and soldiers out of betrayal! They are outside of every right, outside the people law; in a war against another army they would be massacred without mercy. Who could keep the men [from retaliating] and prevent a summary justice? And yet, have you seen our soldiers? [...] And then," he added after a short pause as he thought back to what I had said to him shortly before, "and then they tell us we are barbarians."]

After the verbal response, the captain offers the practical demonstration that Japanese are not as inhuman as they are often regarded, thereby inviting Western readers to revise their assumptions. In his book *Cosmopolitanism*, Anthony Appiah draws attention to the surprising results obtainable from cross-cultural communication when the "Other" is no longer thought of as an imaginary figure, but is present and communicating with his/her own voice:

> The problem of cross-cultural communication can seem immensely difficult in theory, when we are trying to imagine making sense of a

stranger in the abstract. But the great lesson of anthropology is that when the stranger is no longer imaginary, but real and present, sharing a human social life, you may like or dislike him, you may agree or disagree; but, if it is what you both want, you can make sense of each other in the end. (Appiah, 2006: 98–99)

By introducing the real voice (albeit with the translation's limitation) of the Japanese captain Barzini is moving his readership away from an imaginary notion of the Japanese to an experiential one. His attraction to the Japanese people results in a demonstration that it is possible to make sense of its society by virtue of being interested in their alternative way of thinking and their moral values.

However, in his attempt to bridge the differences, Barzini does not only spark interest in what Italians and Japanese do not share, but he is especially interested in building on common traits and similar political values. Barzini clearly praises Japan for its patriotism, its bold military ambitions, the impeccable organization and the state-of-the-art technology that allowed a country of a territorial scale comparable to that of Italy to become a dominant power in Asia:

> La forza soverchiante dei russi potrà aver ragione col tempo della sapienza e del valore giapponesi? Chi sa. La macchina più perfetta può venire schiacciata da una montagna che vi si abbatte sopra. Ma finora gli avvenimenti sembrano provare il contrario. E questo è molto istruttivo. Quei paesi del mondo che non sentono di possedere la potenza della montagna, dovrebbero interessarsi al come è fatta la "macchina." (Barzini, 1959: 206)

[Can the overwhelming strength of the Russians eventualy prevail over the Japanese wisdom and virtue? Who knows. The most perfect car can be crushed by a mountain that crashes over it. But so far the events seem to prove otherwise. And this is very relevant. Those countries in the world that do not feel they possess the power of the mountain should be interested in how the "machine" is made [...]]

Inevitably, Barzini's readers are invited to interpret the rising power of Japan as a demonstration of what Italy could also do, provided that the country was united under the same goal. However, Barzini is not overly fond of diverting the reader's attention to abstract projections of political scenarios;

instead he determines to prove his point by showing similar mental traits that individual Japanese have in common with Italians, in particular with those who share a nationalistic ideology. In other words, he is more interested in building empathy for the ordinary Japanese, disproving the idea that such political enterprise has been carried out by "efficient machines" deprived of any human quality. Barzini for example is eager to glimpse the "human side" of the Japanese soldiers, as they are celebrating the fall of Port Arthur with joy and euphoria, and he even joins them as they chant patriotic rhymes: "Avanti! Avanti! Tutti uniti / finché il nemico non è sconfitto!" "Tutti acclamano, ed io, dal carro cinese, unisco di cuore agli altri il mio grido" (Barzini, 1959: 310–11). ["Let's go! Let's go! All united / until the enemy is defeated!" "Everybody applaud, and I, from the Chinese chariot, unite my heart to others."] He goes on to stress how mutual this admiration is, as he explains to his readers the special attention that the Japanese reserve for Italy insofar as it is considered the nation that today carries on the legacy of the Roman Empire, posing as a model both for Japanese aesthetic sensibility and their nationalistic ambitions:

> Su tutte le persone colte del Giappone l'Italia esercita un fascino, che somiglia molto a quello che il Giappone irradia sopra di noi. Essi sanno che l'Italia è bella, fiorita, luminosa, che è il paese delle arti, che ha dominato il mondo, che è stata la culla della civiltà occidentale. Nelle scuole giapponesi si insegna la storia di Roma. Questo popolo che ammira e ama due cose sole, la bellezza e la gloria, ha verso di noi una grande simpatia e un sentimento naturale d'amicizia. (Barzini, 1959: 259)

> [To all the educated people of Japan, Italy has a fascination, which is very similar to what Japan radiates above us. They know that Italy is beautiful, flowery, luminous, is the country of the arts, has dominated the world, has been the cradle of Western civilization. The history of Rome is taught in Japanese schools. This people who admire and love two things alone, beauty and glory, have a great sympathy and a natural feeling of friendship toward us.]

Insisting on the mutual feeling of "simpatia" ("sympathy") and "fascino" ("attraction"), Barzini strikes the emotional chord in the reader's mind with the intention of building a sense of solidarity and brotherhood beyond – and notwithstanding – the pan-Japanese ideology that he is describing.

Cognitive approaches to literature have illustrated the important role of "empathy" in engaging readers in affective feelings toward distant others, whether the boundaries are those of family, gender, social class, or nation.⁹ The caveat here is that Barzini is seeking common ground only whenever there is a nationalistic ideology that seems to exclude any other foreigner. Nationalism can be (but is not always) in opposition to cosmopolitanism: to extol the Japanese for their patriotism can be conducive to a discourse that compares one form of parochialism with the "Other." However, Barzini's brand of cosmopolitanism has very little to do with the abstract idea of being a rootless "citizen of the world," beyond, and despite, any sense of allegiance to the home country. In this sense, his cosmopolitan ideal is not in conflict with patriotic values and with the feeling of being emotionally attached to a place called "home." In fact, Barzini's cosmopolitan feelings are best described using Anthony Appiah's notion of "rooted cosmopolitanism," which is the title of the final chapter of his book on *The Ethics of Identity* (2005). According to this view, there is nothing chauvinistic about being in love with the place we are from, provided that we are open to appreciate and to value other places and cultures on their own terms, without denying the right of other people to be proud of their own country as much as we are proud of ours. According to Barzini, as the Japanese, despite their enthusiastic patriotism, admire Italy for its past history and for its artistic treasures, so the Italians should admire the Japanese for being a young, aspiring nation, regardless of the obvious differences and without dismissing their own patriotic feelings. Barzini knows that one of the reasons that restrains Italians from an emotional attachment to Japanese culture is the issue of race. The so-called "yellow peril" is a culturally rooted concept that the West applied first to Mongolian people, then to the Chinese and, finally, especially after the Sino-Japanese War, to the Japanese as well.¹⁰

Barzini is keen to defuse the idea that a racial divide would hamper the possibility of a cross-cultural encounter: "Spogliamoci dei nostri pregiudizi di razza e giudichiamo serenamente. Il Giappone offre ora al mondo uno spettacolo meraviglioso. Esso dà un grande esempio di coraggio, di serietà,

---

9   Patrick Colm Hogan, 2003, *Cognitive Science, Literature, and the Arts: A Guide for Humanists* (London: Routledge): 283–324. For an approach to cognitive studies in relation to literature, see Lars Bernaerts et al. (editors), 2013, *Stories and Minds: Cognitive Approaches to Literary Narrative* (London: University of Nebraska Press).
10 See Michael Keevak, 2011, *Becoming Yellow: A Short Story of Racial Thinking* (Princeton, NJ and Oxford, UK: Princeton University Press). On page 135 Keevak comments: "The Yellow Peril, it was often argued, was little more than an invention of the Western powers jealous of Japan's own imperial aspirations."

di virtù civile" (Barzini, 1915: 73) [Let's get rid of our race prejudices and judge peacefully. Japan now offers the world a marvelous spectacle. It gives a great example of courage, of seriousness, of civil virtue]. Furthermore, he warns his readers away from Eurocentric approaches that deem naturally inferior any non-Western civilization: "Dell'anima giapponese non è stata compresa che quella parte infima che collimava con la nostra, che rispondeva a sentimenti nostri, la parte comune all'anima di tutti gli uomini" [Of the Japanese soul it was not understood that the small part that collimated with ours, which responded to our feelings, the part common to the soul of all men], "Abbiamo visto il Giappone come lo ha visto Pierre Loti, senza capirlo" (Barzini, 1915: 123, 124) [We saw Japan as Pierre Loti saw it, without understanding it].

"Patriotic cosmopolitanism" is more appropriate than nationalism to describe Barzini's motivations in introducing Italians to such a geographically remote nation. Barzini's cosmopolitan views require both Japanese and Italians to love their nations, as the condition that sparks curiosity and intellectual openness for what is different, or not immediately assimilated to one's own view. The nationalistic discourse is here depleted of one of its main features, that is, the appraisal of war as a means for territorial expansion and of glory for the nation. To be sure, Barzini is relentless in his condemnation of the conflict. At the end of a bloody battle Barzini comments:

La Russia vuole la Manciuria, il Giappone non consente, e tale questione si risolve con la condanna a morte di decine di migliaia d'uomini che non hanno mai pensato né all'una cosa né all'altra. Vi è un'assurdità scellerata così evidente, e pure così insanabile, che si rimane accasciati dalla rivelazione di questo gran male che non si cura: l'ingiustizia è la gran legge dell'umanità, fatale, inesorabile, eterna. (Barzini, 1959: 276)

[Russia wants Manchuria, Japan does not allow this to happen, and this issue is resolved with the death sentence of tens of thousands of men who have never thought of either one thing or another. There is a heinous absurdity so evident, and yet so incurable, that we become discouraged by the revelation of this great evil that cannot be cured: injustice is the great law of humanity, fatal, inexorable, eternal.]

Admiration for Japanese virtues does not mean, for Barzini, endorsing the logic of war. In contrast with the more usual way in which the West looked at the Japanese as masters in conducting warfare, eager to expand their empire, Barzini argues that the ceasefire with Russia and the subsequent peace resolution was possible largely thanks to Japanese efforts to prioritize the end of the conflict over their claims for new territory:

> Un giorno sapremo quanta parte l'energico Presidente americano [Theodore Roosevelt] ha avuto all'ultimo momento, e quale influenza avrà esercitato sui giapponesi la considerazione che nessun'altra vittoria, per quanto grande, avrebbe potuto indurre la Russia a pagare l'indennità, mentre poi la continuazione della guerra avrebbe aperto più larghe e forse irreparabili brecce nella finanza della nazione. Ma anche se è così, l'estrema rinunzia giapponese non perde troppo del suo valore, perché simili preoccupazioni verso il paese e verso il popolo, simili premure di risparmiargli sangue, lacrime e denaro, avrebbero pur dovuto animare gli avversari rimasti invece inesorabili. Il Giappone ha tutto il merito della pace, conquistata con un eroismo di più. (Barzini, 1959: 377)

> [One day we will find out how much influence the energetic American President [Theodore Roosevelt] has exercised at the last moment, and what influence will have exercised on the Japanese the consideration that no other victory, however great, could have induced Russia to pay the indemnity; while the continuation of the war would have opened wider and perhaps irreparable wounds in the nation's finances. But even if it is so, the extreme Japanese renunciation does not lose too much of its value, because similar worries about the country and the people, similar care to spare blood, tears and money, should have had [the effect of] animating the opponents, who remained instead inexorable. Japan has all the merit of peace, conquered with one more gesture of heroism.]

8. The Unavoidable Distance

Despite these efforts to promote a more complex image of the Japanese, the reception of Barzini's reports produced unintended consequences. The articles did not foster any anti-war spirit; in fact, it was quite the opposite reaction that predominated. Indeed, Barzini's cosmopolitan sympathy for Japan ultimately fueled a nationalistic propaganda at home, fostering national isolationism, rather than cross-cultural opening. Obviously, the Italian political spectrum offered a variety of voices and views in response to the Manchurian War, but a general sense of Japanophilia in Italy (as well as in much of Europe[11]), favored those who saw in the Japanese victory an argument in favor of Italian colonialism. While leftist-oriented political magazines, such as *L'Avanti*, welcomed the military rise of Japan as a powerful stronghold against the invasion of Western capitalism in Asia, right-wing intellectuals (writing for *Il Regno, Hermes* and *Il Leonardo*), together with contributors to the literary magazine *Il Marzocco*, took Japan as an example of heroic patriotism and as a modern imperialistic nation. While Barzini considered the Japanese decision to declare war a necessary act of defense in response to the Euro-American colonialist agenda, Mario Morasso glorified the spirit of dominion that drive the Japanese army toward future conquests: "Che semina meravigliosa la guerra che or si combatte e che infaticabili, che prodighi seminatori i buoni giapponesi!" (Morasso, 1990: 210–11) [What a marvelous sowing the war is, which is now fought, and how tireless and generous the good Japanese sowers are!]. Similarly, Alfredo Oriani celebrated the Japanese soldiers as founders of a modern pagan religiosity that poses the cult of the nation as supreme ideal: "Una immensa forza anima la loro [dei giapponesi] coscienza, l'ebrezza della modernità così brevemente conquistata li esalta: ognuno si sente come un verso nel poema nazionale" (Oriani, 1921: 229) [An immense force animates the Japanese soldiers' consciousness, the inebriation of modernity so briefly conquered exalts them: each one feels like a verse in the national poem].[12]

In the transition from the liminality of the "translation zone," where the journalist/translator is exposed to a multiplicity of languages, to the "reception zone," where the complexities of the Russo-Japanese war boil down to an aesthetic and political Japanophilia, something important has been lost. A collective national narrative of events ultimately comes to subsume Barzini's

---

11 Donald Keene notices that at the origin of the Western respect and appreciation for Japan is the victory in the Sino-Japanese War: "The Sino-Japanese War undoubtedly produced a change of opinion about Japan in the West. Few experts predicted that Japan would win the war against the mighty continental power, and when the initial victories proved not to be flash in the pan, it was grudgingly admitted that the much decried 'superficial modernization' was in fact genuine. Okakura Kakuzō wryly commented that as long as Japan indulged in the gentle arts of peace she had been regarded as barbarous, but victory in war had indulged the foreigners to call Japan civilized": Donald Keene, 1971, *Landscapes and Portraits: Appreciation of Japanese Culture* (Tokyo and Palo Alto: Kodansha International): 294–95.
12 For an analysis of Japan as founder of a national religion see Emilio Gentile, 1993, *Il culto del littorio: La sacralizzazione della politica nell'Italia fascista* (Bari: Laterza): 28–29.

individual narrative, notwithstanding his being the only Italian reporter present on the battlefield and one of the most popular Italian journalists of the time. His cosmopolitan message fades away, replaced by the rhetoric of Japan as a nation of fearless samurai warriors. What is missing is Barzini's individual ethical stance against the war, which he develops on the ground as the violence is unfolding. The reports from Manchuria offer a prime example of the extreme situation that Barzini was experiencing, and problems related to the subsequent interpretation of it. But exactly what is an extreme situation? Giorgio Agamben has provided a reflection on the "paradigm of the 'extreme situation'" that helps to explain Barzini's narrative impasse and the difficulties in negotiating an ethical judgment of his experience. In a "limit," or "extreme," situation, Agamben points out, the general tendency of those affected is to accept it as normal and operate according to this new level of reality. He refers to the example of Nazi concentration camps, in which prisoners/workers showed the "tendency of the limit situation to become habit" (Agamben, 1999: 49). By becoming habitual, the "limit situation" surrenders its prerogative of being "extreme"; in fact it turns into its opposite, becoming "normal" to the point that the distinction between what is normal and what is extreme vanishes in the mind of the witness. The paradox of accepting as ordinary a situation in which dead bodies are seen everywhere on the battlefield is recurrent in Barzini's reports. For instance, in the midst of the Battle of Mukden, where he was present as the only Western reporter, he is surprised by the soldiers' adaptability to the level of violence: "Non v'è un solo soldato che non tremerebbe di terrore al trovarsi di fronte a dei fucili che sparano. Eppure tutti insieme sono eroi. È perché la guerra diventa un lavoro; un lavoro che tutti fanno perché lo fanno tutti. L'adattabilità umana è sorprendente" (Barzini, 1959: 327) [There is not a single soldier who would not be terrified of being confronted with shotguns. Yet all together are heroes. It is because war becomes a job; a job that everyone does because everyone does it. Human adaptability is surprising]. He has a similar thought while he is describing the scene of the Battle of Liaoyang: "Penso che una battaglia è meno terribile a vedersi che a immaginarsi" (Barzini, 1959: 268) [I think that a battle is less terrible to see than to imagine].

When the nature of the conflict is unproblematically accepted and becomes a habitus in the mind of the soldiers, the task of the correspondent/translator becomes the negotiation of an ethic for himself, resisting the pressure of terming the situation as simply unavoidable, thus necessary. In Moira Inghilleri's words: "Translators operating in limit situations have found themselves having to negotiate the ethical for themselves; they have had to define or redefine themselves in the face of violence, torture and human suffering" (Inghilleri, 2009: 210). The ethical task of the reporter and translator is not limited to providing the most correct and informative dispatches from the war zone, but it also implies a moral obligation related to the effect that the circulation of information can produce in the audience at home. In the face of violence Barzini chooses not to support the motivations of the conflict or to take a stand for either side. In fact, despite his obvious sympathies for the Japanese, Barzini gives voice and dignity to the Russian army as well, by extensively interviewing them and reporting their thoughts in translation. If the ordinary Russian POWs are described as brave, although simple-minded, revealing their peasant-like profile beneath the uniform, the military officials are extolled for their courage and devotion to the cause. An interview with a Russian general after the loss of Port Arthur allows Barzini to absolve the behavior of the Russian army during the war and to suggest that the responsibility must be directed toward the autocracy of the empire: "Penso che il sangue di Port Arthur non sarà versato invano, se a seimila miglia da qui potrà far schiudere le vecchie porte d'un Impero alla Libertà" (Barzini, 1959: 320) [I think that the blood of Port Arthur will not be shed in vain, if six thousand miles from here can it open the old doors of an Empire to freedom].

While the violence in the conflict zone is unleashed with no restraints, Barzini is able to detach himself from the irrational scene and to elaborate an ethical message that grants admiration of and sympathy for the Japanese army, on one hand, and dignity and piety to the Russian soldiers on the other. By insisting on the human suffering and on the horrific images of death, Barzini delivers a straight condemnation of the war as a means of territorial expansion. If his reports and translations are not simple accounts of facts, but politically and morally motivated, why did the reception of these articles not challenge the prevailing nationalistic discourse in Italy?[13]

---

13 See for instance Enrico Corradini's glorification of the Russo-Japanese war: "The cannon that thunders over Port Arthur brings confirmation, with its rude and decisive voice, of ideas and passions dear to us. Truly this great war seems tailor made for us. Just as from all sides we were accused of being wild Utopians [and] the facile sneers of the 'pioneers of progress' relegated us to the savage past [and] called us out of tune with the times, here are two great empires, which pass for civil in men's opinions and in the text books, that have felt the need to come to blows" (Enrico Corradini, 1904, "La conferma del cannone," Il Regno, quoted in Norberto Bobbio, 1995, Ideological Profile of Twentieth-Century Italy, translated by Lydia G. Cochrane (Princeton, NJ: Princeton University Press, 1995): 51).

A valid answer to this question is in Mona Baker's social narrative theory, as it is elaborated in her book *Translation and Conflict* (2006). In this interdisciplinary essay Baker draws on narrative theory to explore the effects of translation in building competing narratives, showcasing the influential role of the translator/interpreter in the circulation of narratives that construct a conflict (including but not limited to war).

Borrowing from social theorists Margaret Somers and Gloria Gibson, Mona Baker examines four types of narratives that construct our understanding of events and our view of the world in which we live: personal narratives "are narratives of the self"; public narratives are "stories that emerge within any social grouping, from the family to the classroom, workplace, and the media; disciplinary narratives" and "the theoretical and historical accounts that circulate in any field of knowledge"; and metanarratives are the "exceptionally powerful and resilient narratives" (Baker, 2016: 248) in which the contemporary world is embedded (e.g. progress, industrialization, globalization, etc.). Baker points to the fact that the first two typologies are usually interdependent, as personal narratives "are dependent on and informed by the collective narratives in which they are situated. But they are also crucial for the elaboration and maintenance of the same narratives" (Baker, 2006: 29). Barzini's reports from Manchuria offer a sample case of interdependence of ontological and shared narratives, in which the former draws on and reinforces the latter. In fact, Barzini's personal way of making sense of the events of the war, as above described, inevitably intersects with stories about Japan and Russia that were circulating in Italy at the turn of the century. Even though Barzini presents the Japanese people with a "human face," engaged in defending their country from Western colonialism and, therefore, violent out of necessity, not by nature, there are parts in which he yields to the "aesthetic of the warrior," which informed the East Asian army's fascination with nationalism. According to this form of rhetoric, created under the spell of a reading of Nietzsche,[14] the Japanese soldiers are the modern reincarnation of the barbaric troops that once ravaged Europe. They are the manifestation of a Dionysian spirit, that is, a pagan primordial force of aggression that sooner or later will prevail over the European nations by defeating their weak ideals of peace. Mario Morasso had no doubt that one day "è ai giapponesi che noi saremo debitori per una prossima virilizzazione dell'Europa, è ai giapponesi che noi dobbiamo il veder ignominiosamente

---

14 The cult of Nietzsche in Italy began in the last decade of the nineteenth century as French and Italian translations of Nietzsche's works started to circulate on the peninsula.

smentiti tutti i viscidi oroscopi dei falsi profeti della pace, della fratellanza e di altri simili ubbie" (Morasso, 1905: 221) [It is to the Japanese that we will be indebted for a future virilization of Europe, it is to the Japanese that we must ignominiously see denied all the slimy predictions by the false prophets of peace, brotherhood and other similar superstitions]. Certainly Barzini would not subscribe to this idea, nevertheless he communicates his fascination with the heroic attitude of the Japanese soldiers, such as their perception that serving in the front line is an honor and on the rear positions as an humiliation.[15] He is seduced by their patriotism and contrasts the Russian patriotism of Christian origin ("il patriottismo qui nasce dalla fede," Barzini, 1959: 190 [patriotism here comes from faith]), considered week and irrational, with what he perceives as stronger and more rational Japanese patriotism, which originates from the sentiment of the people for the homeland. Enrico Corradini later developed the same idea in an article that considers Japan as a model of country in which the cult of the nation has achieved the status of a religion.[16] Overall, even if not explicitly, Barzini alludes to the fact (as we have seen above) that Japan represents an ideal for Italy in regard to what extent technology, organization and patriotism can push a small country to become an imperialistic nation, in perfect alignment with the narrative that circulated among Italian nationalists.

Barzini's ontological narrative is informed by the shared narratives about Japan circulating in Italy, despite the author's departure from them. Indeed, pre-existing collective narratives exercise a constraint on the individual who dwells among them precisely because they are situated in the language – that is in "symbols, linguistic formulations, structures and vocabularies of motives" (Ewick and Silbey, 1995: 211–12) and, in fact, they dissolve when the ontological narrative is translated into a different language. Of course, the opposite is also true, that is, that personal stories can indent dominant narratives to the point of undermining their foundations and requiring an alternative narrative to become mainstream. Baker offers the example of feminists aiming to change the social image of women by publishing many suppressed or neglected female stories. In other words, an alternative shared narrative gains currency in society only as a result of many individual stories converging toward a common narrative being told over and over. Barzini's unprecedented and unique experience in Manchuria must negotiate a

15 See Sweeney, 2015, "'Narrative is a thread, and the truth is a fabric': Luigi Barzini and the Russo-Japanese War," *American Journalism*, 32: 41–59 (56).
16 See Enrico Corradini's article "Una Nazione" in *Il Regno*, June 19, 1904.

gulf of incompatibility with the expectations of the target audience as a condition for his stories to be believed and become popular. Nevertheless, his numerous translations and descriptions from the battlefield posed a significant challenge to pre-existing images of Japan as well as to the rhetoric of war, paving the way for an ethic of diversity that extends beyond racial and cultural biases.

9. A Leopard Woman

Women writers who journeyed to the East were not a rarity at the turn of the twentieth century. Some were employed as teachers, governesses, or diplomats' wives; others were simply pleasure-seekers or those interested in doing research in the field.

This last category includes Marie Stopes (1880–1958), better known as a campaigner for women's rights, who went to Japan in 1907 to study fossils and coal mines.[17] The American writer Alice Mabel Bacon (1858–1918) was also in Japan from 1900 to 1902, having been invited by the Meiji government to establish the Tokyo's Women's Educational School. Bacon wrote extensively about her journey and eventually became a specialist in Japanese culture.[18] Almost all of these women writers were British and "white, middle or upper class, and with the means to travel" (Foster, 1990: vii).

Considering that most of these travelers were representatives of colonialist countries and their views reflected Victorian values, the case of Baronessa di Villaurea's (Palermo, 1870–1963) travelog *Al Giappone, impressioni di una viaggiatrice* ("In Japan, impressions of a traveler," 1914) is all the more interesting. Until very recently there was very little information available about her life. Born in Palermo on March 2, 1870 in a highly educated family in which French was the language spoken at home, Angelina Fatta was also fluent in both English and German.[19] At the age of twenty-three she married Francesco De Michele, "barone di Villaurea," and with her husband lived in

---

17 Marie Stopes, 2010, *A Journal from Japan: A Daily Record of Life as Seen by a Scientist* (Glasgow, Bombay and London: Blackie & Son).
18 See at least Alice Mabel Bacon, 1892, *Japanese Girls and Women* (Boston and New York: Houghton, Mifflin and Company).
19 See Luisa Reina, 2012, "Villaurea e le altre. Racconti di italiane in Oriente" in Federica Frediani and Ricciarda Ricorda (editors), *Spazi, Segni, Parole: Percorsi di viaggiatrici italiane* (Milan: Franco Angeli): 145–59.

Sicily in a socially elevated environment, cultivating an interest in painting, writing, philanthropy, and travels. Norway, Egypt, the Austro-Hungarian Empire, Germany, Greece, England and Palestine are among the destinations that the baroness visited during her life.

While research in archives will provide more insight into this unique case of an Italian woman writer and traveler in Japan from that time period, for now we can assume that the purpose of her journey to Japan was probably related to the exceptional presence in Palermo of the Japanese painter Otamà Kiyohara (1861–1939, also known as Kiyohara Tama or Eleonora Ragusa).

Otamà was a young painter apprentice whose life changed the day she met the Italian sculptor Vincenzo Ragusa (1841–1927). Ragusa moved to Japan for a few years (1876–82), along with the painter Antonio Fontanesi and the architect Vincenzo Cappelletti, to open a school of Western art at the invitation of Emperor Mutsuhito. Upon his return to Palermo, Ragusa opened a *Scuola di Arti Orientali* (School of Oriental Arts), employing Otamà's relatives as instructors. Eventually the experiment of introducing Eastern art in Sicily failed, apparently because of lack of raw material, but Otamà remained in Sicily to marry Ragusa and spent the next fifty years in Palermo until she returned to Japan a few years before her death. In Palermo, Otamà was a well-known artist who introduced many apprentices to the secrets of her art, with many Palermitan families owning her artwork.[20] It is very likely that Otamà sparked Fatta's interest in Japanese society and culture. Indeed, while in Tokyo, the *Baronessa* visited the Japan Art Academy (*Nihon Geijutsu-in*) and attended the *Taiheiyō Gakai* (Pacific Society) exhibition of May 1908.[21] The rising Western-style painter Hiroshi Yoshida (1876–1950) guided her

---

20   "Il rapporto che Eleonora Ragusa instaurava con i propri allievi, sia ragazze che ragazzi, diventava nel tempo un legame profondo di affetto ed amicizia, che coinvolgeva anche le loro famiglie. Lo testimonia il fatto che anche dopo il suo ritorno in Giappone fra loro si mantennero intensi rapporti epistolari. Nelle dimore di tante famiglie palermitane si conservano opera di Otamà, ma anche dei suoi allievi, debitori alla maestra di modi garbati e di tenzione alla straordinaria bellezza delle forme della natura": Maria Antonietta Spadaro, 2002, *Otamà Kiyohara/Eleonora Ragusa: "Una favola fin de siècle"* (Palermo: Gruppo Editoriale Kalos): 8. See also Maria Antonietta Spadaro, 2008, *O'Tama e Vincenzo Ragusa: echi di Giappone in Italia* (Palermo: Gruppo Editoriale Kalos).

21   Yoshida Hiroshi was a founder member in 1902 of the *Taiheiyō Gakai* (Pacific Ocean Painting Circle), which gathered Japanese painters coming back from overseas with the intention of introducing a Western style of painting in Japan. *Taiheiyō Gakai* was openly in contrast with a second group of painters, Hakubakai (White Horse Society), which was also, paradoxically, pursuing a Westernization of the style.

through the works of art as he was able to communicate in English, having traveled twice already to the United States, where he sold his watercolors in large quantities and his exhibitions drew significant crowds. The economic success of his second American tour, from 1903 to 1906, provided him with the financial means to explore Europe, including Venice, before returning to Japan in 1907, when he married his wife Fujio (1887–1987), a painter herself and the daughter of Yoshida Kasaburō, Hiroshi's stepfather. Villaurea had the opportunity to admire Fujio's and Hiroshi's canvases exposed at the sixth Taiheiyō Gakai Exhibition, with particular regard to the European samples: "Le sue tele e quelle della moglie sua occupano varie pareti, sono paesi, Venezia vi si ripete" (Villaurea, 1914: 91) [His canvases and those of his wife occupy various walls, various countries are represented, Venice is repeated].

The aesthetic response that Villaurea offers to her readers is indicative of her idiosyncratic approach to Japan. While she cannot help noticing the remarkable effort that Yoshida put into absorbing the European style of painting ("Egli ha viaggiato, copiando dal vero con certo successo, ed è naturalmente occidentale, fino al midollo dell'osso," Villaurea, 1914: 91) [He has traveled, copying from life with some success, and is naturally Western, to the core]), she is also critical of a pictorial technic that unabashedly distances itself from the local tradition. In fact, what she admires in Hiroshi's art is the Japanese "original naivete" that is still perceptible behind the ostentatious façade of his foreign style. Yet as she will often repeat in similar situations in which the Japanese tradition is perceived as declining, for her it is only a matter of time before the rampant Western influence will take over, destroying the uniqueness of Japanese art: "Essi dimenticano difficilmente la loro ingenuità originaria e per distruggerla hanno bisogno di lunghi anni di dimora, nei centri artistici europei" (91) [They hardly forget their original ingenuity and in order to destroy it they need long years of residence in the European artistic centers]. Her encounter with Hiroshi Yoshida will make a deep impression that establishes her view of Japan in which her fickle sentiment toward Westernization is posed in contrast with an allegedly pure Japanese origin.[22]

---

22 For more information about Yoshida Hiroshi and his wife Yoshida Fujio in relation to their American and European tour see Laura W. Allen et al. (editors), 2002, *A Japanese Legacy: Four Generations of Yoshida Family Artists* (Minneapolis, MN: Minneapolis Institute of Arts; Chicago, IL: Art Media Resources). Also, Shippitusha Ogura Tadao… et al. (editors), 2016 (1991, 1st edition) 吉田博全木版画集 = *The Complete Woodblock Prints of Yoshida Hiroshi* (Tōkyō: Abe Shuppan).

It remained unusual for an Italian woman at the dawn of the twentieth century to not only venture on a journey to the Far East, but also to publish a book about it. Views on the inferiority of women in Italy were even stronger than in British-American culture, and the southern mores were especially retrograde compared to the rest of the country. Even well-educated and upper-class women, as the baroness certainly was, were somehow bound to the role of housewife and housekeeper:

> Richer women had considerably more leisure time but much of it was spent at home, doing things like sewing, reading, receiving guests and hosting family parties. The situation was, however, changing a little. Middle- and upper-class women who, fifty years earlier, would rarely have set foot outside the house, because of the danger of their reputation, were increasingly beginning to go out. Admittedly, Italian women were less advanced in this respect than women in some other countries: American women living in Italy were seen as almost surreally emancipated in their disregard for "proper" behavior. (Willson, 2010: 14)

It is also true that at the time of Villaurea's journey to Japan things were slowly starting to change for Italian women. Feminist organizations such as *Unione femminile nazionale* (National Female Union) founded in 1905, or *Consiglio Nazionale delle Donne Italiane* (National Council of Italian Women) founded in 1908 encouraged gender awareness and social rights. Magazines specifically addressing women readers, such as *La donna* and *Vita femminile*, served the same purpose. At the time that Fatta traveled to Japan, Italian feminist movements were engaged in a political battle to obtain the right to vote; though the 1912 electoral reform did not achieve this goal they were able to draw public attention to the suffrage movement.

The example of Angelina Fatta highlights a combination of conservative and progressive elements. On the one hand, her independent travel in the Far East qualifies her as a pioneer of Italian female writers who adventure to "exotic" places. While she travels in the company of her husband (Reina, 2012: 151), she does not fall into the role of a dutiful wife following her spouse. Rather the opposite, since she apparently controlled the itineraries of their journeys and her East Asian travelog does not mention her husband at any point. By documenting her journey using her personal Kodak camera, she is also part of a vanguard of new travel writers who are embracing a technology that was introduced in Italy only a short time earlier, in 1905 (Reina, 2012: 157). Writing during her journey is not a private pastime, but in choosing popular destinations, such as Japan after the Russo-Japanese war, or, later on, a pilgrimage to Palestine, she sought to articulate for readers the rising of the East Asian country (especially during the time of Puccini's *Madama Butterfly* becoming a major hit in theaters around the world).[23] In Dacia Maraini's words, the choice to travel to the Far East breaks with the convention of traveling with a male figure (Ulysses' adventures versus Penelope patiently at home), whose constraining authority limits women's freedom of movement like a pair of tight shoes.[24]

Yet Fatta's choice of hiding her personal identity by adopting "Baronessa di Villaurea" as her *nom de plume* betrays her lack of confidence in the status of being a "woman writer" and her belief that only her social status (*baronessa*) can grant her the authority to write. Also, her laudable initiative of devolving the revenues from the book sale to the cause of orphans in her hometown (as stated on the book cover) further demonstrates her need to subordinate her role as a writer to a more socially acceptable profile as a woman involved in philanthropy and fundraising. These conflicting elements of traditionalism and reformism, or respect for the past and tension about the future, play a major role in Villaurea's account of Japan. Their importance lies in the overall image of Japan itself, as a country engaged in a contrasting dynamism of traditional and progressive cultural streams:

> Attività, pazienza, resistenza al lavoro, quante attitudini prodigiose manifesta questo popolo sempre ilare! Popolo eccezionale! Bisogna studiarlo e vederlo da presso, lento ed attivo ad un tempo; pare immobile come il sole della sua bandiera, e cammina invece intorno al progresso,

---

23 Angelina Fatta's second book *Sulla terra della redenzione: Palestina* (Palermo: Scuola Salesiana del Libro, 1933) is published in the name of Angelina di Villaurea. The book offers a Christian view of the Holy Land for Catholics, and in fact the book is published with the Vatican's *imprimatur*.

24 "How strange that after forty years one is still wearing the same shoes one was born with. How stupid that without one even being aware of it or concerned about it they've always been a size too narrow. Look at your own feet and you'll see: they are covered with corns because of the way your shoes pinch you and restrict your circulation. Haven't you ever noticed that walking has always been painful even when it seemed quick and easy. But then – take off your shoes and you'll find you can't walk because the way you walk has become part of your whole life-style and perception of the world. So we women live our lives in a world that has been created without us and acts against us. But we also have a sadistic love–hate attitude toward this culture as we always have towards those who tyrannise over us" (Dacia Maraini, *Letters to Marina*, quoted by Sartini-Blum: 155).

alla civiltà, in una corsa misurata, flemmatica, continua, eppure forse appena percettibile. (Baronessa di Villaurea, 1914: 62–63)

[Activities, patience, resistance to work, how many prodigious attitudes this always hilarious people manifests! Exceptional people! We must study them and see them from near, as being slow and active at the same time; they seem as still as the sun of their flag, and instead they walk on progress, on civilization, in a measured, phlegmatic, continuous, yet perhaps barely perceptible race.]

The combination of tradition and change is a trademark of the Meiji period (1868–1912); in this sense, Villaurea is giving a personal account of the rapid transformation that Japan has been undergoing since imperial rule was restored. If the rediscovery of old traditions and values, such as a belief in the divine ascendancy of the emperor, were part of the restoration project, the government also made a simultaneous conscious effort to incorporate a wide range of Western knowledge, the lack of which was holding Japan back from becoming a legitimate peer among other superpowers. This policy of Westernization included economic, political and administrative reforms, such as the opening of the trade market or the elimination of the samurai class, but it also involved the society as a whole: "Western dress became fashionable among progressives, and in 1872 became compulsory for government officials (including on ceremonial occasions) and civil servants such as postmen. Western-style haircuts also became increasingly fashionable, and a popular symbol of modernity" (Henshall, 2004: 79). How Western style impacts tradition is the focus of Villaurea's examination of Japanese women:

La giapponese di oggi va semplificando sempre più la sua capigliatura, sino ad accostarsi al moderno rigonfiamento del nostro stile.
 Guai a lei se la moda dovesse invaderla di più! Quanto del suo fascino non andrebbe perduto! Io temo tutto!
 Finché la donna conserverà un po' di buon senso, è sperabile, non seguirà l'innovazione maschile, non si spoglierà del *kimonò*!
 Infatti fuori di qualche deplorevole cattivo esempio a corte, di questo buon senso pare sinora con istintiva femminilità, guidata la graziosa giapponesina! Per confortarla assicuriamola, come noi signore di occidente saremmo ugualmente sgraziate e mal vestite nel loro *kimonò*. (126–27)

[Today's Japanese woman is increasingly simplifying her hair, until it approaches the modern swelling of our style.

Woe to her if fashion were to invade her more! How much of her charm would be lost! I fear everything!

As long as the woman retains some common sense, it is hopeful that she will not follow the male innovation, she will not get rid of the kimonos!

In fact, except for some deplorably bad example at court, this common sense seems so far to be guiding with instinctive femininity the pretty Giapponesina! To comfort her, let us assure her, as we ladies of the West would be equally ungraceful and ill dressed in their kimonò.]

While striking an ironic tone ("la graziosa giapponesina") to defuse her anxiety in the eyes of the Italian audience, the *Baronessa* ends up revealing her discomfort about the social transformation that she is witnessing in Japan. From her perspective, Japanese women live on the cusp of tradition and change; they occupy a liminal space that creates uncertainties for the Italian observer, who is hesitating between expressing her feminist solidarity toward women rights and betraying a certain penchant for the *status quo* characteristics of her social group. Indeed, up to a certain point, Villaurea welcomes the transformation of relationships that the process of the country's modernization is generating within the household, ultimately aligning Japan more closely with the Western contemporary feminist movement:

A conti fatti io credo che c'è da ringraziare la provvidenza quando non si nasce donna al Giappone.

Decantata per la dolcezza, per la mansuetudine, la pieghevolezza del carattere, per le grazie, le moine, i sorrisi, lo credo bene, costituisca l'ideale fra tutte le mogli del mondo.

Vivere senza contrasti e senza esigenze, fra i sorrisi e le moine affettuose di una donnettina premurosa, ed osservarla, fragile come un giunco, spezzarsi in un inchino sino a terra, per offrire una tazza di thé od un paio di pantofole al marito, e sentire il proprio nome preceduto da un signor padrone, c'è di che portare al paradiso della beatitudine, il facile orgoglio maschile.

Così è stata finora la condizione della donna ... ma col nuovo Giappone?! (93–95)

[Over all, I believe that there is providence to thank when a woman is not born in Japan.

Praised for the sweetness, for the meekness, the flexibility of her character, for her graces, her wheedling, her smiles, I believe it well, she constitutes the ideal among all the wives of the world.

To live without contrasts and without demands, amid the smiles and affectionate tendencies of a caring little woman, and to observe her, as fragile as a reed, to break in a bow to the ground, to offer a cup of tea or a pair of slippers to her husband, and to hear one's name preceded by a master lord, is enough to bring the easy male pride to the paradise of bliss.

So has the status of women been so far ... but in the new Japan?!]

Here the ironic tone stresses not only the inferiority of the Japanese woman compared to her Western counterpart, but also her reduction to the stereotype diffused by Pierre Loti's *Madame Chrysanthème*. Dismissed as commodities or dolls in the hands of selfish men, Japanese girls are far from experiencing the freedom of their Western counterparts. At the same time, Villaurea seems to predict a resurgence of female self-awareness in the immediate future. By ending the above passage with an open question ("ma col nuovo Giappone?!"), the baroness alludes to a different scenario, a big leap toward a revolution in gender roles: in fact, she already begins to observe [emerging the first timid feminists, those who will one day swell the legions, banner flying, will claim for their sisters, sold to the barbarous male servant, the law of individual human freedom] "uscire le prime timide femministe, quelle che un giorno ingrossate a legioni, vessillo spiegato, sapranno rivendicare per le loro sorelle vendute al barbaro servaggio maschile, la legge di umana liberta individuale" (96). Indeed, the first Japanese feminist movement was on the rise and during the years between 1911 and 1916 a literary journal titled *Seitō* ["Bluestocking"] hosted the articles of five women in Tokyo challenging the traditional views of modern Japanese womanhood.

It would be wrong to identify Villaurea as an activist for women's rights since her consideration of women's status in Japan is not always critical; at times it unexpectedly leaves room for melancholia about the ongoing transformation of gender relations. We find statements scattered throughout the book in striking contradiction to claims of individual freedom:

Giacché il vecchio deve a poco a poco fatalmente scomparire rasseg-niamoci nobilmente ad accettare anche la donna nuova. E quasi a consolarmene pensavo: quale contrasto fra questa gioventù attiva e sana e l'altra di quel lontano quartiere del vecchio Giappone dello *Yoshiwara!* (96)

[Since what is outdated must gradually fatally disappear, let us resign ourselves nobly to accepting the new woman too. And almost to console myself I thought: what a contrast between this active and healthy youth and the other from that distant neighborhood of old *Yoshiwara* Japan!]

Further down, she adds the ironic comment: "Penso, che ne farà di esse la futura civiltà galoppante? Non riesco a realizzare un Giappone con la donna nuova. Oh! poveri futuri turisti" (123) [I think, what will the future galloping civilization make of them? I cannot imagine a Japan with the new woman. Oh! poor future tourists]. Beneath Villaurea's feminist veneer exists a condescending, if not opposing, view of the new Japanese woman. She seems to be especially attracted to women who opt for tradition. Indeed, she tries to find them in Tokyo, at the Women's Educational School where they receive their education. As Alice Mabel Bacon points out, this school was "one of the most conservative and anti-foreign of the Tokyo schools, – a school for noble girls, under the management of the Imperial Household Department" (v). Villaurea is quite impressed by the school environment:

Confinata al limite estremo della città ... è l'università delle ragazze, una dimostrazione di quanto di più completo ed evoluto si può immaginare in fatto di educazione femminile dà l'illusione di trovarsi molto lontano dall'Asia estrema, piuttosto in pieno Nord, Scandinavia o Olanda, dove la donna impara con l'istruzione, il rispetto e il controllo di se stessa, senza l'umiliante condizione creata dalle nostre vecchie abitudini, che costituiscono intorno alla ragazza, una gabbia preservativa per la sua onestà.

Mille e duecento ragazze fra interne ed esterne vivono in questi sani ed igienici ambienti, divisi a vari padiglioni e seminati a mezzo a vastissimi giardini ...

Ma io dimenticavo ... qui l'educazione maschile non è quella dei nostri evoluti paesi. Nessuno si occupa di disturbare o portare offesa alla gentile studentessa, che va tranquillamente e dignitosamente per la sua via.

Si vuole questa ostentata indifferenza maschile per il gentil sesso, attribuire non a educazione acquisita, ma all'atavica continuazione di quel disprezzo per l'amore, ricavato dalle antiche leggi della cavalleria giapponese, il *Bushido*. (92)

[Confined at the extreme edge of the city ... it is the girls' university, a demonstration of the most complete and advanced imaginable institution in terms of female education – it gives the illusion of being very far from extreme Asia, quite in the middle of the North of Europe, such as Scandinavia or Holland, where the woman learns through education, respect and control of herself, without the humiliating condition created by our old habits, which constitute, a cage around the girl to protect her modesty.

Twelve hundred girls between inside and outside live in these healthy and hygienic environments, divided into various pavilions and disseminated among vast gardens ...

But I forgot... here male education is not that of our advanced countries. No one takes care of disturbing or offending the kind student, who goes quietly and with dignity on her way.

We want this ostentatious masculine indifference to the fair sex to be attributed not to acquired education, but to the atavistic continuation of that contempt for love derived from the ancient laws of the Japanese cavalry, the *Bushido*.]

By observing examples of women with a social and cultural pedigree similar to her own (noble and highly educated girls), Villaurea is inevitably drawn into comparing of them with herself and with the position of Sicilian women at the turn of the twentieth century. The typical portrait of the subjugated Japanese woman is replaced by the image of an unconventional female whose education allows her to gain self-control and a certain degree of independence. For Villaurea, this unexpected positive example of femininity is a crystallizing moment that enables her to reflect on gender disparity in Southern Italy in regard to freedom and respect. In many parts of Italy, a wide gap existed between politics aimed at implementing mass education and reality. At the dawn of Italian unification, the so-called Casati Law (1859) introduced an advanced public education system that provided elementary instruction for children of both sexes. Despite a decline in female illiteracy, the social reality of the time – especially in regions like Sicily– underscored a situation similar to what Villaurea describes in the above passage. At the turn of the century in the South of Italy:

The continuing gender disparity was partly because girls were more likely to be denied schooling, as their "need" for education was considered less important. Some parents, moreover, kept daughters at home because of fears of their morality. (Willson, 2010: 16)

As a member of the noble Palermitan class Villaurea realizes that her education, although advanced when compared to the average Sicilian woman, cannot match the level of her Japanese counterpart. Nevertheless, Villaurea does not take this as a cue to make the case for social reform toward more equal gender relations because she has an ultimately conservative spirit that limits her openness to the feminist cause.

My conclusion is that Villaurea's hesitation to condemn the gender roles in Japan lies in her anxiety regarding social change that could undermine the social prestige of the noble class to which she belonged. In her observations about social relations in Japan the baroness expresses an identification with conservative gender roles that coincides with an analysis of class status:

Lo spirito di sottomissione ereditario nella classe inferiore, non contaminato ancora da moderna utopistica livellazione sociale, non conosce ribellione, ed accetta il lavoro con serena rassegnazione. L'umile ignora la piaga dell'odio verso il superiore, e gli dimostra rispetto, sottomissione e spesso un attaccamento perduto nei nostri paesi da anni e anni. (118)

[The spirit of hereditary submission in the lower class, not yet contaminated by modern utopian social leveling, knows no rebellion, and accepts work with serene resignation. The humble ignore the plague of hatred towards the superior, and show him respect, submission and often an attachment lost in our countries for years and years.]

Villaurea's preference for an ultraconservative policy and her anxiety regarding a subversion of power relations represent an aristocratic sentiment that the Sicilian writer Giuseppe Tomasi di Lampedusa (1896–1957) expressed in the novel *Il Gattopardo* (*The Leopard*), 1958. *The Leopard* is the story of the elderly Sicilian prince of Salina, Don Fabrizio, at the time of Italian unification in 1861. Don Fabrizio is the last representative of the old aristocratic order threatened by the depredation of Garibaldi's campaign to unify Italy. His properties are crumbling and his power is being undermined by the new bourgeoisie class taking over Sicily's feudal administration by its establishment of democratic policy. Don Fabrizio, the Leopard, is a giant whose death, as well as that of his class, is approaching; the novel is dominated by his "feeling of an immobilized present animated and enlarged by a sustained reflection on the past" (Said, 2006: 98). An analogous feeling of melancholy and longing for an irrecoverable world must be considered when reading Villaurea's journal on Japan. As a representative of a social class that has been losing prestige and authority since the unification of Italy, the Sicilian baroness cannot help but project her anxiety onto her analysis of the social transformation that Japan was undergoing at the time of her visit. What she is searching for is an ossified image of Japan, a confirmation of an immobile representation nourished by literary and visual sources. Here, for instance, is her first impression upon arrival:

> Giappone! Ma ecco, accade in me un fenomeno stranissimo! A dispetto di tanto mare percorso e di tanta attesa, io non riesco a convincermi di essere arrivata! Sono i quadri raccolti nella mia fantasia ad animarsi, a vivere?
>
> Tutto è allucinazione! Un'allucinazione che fa muovere il mio Giappone, quello della mia costruzione, del mio sogno! Possibile sia ancora il reale rimasto così intatto? (47)

[Japan! But here, a very strange phenomenon happens in me! In spite of having covered so much sea and after having waited for so long, I cannot convince myself that I have arrived! Are the paintings collected in my imagination to come alive, to live? Slender bridges between two twisted trees, wooden houses lined with paper-pane shutters through narrow streets ... little women folded in kimonos with a wide belt ... All is hallucination! A hallucination that makes my Japan move, that of my construction, of my dream! Is it possible that the real is still so intact?]

The reality that she describes is filtered by memories of *Madame Chrysanthème* (1887), the best-selling novel written by the French author Pierre Loti (1850–1923), which features the stereotype of the charming, graceful and, above all, complacent Butterfly. The real Meiji Japan's impact on Villaurea draws her attention to a new kind of Japanese woman, as well as a new society that is trying to move away from its feudal past. Nevertheless, Villaurea's noble resignation ("Rassegnamoci nobilmente ad accettare la donna nuova," 123) expresses a conflict between continuity and change that is rooted in her social status as a Sicilian baroness.

Works Cited

Agamben, Giorgio. 1999. *Remnants of Auschwitz: The Witness and the Archive*, translated by Daniel Heller-Roazen. New York: Zone Books.
Appiah, K. Anthony. 2005. *The Ethics of Identity*. Princeton, NJ: Princeton University Press.
—. 2006. *Cosmopolitanism: Ethics in a World of Strangers*. New York: W.W. Norton.
Apter, Emily. 2006. *Translation Zone. A New Comparative Literature*. Princeton, NJ: Princeton University Press.
Baker, Mona. 2006. *Translation and Conflict: A Narrative Account*. London and New York: Routledge.
—. 2016. "Narrative Analysis." In *Researching Translating and Interpreting*, edited by Claudia V. Angelelli and Brian J. Baer, 247–56. London and New York: Routledge.
Barzini, Luigi Sr. 1915 [1906]. *Il Giappone in armi*. Piacenza: L'arte bodoniana.
—. 1959. *Avventure in oriente*, edited by Luigi Barzini Jr. Milan: Arnoldo Mondadori Editore.
Bassnet, Susan and Lefevere, André. 1998. *Constructing Cultures: Essays on Literary Translation*. Clevedon; Philadelphia: Multilingual Matters.
Clark, Steve. 2015. "'A Study rather than a Rupture': Isabella Bird on Japan." In *New Directions in Travel Writing Studies*, edited by Julia Kuehn and Paul Smethurst, 17–34. New York: Palgrave Macmillan.
Clifford, James. 1997. *Routes: Travel and Translation in the Late Twentieth Century*. Cambridge, MA: Harvard University Press.
Corradini, Enrico. 1904. "La conferma del cannone," *Il Regno*. Quoted in Norberto Bobbio. 1995. *Ideological Profile of Twentieth-Century Italy*, translated by Lydia G. Cochrane. Princeton, NJ: Princeton University Press.
Cronin, Michael. 2000. *Across the Lines: Travel, Language, Translation*. Cork, Ireland: Cork University Press.
—. 2003. *Translation and Globalization*. New York: Routledge.
Culler, Jonathan. 1981. "Semiotics of Tourism," *American Journal of Semiotics*, 1 (1/2): 127–40.
Cuomo, Daniela. 2003. "Esordi e sviluppi della stampa italiana sul Giappone." In *Italia – Giappone, 450 anni*. Vol. 1, 256–61, edited by Adolfo Tamburello. Rome; Naples: Istituto Italiano per l'Africa e l'Oriente – University of Naples "l'Orientale."
Ewick, Patricia and Silbey, Susan S. 1995. "Subversive Stories and Hegemonic Tales: Toward a Sociology of Narrative." *Law & Society Review*, 29(2): 197–226.
Forsdick, Charles. 2000. *Victor Segalen and the Aesthetic of Diversity: Journeys between Cultures*. Oxford and New York: Oxford University Press.

Foster, Shirley. 1990. *Across New Worlds: Nineteenth-Century Women Travelers and their Writings*. New York: Wheatsheaf.
Geertz, Clifford. 1993. "Found in translation. On the social history of the moral imagination." In *Local Knowledge: Further Essays in Interpretive Anthropology*, 36–54. London: Fontana.
Henshall, Kenneth. 2004. *A History of Japan from Stone Age to Superpower*. 2nd edn. New York: Palgrave Macmillan.
Hokenson, Walsh J. 2004. *Japan, France, and East–West Aesthetics: French Literature, 1867–2000*. Madison, NJ: Fairleigh Dickinson University Press.
Inghilleri, Moira. 2009. "Translators in war zones: ethics under fire in Iraq." In *Globalization, Political Violence and Translation*, edited by Esperanza Bielsa, Christopher W. Hughes, 212–23. New York: Palgrave Macmillan.
Keene, Donald. 1971. *Landscapes and Portraits: Appreciation of Japanese Culture*. Tokyo and Palo Alto: Kodansha International.
Keevak, Michael. 2011, *Becoming Yellow: A Short Story of Racial Thinking*. Princeton, NJ and Oxford, UK: Princeton University Press.
Knightley, Phillip. 2004. *The First Casualty: The War Correspondent as Hero and Myth-Maker from Crimea to Iraq*. Baltimore and London: Johns Hopkins University Press.
Morasso, Mario. 1905. *L'Imperialismo nel XX secolo: La conquista del mondo*. Milan: Fratelli Treves Editori.
—. 1990. *Scritti sul Marzocco, 1897–1904*, edited by Piero Pieri. Bologna: Printer.
Oriani, Alfredo. 1904. "Fit via vi." *Il Marzocco*, March 8, 1904. In Alfredo Oriani. 1918. *Fuochi di bivacco*, 256–61. Bari: Gius. Laterza & Figli.
—. 1921. *Punte secche: Seconda serie di Fuochi di bivacco*. Bari: Gius. Laterza e Figli.
Pecorini, Daniele. 1935. *Japanese Maple*, translated by Hilda Bonavia. London: Geoffrey Bles.
—. 1937. *Foglia d'acero: scene di vita in Corea ed in Giappone durante la guerra russo-giapponese (1904–1905)*. Rome: Palombi.
Polezzi, Loredana. 2001. *Translating Travel: Contemporary Italian Travel Writing in English Translation*. Burlington: Ashgate.
Reina, Luisa. 2012. "Villaurea e le altre. Racconti di italiane in Oriente." In *Spazi, Segni, Parole: Percorsi di viaggiatrici italiane*, edited by Federica Frediani, Ricciarda Ricorda, 145–59. Milan: Franco Angeli.
Robbins, Bruce. 2009. "Comparative Cosmopolitanism." In *The Princeton Sourcebook in Comparative Literature. From the European Enlightenment to the Global present*, edited by David Damrosch, Natalie Melas, Mbongiseni Buthelezi, 309–28. Princeton and Oxford: Princeton University Press.
Sartini-Blum, Cinzia. 2008. *Rewriting the Journey in Contemporary Italian Literature*. Toronto: University of Toronto Press.

Said, Edward W. 2006. *On Late Style: Music and Literature against the Grain*. New York: Pantheon Books.

Spadaro, Maria Antonietta. 2002. *Otamà Kiyohara/Eleonora Ragusa: "Una favola fin de siècle."* Palermo: Gruppo Editoriale Kalos.

Sweeney, Michael S. 2015. "'Narrative is a thread, and the truth is a fabric': Luigi Barzini and the Russo-Japanese War." *American Journalism*, 32: 41–59.

Tarling, Nicholas. 2015. *Orientalism in the Operatic World*. Lanham, Boulder, CO, New York and London: Rowman & Littlefield.

Venuti, Lawrence. 1995. *The Translator's Invisibility: A History of Translation*. London and New York: Routledge.

—. 2009. *From "Translation, Community, Utopia." The Princeton Sourcebook in Comparative Literature: from the European Enlightenment to the Global Present*, edited by David Damrosch, Natalie Melas and Mbongiseni Buthelezi, 358–79. Princeton: Princeton University Press.

Villaurea, Baronessa di. 1914. *Al Giappone: impressioni di una viaggiatrice*. Palermo: Officine tipo-litografiche.

Willson, Perry. 2010. *Women in Twentieth-Century Italy*. New York: Palgrave Macmillan.

CHAPTER TWO

Mussolini in Japan: Japanese Representations in the Age of Fascism

> Ma la loro massima forza è morale. È nella compattezza delle loro volontà, nella sublimazione del sacrificio per la Patria, per cui chi muore in guerra diviene una specie di nume tutelare. Gli eroi sono eterni. Il loro spirito entra nell'anima del combattente e li infiamma.
>
> (Luigi Barzini, *Perché il Giappone vince*)

1. One Country, Multiple Narratives

In this chapter I examine the literature of Italians traveling and living in Japan during the twenty years of the Fascist era (1923–43), as I identify in the Axis alliance between Italy and Japan (1937–43) a fundamental shift in the mode of representing Japan through travel writing. This historical event is the watershed that separates the chapter into two sections. Before the ratification of the military alliance, a nationalistic approach informed by a sense of Italian cultural supremacy defined the attitude of Italian writers who landed in the East Asian country. The writings of this period are more likely to stress anthropological differences based on the supposedly unfathomable character of the Japanese society, and to adopt a language of racist and sexual biases. By contrast, I argue that during the years of the military alliance between Mussolini's Italy and Hirohito's Japan, a narrative aimed at promoting commonalities and mutual goals with Japan took place in Italy. The first part analyses the body of literature devoted to Japan with an Orientalist narrative, based on the "'territorial either/or' theory of identity" (see Introduction p. 4). Such a binary construction is based on the use, often blatant, of racist rhetoric to denigrate the Japanese "Other" and, by contrast, to make the case for the "natural" superiority of the Italian visitor. Charles Burdett has contextualized this type of identity theory discourse at the time of the Fascist regime, when manipulating the press for political purposes was an ordinary practice. When collective identity is under the influence of a regime and the traveler is a journalist working to serve the purposes of political propaganda, travelogs become a useful source for discovering the apparatus of enforced images and ideas. As Burdett puts it:

> The question that travel writing provides a medium to explore, whether it concerns the limits of personal autonomy, the coercive power of collective versions of identity or the problems that attain to representing other cultures and people, assumes an undeniable importance in the context of a regime that attempted to enlist large swathes of the population in its drive to transform the whole of society, and which pursued an increasingly aggressive and expansionist foreign policy. (Burdett, 2007: 9)

During the so-called *Ventennio*, as Burdett argues, travel literature was connected to journalism, whose main role was to mold public opinion in order to meet the goals of an aggressive foreign policy. Most of the writers I consider in the following pages were sent to Japan as correspondents for national newspapers: Giovanni Comisso worked for *Corriere della Sera*, Arnaldo Cipolla was hired by *La Stampa*, while Mario Appelius published his articles in *Il Popolo d'Italia* and Ercole Patti in *Gazzetta del Popolo*. After their first appearances in national dailies, the reports from Japan were collected and published in book form by well-known publishing houses like Mondadori, Bompiani or Treves. Since the authors of the reports were also freelance writers, the transition of the travelogs from newspapers to book form sometimes involved the creation of a plot and consequently the transformation of written accounts of journeys into travel literature or novels. For example, this was the case with Ercole Patti's *Ragazze di Tokio* (1934) and Giovanni Comisso's "Amori d'Oriente" (1949). All these authors had in common a limited knowledge of Japan and were unacquainted with the local language, making them ideal profiles of Orientalist writers.

In the second part I concentrate on the period of the Axis alliance, which I approach from two opposing perspectives: on the one hand, I focus on a propaganda-driven narrative of Japan as a country that shared with Italy the same vision of a prestigious and glorious future, the same deification of its leader, the same collective belief in patriotic faith and a set of core ethical values. I focus in particular on the cultural apparatus organized by the government to support its military agenda. On the other hand, because of the political ties between the two countries, I am interested in the flow of ideas, people, cultures and languages between Japan and Italy that took place during the alliance, beyond the political propaganda. Therefore, this second part of the chapter is organized around two potentially antithetical concepts: one is nationalism and the other is transnationalism. First, I will offer examples of how a Fascist political ideology bolstered the unlikely alliance between two nations that had until then little history of diplomatic relations on record: by removing obvious differences, they managed to advance the political agenda of both countries. Then, I will move to two different cases of transnational relations that exceed the nature of propaganda-based relationships. The first one is represented by the works of Pietro Silvio Rivetta (1886–1952), whose deep knowledge of Japanese culture and language deserves a different approach, one that emphasizes more his role as translator and mediator of Japanese culture in Italy and less his service for the Fascist regime. Finally, I will concentrate on the case of Arundel Del Re (1892–1974), who was an Italian immigrant to Japan in the 1920s, but who remained aloof from the politics of the Italian regime and connected to a transnational network of people and countries. Whereas the nationalist propaganda of the war period fabricated a fanciful Italo-Japanese sense of brotherhood, both Silvio Rivetta and Arundel Del Re, by contrast, appealed to a notion of "relational Orientalism" (see Introduction pp. 4–5) to absorb and promote Japanese culture, while at the same time acknowledging differences. By showing contrastive examples of nationalism, propaganda and transnationalism I hope to offer a glimpse of the heterogeneous movement of people and ideas between Italy and Japan under Mussolini's regime.

2. A Disneyland for Sexual Escapades

During the years preceding the Axis alliance, travel writings about Japan show a redundant nationalistic element in their accounts. In Angelo Pellegrino's words:

> Un popolo di poeti, di artisti, di eroi, di santi, di pensatori, di scienziati, di navigatori, di trasmigratori. Il fascismo è il grande momento dei Fraccaroli, dei Vergani, dei Cipolla, e di tanti altri "trasmigratori" inviati

speciali del regime. Va da sé, l'atteggiamento generale degli inviati speciali durante il Ventennio è fortemente nazionalistico. Pieni di italocentrica sufficienza, essi affrontano le diverse culture orientali con lo scopo spesso palese di denigrarle. Con varie sfumature, il loro atteggiamento è sostanzialmente riduttivistico. Va esaltata la patria fascista, il mezzo è l'ironia e il discredito delle cose degli altri paesi, massime dei paesi orientali, allora ancora lontani dall'essere nazioni, quasi tutti sotto il giogo coloniale di potenze avverse alla politica del fascismo. (Pellegrino, 1985: 34)

[A people of poets, artists, heroes, saints, thinkers, scientists, navigators, migrants. Fascism is the great moment of Fraccaroli, Vergani, Cipolla, and many other "migrants," who were special reporters at the service of the regime. It goes without saying, the general attitude of special reporters during the twenty years is strongly nationalistic. Full of italocentric sufficiency, they face the different oriental cultures with the often evident aim of denigrating them. With various nuances, their attitude is essentially reductive. The fascist homeland has to be exalted, the means is the irony and the discredit of the things of the other countries, especially Eastern countries, then still far from being nations, almost all under the colonial yoke of powers opposed to the politics of fascism.]

Among those reporters there were also anti-fascist writers, who walked the fine line between subservient respect for the regime and the dissimulation of their political views. Giovanni Comisso from Veneto and Ercole Patti from Sicily belong to this category as they traveled in Asia in the early 1930s working as special correspondents for important national papers, while writing their fictional stories. They both revisited their articles in order to republish them as semi-fictional novels, whose titles stress the sexist image of Japan as an erotic Disneyland: Ercole Patti's *Ragazze di Tokio* (1934) ["Tokyo girls"] and Giovanni Comisso's *Amori d'Oriente* (1949) ["Oriental loves"].[1] The reduction of Japan to a country worthy only of sexual exploitation is a clear metaphor for a nationalistic ideology intent on looking at the "observed country" from a perspective of dominion and superiority.[2] Beyond the sexual

---

1   The sexual innuendos are once again included in the title of the new edition of his journalistic reports from Asia: Giovanni Comisso, 1958, *Donne gentili* ["Kind women"] (Milan: Longanesi).
2   The perspective of the Western observer whose point of view emphasizes the superiority of his civilization over the observed Eastern civilization is a cornerstone of

metaphors, Comisso and Patti deploy other rhetorical devices to diminish the Land of the Rising Sun in the eyes of the Italian reader. What makes their case of special interest is the transition of their accounts of Japan from the anthropological and sociological style of journalistic prose to the creative realm of fiction, with all the freedom that such rewriting entails.

Between 1931 and 1932 the young Sicilian novelist Ercole Patti (1903–76) was employed as a reporter in Asia by the daily newspaper *Gazzetta del Popolo*. The itinerary of his tour included countries whose political and military turmoil drew the attention of the international community: India, under the effect of Gandhi's non-violent resistance movement, but also China and Japan, whose diplomatic relations had broken down when Japanese army forces clashed with Chinese troops in Manchuria in September 1931.

These articles were later collected in a travelog titled *Ragazze di Tokio: viaggio da Tokio a Bombay* (1934) ["Tokyo girls: journey from Tokyo to Bombay"], which was republished in a new edition titled *Un lungo viaggio lontano* ["A long journey away"] in 1975.

From the point of disembarking in Yokohama, Patti immediately seems unsympathetic to the people observed along his journey, as well as uneasy about the places he visits. He describes the predominant trait of local inhabitants as a deeply aggressive feeling expressed with a seamless smile: "È il Giappone che ride sempre e in certi momenti il sorriso, a furia di resistere sulle labbra per tanto tempo, assume un'aria feroce e ossessionante" (Patti, 1975: 13) [It is Japan that always laughs and at certain times the smile, by

---

Said's Orientalist theory. Giuliana Benvenuti observes this phenomenon in the accounts of Italian travelogs in the Orient: "Nel resoconto novecentesco possono alternarsi, ovvero convivere, diverse modalità di descrizione, se di una estetica dell'eccentrico e dell'ignoto sarà erede Gozzano, con la sua ripresa dell'esotismo ottocentesco, con 'l'enfasi sullo 'stridore' dell'India, di un atteggiamento illuminista sarà erede Moravia, ma in ogni caso, la 'struttura di atteggiamento e di riferimento' di questi autori è ancora in larga misura quella che Said considera propria dell'imperialismo, poiché l'osservatore, qualunque estetica privilegi, si sente superiore in termini di conoscenza rispetto agli osservati, anche quando percepisca questa superiorità conoscitivo-razionale come un peso, un fardello, una gabbia": Giuliana Benvenuti. *Il viaggiatore come autore: L'India nella letteratura italiana del Novecento* (Bologna: Il Mulino, 2008): 48. For the analysis of Patti and Comisso's sexual accounts see Angelo Pellegrino, 1985, *Verso Oriente: Viaggi e letteratura degli scrittori italiani nei paesi orientali (1912–1982)* (Rome: Istituto dell'enciclopedia Treccani): 62: "Oggi si direbbe che il duo Comisso-Patti s'è portato com'era proprio del tempo, cioè da bravi maschilisti italici, posseduti da un'idea del femminile – perché no? – un tantino fascista."

dint of resisting on the lips for a long time, takes on a fierce and obsessive air].
The perception of being in a place that stands apart from common humanity
is elaborated in the following passage, in which the Japanese are described as
a sort of machine:

> I giapponesi escono di casa calmi, rassettati, col cappello duro e il *tight*
> ben spolverati, le scarpe lucide, la pace nel cuore, formidabili, freddi,
> imbattibili e vanno a fabbricare le potenti corazzate, i grattacieli, le
> grandi motonavi, organizzano l'esercito, invadono lentamente la Cina,
> con una precisione sconcertante e sulle labbra un sorriso che fa venire i
> brividi. I loro cervelli, non geniali, ma sicuri e garantiti, funzionano come
> cronometri. (Patti, 1975: 38)

> [The Japanese leave the house calm, tidy, and tightly dusted, in a hard hat
> and shiny shoes, with peace in their heart, formidable, cold, unbeatable
> and go to make powerful battleships, skyscrapers, big ships, organize the
> army, slowly invade China, with a disconcerting precision and a smile
> on the lips that makes you shiver. Their brains, not brilliant, but safe and
> guaranteed, work as chronometers.]

The Japanese individual is portrayed as a person lacking in human
emotions, whose efficiency is compared to that of a ruthless robot.

In Patti's view, even the behavior of Japanese youth stands outside the
definition of "typical, commonly accepted behavior." This is his conclusion
after a night spent in a Tokyo bar:

> I giovanotti giapponesi hanno una maniera di divertirsi che contrasta
> singolarmente con quella dei giovanotti di tutte le razze. Essi siedono
> lunghe ore al "cafè," in atteggiamenti di abbandono, tranquillo e
> domestico, chiacchierando del più e del meno, masticando bruscolini e
> sorseggiando birra. Non ce n'è uno che allunghi la mano per carezzare
> una ragazza. Parlano e ridono continuamente. Non ho mai capito che
> cosa abbiano tanto da ridere. La loro serata trascorre lieta e uguale fra
> luci variopinte, canzoni cavernose di grammofoni, insipide sigarette col
> Fusjiama sulla scatola, risatine.
>
> Soggiogato da quell'inesorabile crepitare di sorrisi pullulanti in tutta
> la sala, ad un certo punto, trascinato pei capelli, fui costretto a mettermi
> a ridere anch'io. Non c'era altro da fare. Guardandomi nello specchio
> che avevo accanto mi sorpresi con un sorrisetto dolciastro sul labbro. Il

Giappone è terribile: ti piega ai suoi voleri e ti impone le sue usanze senza che tu te ne accorga. (Patti, 1975: 45)

[Japanese youngsters have a way of having fun that contrasts individually with that of youngsters of all races. They sit long hours at the "cafè," in attitudes of abandonment, quiet and domesticity, chatting about this and that, chewing tiny tidbits and sipping beer. There is not one who extends his hand to caress a girl.

They talk and laugh continuously. I've never understood what they have so much to laugh about. Their evening passes happily and equably between colorful lights, cavernous songs of gramophones, insipid cigarettes with mount Fuji on the box, giggles.

Subjugated by that inexorable crackle of smiles that swarmed across the hall, at one point pushed to the limits, I was forced to laugh too. There was nothing else to do. Looking at myself in the mirror that was next to me I surprised myself with a sweet little smile on the lips. Japan is terrible: it bends you to its will and imposes its customs without you noticing it.]

What is more typical than a group of young teenagers talking, smiling, and drinking beer in a bar at night? But for Ercole Patti a standard norm of behavior must include things like man's sexual body language: "Non ce n'è uno che allunghi la mano per carezzare una ragazza" [There is not one who extends his hand to caress a girl]. Moreover, without any regard for the fact that he does not know the language, Patti does not refrain from commenting on the frivolity of the smiling faces. His sense of exclusion is well represented by his unmotivated smile reflected on a mirror, in an attempt to convince the reader that the other smiles are as meaningless as his own. Facing the complexities of a foreign culture without having the linguistic knowledge to transcend the communication barrier, Patti's experience falls into the category of the "semiotic" traveler, who, according to Michael Cronin, relies on his five different senses to overcome his linguistic limitations. "What semiotic transcendence assumes, of course, at some level, is that there is a common humanity that makes communication possible and that we are not irredeemably bound by the circumstances of our birth into a particular language" (Cronin, 2000: 89). The semiotic instruments that Patti adopts are used not as a communicative system, but rather as an interpretative method aimed at stressing the differences between the two cultures, rather than the common humanity.

The process of alienation from Japanese society is completed when Patti uses animal metaphors to describe the persons he meets. The allegedly cruel gaze of a bystander is compared to a grim-faced teddy bear: "Un uomo basso e tozzo mi guardò a lungo di sotto le falde del cappello duro, con due occhi neri, fermi e crudeli da orsacchiotto di stoppa col fischietto sulla pancia" (47) [A short, squat man looked down at me from under the brim of his hard hat, with two black, stiff and cruel eyes like a teddy bear with a whistle on his stomach]. Other bystanders' smiles are compared to those of imaginary tigers: "Partimmo sotto lo sguardo di due giovanotti che si erano fermati a guardarci con taciti sorrisi da tigre" (47) [We left under the gaze of two young men who had stopped to look at us with tacit tiger smiles]. Finally, Patti attains his goal of meeting a prostitute, whose movements are compared first to a cat and then to a sturgeon: "Sotsouko sorride serena e familiare osservando con curiosità e stupore le mie valigie. Va su e giù nella minuscola stanza a passi lenti e molli, come un piccolo gatto. All'improvviso si lancia a capofitto nel letto, con un guizzo, come uno storione" (48) [Sotsouko smiles serene and familiar, looking with curiosity and amazement at my suitcases. It goes up and down in the tiny room with slow and soft steps, like a little cat. Suddenly she throws herself headlong into the bed, with a leap, like a sturgeon]. In general, in *Un lungo viaggio lontano* the point of view of the observer carries a sense of nationalistic superiority over the object of his observation. The chauvinistic tones of this representation are expressed through a complex of metaphors and images, like the persistent image of the "smile," that successfully present a degraded vision.

Giovanni Comisso (1895–1969) was already an accomplished novelist when, between 1929 and 1930, he completed his journalistic reports in Asia for the national daily paper *Corriere della Sera*. A selection of his articles was published in the book *Cina-Giappone* ("China-Japan," 1932), which was later republished under the new title *Donne gentili* (1958). While editing articles for *Cina-Giappone*, Comisso began to write a fictional and autobiographical story based on his Oriental tour. The result was *Amori d'Oriente* ["Oriental loves"], that would be unpublished until 1949.[3] Lorenzo, the alter ego of the author,

---

3 It is interesting to note that immediately after the publication Comisso wrote an article on "La Fiera Letteraria" to mark his distance from the content of the book, saying that it belonged to a previous and outdated period of his career: *"Amori d'Oriente* è semplicemente un mio libro scritto quindici anni or sono e solo ora ha trovato la possibilità di essere pubblicato. È un libro mio, ma scritto da un altro me stesso che oggi considero staccato da me. Non rinnego questo libro, perché allora avrei dovuto distruggerlo. Ma siccome rappresenta il limite massimo della mia possibilità narrativa nella trama degli istinti, ho desiderato venisse pubblicato per avere, io compreso, la misura completa della mia maniera di scrivere. Purtroppo, *Amori d'Oriente* piace: e

is the protagonist of a search for sexual pleasure in the Middle and Far East. The protagonist's intentions are explicit from the outset in the same fashion as we have already seen in Patti's book: "Gli avevano parlato del Giappone come di una terra dove l'abbondanza di donne rende piacevoli tutte le ore del giorno, attendeva il sopraggiungere della notte per avere la possibilità dei primi incontri" (Comisso, 2002: 1031) [They had talked to him about Japan as a land where the abundance of women makes it pleasant all hours of the day, in fact he was waiting for the arrival of the night to have the possibility of the first meetings]. However, Lorenzo must cope with the fact that his sexual appetite cannot be satisfied in a land where women do not live up his expectations:

> Il servo dell'albergo aveva presentato a Lorenzo una delle tanto attese bellezze della città, ma sebbene assai bella di volto, aveva rivelato un corpo patito la cui pelle era cosparsa di cicatrici. L'aveva fatta uscire subito, il suo amico gli aveva spiegato che erano punture fatte con aghi infuocati per guarirla da qualche malattia, come usano in Cina, ma non aveva voluto sapere di altre. (Comisso, 2002: 1029)

> [The servant of the hotel had presented to Lorenzo one of the long-awaited beauties of the city, but although very beautiful in appearance, she had revealed a wrecked body, with scars spread all over her skin. He had let her out immediately, his friend had explained that they were bites made with burning needles to cure her from some illness, as they use in China, but he did not want to know about others.]

Lorenzo is disappointed by the body types he encounters and does not hesitate to express his distaste for the appearance of Japanese women as well as men: "Subito [Lorenzo] si accorse che contrastava con queste [donne] l'aspetto aspro, orrido e a volte malsano degli uomini, vestiti con chimono grigio, scalzi o con zoccoli e cappello all'europea: terrei e occhialuti" (Comisso, 2002: 1031) [Immediately [Lorenzo] realized that he contrasted with these [women] the appearance of sour, horrid and sometimes unhealthy

---

questo mi riconferma l'errore nella narrativa d'istinti" (Giovanni Comisso, "Il libro di un altro me stesso," quoted in Comisso, 2002, "Amori d'Oriente," in Rolando Damiani and Nico Naldini (editors), *Opere* (Milan: Mondadori): 1724). In 1954 an English translation of *Loves of the Orient* was published in New York by the publishing house Bridgehead Books, but American censorship intervened to stop distribution.

men, dressed in gray kimono, barefoot or with hooves and European hats: ashen and bespacted men]. Even his meeting with a prostitute generates frustration in Lorenzo, who ends up blaming the two women protagonists because of their irreconcilable diversity:

> La porta si aperse, una vecchia occhialuta e con i denti d'oro gli fece un grande inchino, pregandolo di togliersi le scarpe, salì una scaletta di legno e si trovò in una stanza dove si sentiva un fastidiosissimo fonografo con voci nasali e continue. La vecchia gli offerse alcuni cuscini e gli mise accanto l'occorrente per fumare, facendogli segni di avere pazienza. Pertanto il fonografo non smetteva diventando sempre più irritante. [...] La porta si aperse ed entrò una ragazza vestita e pettinata all'europea, che lo salutò in inglese, e tra sorrisi artefatti e altre parole in giapponese lo indusse a sedersi sui cuscini. Anche questa ragazza non aveva nulla di notevole, Lorenzo era ormai deciso di adattarsi, ma il fonografo, dopo un attimo di tregua, aveva subito ripreso pettegolo e insistente. Fece segno di fare tacere questa musica, la ragazza gli rispose che non si poteva, perché il fonografo non era in quella casa, ma in una di fronte. La musica non finiva più, Lorenzo volle sapere dove fosse la stanza per fare l'amore, si sentì rispondere che era quella. Il fonografo non accennava a smettere. La ragazza non accennava a spogliarsi. La vecchia voleva pagasse prima [...] Lorenzo ne ebbe abbastanza. Le donne dovettero accorgersi che era in grande furore, perché al suo cenno di aprire la porta, si affrettarono umili senza dire una parola. (Comisso, 2002: 1032–33)

[The door opened, an old bespectacled lady with gold teeth made him a big bow, begging him to take off his shoes; he climbed a wooden ladder and found himself in a room where he felt an annoying phonograph with nasal and continuous voices. The old woman offered him some cushions and gave him all he needed to smoke, while showing signs that invited him to be patient. However the phonograph did not stop becoming more and more irritating [...] The door opened and a girl entered dressed and combed in European style, she greeted him in English, and while giving him artificial smiles and using other words in Japanese she persuaded him to sit down on the cushions. Even if this girl had nothing remarkable, Lorenzo had now decided to adapt, but the phonograph, after a moment of respite, had immediately resumed with its intrusive and insistent noise. He signaled to silence this music, the girl replied that it could not be done, because the phonograph was not in that house, but in a different one across the street. The music no longer ended, Lorenzo wanted to know where the room to make love was, they told him that he was already in the designated room. The phonograph showed no signs of quitting. The girl did not make any move to undress. The old woman wanted him to pay first [...]

Lorenzo had had enough. The women must have realized that he was in great fury, because at his nod to open the door, they hurried humbly without saying a word.]

Here, Lorenzo's distaste for the unappealing body of the prostitute comes with a deeper frustration due to a lack of communication and a deep awareness of an unbearable diversity. The image of the gramophone and its obnoxious sound vividly expresses this distance that cannot be bridged. The cacophonic sound stands for how Lorenzo perceives the Japanese "Other." The location of the gramophone outside the room – that is, in an inaccessible and unknown space – represents the impossibility of reaching out to the source of the music, that is, the core of the Japanese soul.

The conclusion of the journey in the Land of the Rising Sun features another rejection of Japanese customs and culture. After debunking the myth of the "sexy and gracious Jap girl," Lorenzo questions the benefits of the well-known Nippon tradition of a warm bath at dusk. What is generally considered a sublime way to relax turns out to be another tragicomic experience for Lorenzo.

> Discese per il bagno e con sorpresa trovò nella baracca attigua all'albergo due floride ragazze. Una con il sapone in mano e l'altra con la spugna, le maniche del chimono rimboccate lasciavano intravedere braccia poderose, l'acqua era caldissima, esse ridevano. Appena spogliato si fecero vicine e presero a insaponarlo alla schiena. Nessuna grazia raggiava dai loro volti, ma un'indifferenza ostinata. L'aria era minacciosa e l'acqua ostile, non poteva né immergersi, né stare fuori: una specie di furore lo prese.
>
> Allora urlando di chiudere le piccole finestre e di buttare acqua fredda nella vasca, si rivolse verso le ragazze, ma queste, forse credendolo invaso dall'amore, dato uno strillo fuggirono, sbizzarrendo nei piccoli occhi. (Comisso, 2002: 1046)

[He went down to the bathroom and, surprisingly, found two thriving girls in the shed next to the hotel. One with the soap in hand and the other with the sponge, the sleeves of the kimono rolled up gave a glimpse of powerful arms, the water was very hot, they laughed. As soon as they were stripped they came close and started to soap him in the back. No grace radiated from their faces, but a stubborn indifference. The air was menacing and the water hostile, he could neither plunge nor stand out: a kind of rage took over him. Then, as he was screaming to close the small windows and throw cold water into the tub, he turned to the girls, but these, perhaps believing him invaded by an insurgent feeling of love, gave a scream and ran away, squinting with their small eyes.]

The gap between the elements (room temperature too cold, water too hot), the ambiguous morality (Lorenzo's embarrassment about standing naked in front of women), the lack of grace in the girls' mannerisms ("No grace radiated from their faces, but a stubborn indifference") are all conducive to the instinctive reaction of the protagonist, who ends his Japanese adventure in an explosion of rage and a final cry, which is, once again, misinterpreted and taken to be a violent declaration of love. It is clear that Comisso plays with the natural instincts of his character, whose demeanor shows no attempt at understanding and reaching out beyond the differences he encounters. The instinctual reactions underline a sense of dominion and implicitly point out the weakness and "feminine soul" of Japanese society in contrast to the allegedly more virile Italian identity. In the example cited here, the local inhabitants are women willing to serve the newcomer. The protagonist's disappointment and his subsequent intense reaction are meant to emphasize the cowardice and softness of the Asian people.[4]

Neither Patti's *Ragazze di Tokio* nor Comisso's *Amori d'Oriente* were by no means written to endorse a Fascist ideology, as both writers were covertly anti-fascist. Ercole Patti admits in the premise of *Un lungo viaggio lontano* (1975) that his Asian journey was motivated by the need to escape the restrictions of the totalitarian state.[5] In his autobiographical novel

---

4   For this naïveté see, for instance, this example in which the Japanese security system is met with ridicule: "Lorenzo aveva sentito parlare del grande sospetto che i giapponesi hanno verso gli stranieri e si divertiva a eludere tutte le domande mescendogli una birra che finì per fargli reclinare il capo sulla tavola e se ne uscì lasciandolo nel sonno" (Comisso, 2002: 1036).
5   See Graziella Pulce, 2015, "Patti in Giappone: un catanese nell'impero dei segni," *Il manifesto*, July 2. In spite of the imprisonment Patti's antifascism is still questioned. Recently Ruth Ben-Ghiat refered to Patti's actor role as Fascist journalist in Mario Camerini's propaganda film *Il grande appello* (1936) as "the real Fascist journalist Ercole Patti, whose experiences in Djibouti were one source of the story": Ruth Ben-Ghiat, 2015, *Italian Fascism's Empire Cinema* (Bloomington: Indiana University Press): 86.

Roma amara e dolce ("Rome bitter and sweet," 1972), he revisits the three months spent in a Fascist prison in Rome from October 1943 to January 1944[6] when he was accused of conspiring with the partisan resistance. Comisso, on the other hand, was able to disguise his political dissent by virtue of his juvenile participation in the military occupation of Fiume led by the Fascist protégée Gabriele D'Annunzio. His writings during the 1930s show a willingness to comply with the values of the regime by enacting a rhetorical praise of its policies.[7] However, both of them seize the opportunity of traveling in Asia as a way to escape the oppressive surveillance of the regime, even at the cost of limiting their intellectual freedom by working for Fascist journals.

As Derek Duncan points out, the journey to the Orient for the Western traveler is inevitably connected to the geography of erotic imagination and desire: it is a mental space, as well as a material one, where the male colonizer finds a way round the repressive sexual politics at home and enjoys the sense of freedom abroad. Both Patti and Comisso respond to the literature of the "porno-tropics" but in different ways, according to their sexual orientation. Patti's heterosexual character finds an easy avenue through the restrictions of Fascist censorship by reinforcing the association between "virility" and masculinity, on the one hand, and Italian physical superiority on the other; thus addressing anxieties about the perceptions of Italy as a "feminine" colonialist power because of setbacks suffered during the colonial campaign in Africa.[8] Patti's character proves his masculinity through sexual intercourse by reinstating a gender hierarchy, while at the same token acknowledging a racial hierarchy and the Fascist

---

6 See Silvana Grasso, 2006, "La Sicilia tenera di Ercole Patti," *La Repubblica*, November 1.

7 In this regard Derek Duncan mentions Comisso's 1935 introduction to the biography of his mother's brother, Tommaso Salsa, "in which he [...] appears to celebrate Italy's imperial ambition": Derek Duncan, 2002, "Travel and Autobiography: Giovanni Comisso's Memories of the War," in Charles Burdett and Derek Duncan (editors), *Cultural Encounters: European Travel Writings in the 1930s* (New York and Oxford: Berghahn Books): 55. Rolando Damiani, also, points out the existence of Comisso's articles on *Yoga* and *Camicia nera* in which he exploits the theme of the "razza italica" (Damiani, in Comisso, 2002: xxxii).

8 For an analysis of the perceived Italian national identity as "effeminate" following the Adwa defeat and the Fascist attempt to reverse this trope see Silvana Patriarca, 2010, *Italian Vices: Nation and Character from the Risorgimento to the Republic* (Cambridge, UK: Cambridge University Press): 105, 138.

fear of contamination, by belittling the body of the Asian prostitute. The unwillingness to indulge over details about the sexual encounters and erotic phantasies probably represents a parody of the genre of the "sexual exiles"[9] in Asia, but it is also a way for Patti to reckon with the sense of decency required by the Fascist censorship. The explicit bisexual content of Comisso's *Amori d'Oriente*, on the other hand, is one of the reasons that prompted the author to postpone the publication of the novel. Comisso envisions his journey to Asia as escape from the oppressive sexual policies of the regime, predicated upon heterosexuality, reproduction and patriarchy. He pursues an image of the Orient as a refuge for homosexuals as it has been perceived since the end of the nineteenth century by Western travelers, such as Oscar Wilde (1854–1900) and André Gide (1869–1951). Derek Duncan has brought our attention to the play of interpretations included in the multiple rewriting of Comisso's journey in Asia: in *Amori d'Oriente* and *Gioco d'infanzia* ["Childhood game"], the colonialist narrative of the protagonist – a privileged white male European exercising his power to "see" the Oriental "Other" as inferior – lays the ground for the hidden subjectivity of the author to construct an imaginary geography of the Orient as a space to project a phantasy of sexual liberation. The Orient is therefore the frame where the author's private desires are displaced and redirected in an elsewhere that is outside the geography of colonization and military conquest. Rather than an attempt to validate Mussolini's nationalistic views, Duncan concludes, the rewriting of the journey in the Orient must be seen as Comisso's silent critique of the regime. Yet Comisso's *Amori d'Oriente*, as we will see in the next paragraph, is also an Orientalist

---

9   I refer to Jonathan Dollimore's definition of Westerners crossing the boundaries of class and race to travel toward sexual paradises abroad. Dollimore takes a stance in defense of sexual tourism abroad, in response to Said's critique of it, as reaction to the wave homophobia at home: "Sexually exiled from the repressiveness of the home culture [...] homosexuals have searched instead for fulfillment in the realm of the foreign. Not necessarily as a second best: over and again in the culture of homosexuality, differences of race and class are intensively cathected. That this has also occurred in exploitative, sentimental, and/or racist forms does not diminish its significance; if anything, it increases it. Those who move too hastily to denounce homosexuality across race and class as essentially or only exploitative, sentimental, or racist betray their own homophobic ignorance": Jonathan Dollimore, 1991, *Sexual Dissidence: Augustine to Wilde, Freud to Foucault* (Oxford: Clarendon Press; New York: Oxford University Press): 250. All considered, this passage applies well in the case of Comisso's homosexual experience in Asia in its crossing class and racial boundaries, in fact it represents a keen justification of it.

work of ethnography in its effort to deliver an image of the Asian other to the Italian reader, in this reflecting the author's/readers' assumptions, beliefs and values, which mark the difference between the self and the other. In this respect the idea of the Orient is not a seamless space that engenders an all-encompassing erotic phantasy, but its national boundaries play a role in projecting a specific version of stereotyped national characters. In spite of the investment of the author's subjectivity in the narration, in the next section I will argue that, at least in the case of Japan, Comisso's account in *Amori d'Oriente* does not detract from early 1930s Fascist narratives of this country.

3. Virile Forms and Subversive Spirits

The move from *Cina-Giappone* to *Amori d'Oriente* implies the transition from an ethnographic account narrated by the allegedly impersonal voice of the reporter to a fictional story invested by the subjective desires and fantasies of the narrator.[10] Gabriele Schwab has coined the useful notion of "imaginary ethnographies"[11] to describe fictional texts that purport to observe and comment on a foreign culture while blurring the distinctions between reality and fantasy. Whereas in ethnography the process of *Writing Cultures*[12] through fieldwork reports has brought to academic attention the subjective role of the ethnographer in "making" cultures and prompted a debate on to how to minimize such an impact, in literature the process of transfer into language the encounter with a different culture is conceived as an opportunity to measure the public's set of expectations, desires and preconceived notions toward the alien country. In this regard, Comisso's journey to the Orient is a narration in which the subjective forces of imagination impose a selection of places, such as brothels, geisha house, hotels, which are charged

---

10   As Derek Duncan observes *à propos* of *Cina-Giappone*: "The ambivalence of his [Comisso's] involvement with the landscapes he surveys is reflected in his preference for impersonal grammatical structures through which to convey his experiences and his opinions and through which he conceals his own presence and judgment": Derek Duncan, 2006, *Reading and Writing Italian Homosexuality: A Case of Possible Difference* (Aldershot, UK and Burlington, VT: Ashgate): 70.
11   See Gabriele Schwab, 2012, *Imaginary Ethnographies: Literature, Culture, and Subjectivity* (New York: Columbia University Press).
12   I am referring here to Clifford and Marcus's edited volume *Writing Culture: The Poetics and Politics of Ethnography* (Berkeley: University of California Press, 1986).

by the writer's repressed sexual desires:[13] the spaces of the erotic allure remove and replace the historical and cultural dimensions of the territory. The map of sex consumption is born out at the intersection of Orientalism and homoerotics, finding same-sex love in countries that were widely popular destinations for Westerners looking to sidestep repressive sexual policies at home. Therefore, it is in the name of a convergence of public expectation and personal experience that Lorenzo finds his male sexual encounters in India and China: both considered primary destinations of sex tourism (especially homosexual) at the time of Comisso's journey.[14] For the same reason, and crucially, Lorenzo's sexual adventures in Japan are exclusively heterosexual and retain the narrative of virility and sense of sexual potency that characterize the Fascist nationalistic discourse during the 1930s. If the process of rewriting the journey from *Cina-Giappone* to *Amori d'Oriente* constitutes for Comisso a move toward the construction of a self no more connected with the dominant nationalistic discourse, the episodes in Japan represent an exception, as Lorenzo's subjectivity, while visiting the East Asian country, seems to be informed by the ethic of Fascist virilities.[15] In fact, while the

---

13 Comisso is obviously aware of this narrative impulse, as he defines *Amori d'Oriente* "il limite massimo della mia possibilità narrativa nella trama degli istinti" (see 2002: n. 3).

14 Derek Duncan noticed the relation between place and sexual desire in *Amori d'Oriente*, or the metaphorical power of a place in inspiring sexual practices: "Lorenzo's first recognition of the Orient as the place of homosexual desire occurs in Colombo [...] it is, however, in Peking that he becomes more fully aware of his homosexual desire in a gradual mediated movement" (Duncan, 2002: 74). China as a land for homoerotic fantasies was known in Europe since at least the sixteenth century when the Jesuit missionary Matteo Ricci described in an outraged tone the scene that he happened to witness: "There are public streets full of boys got up like prostitutes. And there are people who buy these boys and teach them to play music, sing and dance. And then, gallantly dressed and made up with rouge like women these miserable men are initiated into this terrible vice," quoted from Bret Hinsch, 1990, *Passions of the Cut Sleeve: The Male Homosexual Tradition in China* (Berkeley: University of California Press): 2. For a study that considers the Western imagination on the association of the Muslim world and male homoeroticism see Joseph Allen Boone, 2015, *The Homoerotics of Orientalism* (New York: Columbia University Press). For a study on the British living in China and discovering their freedom in terms of homo/etero sexuality see Patricia Laurence, 2003, *Lily Briscoe's Chinese Eyes: Bloomsbury, Modernism, and China* (Columbia: University of South Carolina Press): 184–98.

15 I refer here to the coercive power of the institutional discourse to "subject" individuals and to constitute them as ethical selves, on the one hand, and on the other, to the "practices of freedom" that individuals can oppose in order to achieve self-formation,

overall journey in *Amori d'Oriente* is predicated upon an image of the Orient as a homosexual paradise, the actual experience in Japan shows very little change compared with the reports. Whereas in his accounts of China and India, for instance, sexuality is not relevant, in Japan Comisso's attention as reporter repeatedly concentrates on women as objects of male desire, or distaste. He even dedicates an article to them entitled *Donne di Chioto* ["Kyoto's women"] assessing their appearance ("Viste da vicino non sono bellezze, la loro dentatura non è perfetta, ma rimangono piacevoli per la grazia dei gesti e per la finezza degli abiti" (Comisso, 1958: 89) [seen from close up they are not beauties, their teeth are not perfect, but they remain pleasant thanks to the grace of the gestures and to the fineness of the clothes], and the level of gender performance that they flaunt to appease the male taste ("Una studiata ingenuità copre infinite scaltrezze, ma difficilmente si scopre l'artificio" (Comisso, 1958: 90) [A studied ingenuity covers endless shrewdness, but it is difficult to discover the artifice]. Finally, Japan is the only station of the Asian journey where Comisso alludes to having a sexual intercourse with a woman. The article introducing the episode, titled *Sorprese della vita errante* ["Surprises of the wandering life"], is reproduced almost uncensored in *Amori d'Oriente*, except that the erotic allusion comes as a surprise since the author's intentions are not revealed up to this point: "Le altre due, quali gheise appartenenti a un ordine inferiore, se ne stavano in disparte; una raccoglieva i piattini di lacca, l'altra versava l'acqua nella teiera sul braciere. Poi chiusero le finestre, e ci lasciarono soli" [The other two, as geisha belonging to a lower order, stood apart; one collected the lacquer plates, the other poured the water into the teapot on the brazier. Then they closed the windows and left us alone].[16] As with Ercole Patti's elliptic rhetoric,

---

as discussed by Michel Foucault in the interview titled "The Ethics of the Concern for Self as a Practice of Freedom" (in Michel Foucault, 1997, *The Essential Works of Michel Foucault, vol. 1: Ethics: Subjectivity and Truth*, edited by Paul Rabinow (New York: New Press): 281–302). For "Fascist virilities" I refer to Barbara Spackman's definition: "Virility is not simply one of many fascist qualities, but rather than the cults of youth, of duty, of sacrifice, of heroic virtues, of strength and stamina, of obedience and authority, and of physical strength and sexual potency": Barbara Spackman, 1996, *Fascist Virilities: Rhetoric, Ideology and Social Fantasy in Italy* (Minneapolis and London: University of Minnesota Press): xii. All these qualities "that characterize fascism are all inflections of that master term, virility" (Spackman, 1996: xii).

16   In *Amori d'Oriente* the passage is only slightly modified: "Le altre due, quali gheishe appartenenti a un ordine inferiore, se ne stavano in disparte, una ramassava i piatti di lacca, l'altra versava l'acqua nella teiera sul braciere. Poi fecero scorrere le vetrate,

Comisso omits to describe the erotic encounter, leaving any assumptions to the reader's fantasy.

The Fascist virility that seamlessly continues to dominate the Japanese section of *Amori d'Oriente* speaks for an enduring narrative that persists even when the author is allegedly free to express his subjective self-identity in fiction. Nevertheless, I maintain that the strategy of alternating a gay identity with a dominant identity does not result in the submission and rejection of the former in favor of the latter. On the contrary, in playing the trope of Fascist virility, Comisso elaborates a critique of it in the form of a frustrated heterosexual character. While reinstating binary differences that are peculiar to a nationalistic discourse, Comisso uses the politics of desire to sabotage the dominant perception of the place.

4. Mussolini's Kimono

When referring to Ercole Patti and Giovanni Comisso's images of Japan we cannot consider their works as products of an explicit nationalist propaganda, oriented to exorcizing the dread of the invincible Japanese army. It must be pointed out that Japan's defeat of China (1894) and Russia (1904) resulted in a perceived anxiety about the so-called "yellow peril" in Europe and America (together with the opposite feeling of sympathy as we saw in the previous chapter); in the 1920s, Italy was part of this phenomenon. As expression of a nationalistic ideology, Italian Fascism adopted racist rhetoric and policies from the outset up to the culmination of the Ethiopian conquest in the mid-1930s and the subsequent anti-Semitic laws. Though the issues of race and racism were vaguely part of Italian Fascist doctrine prior to the Ethiopian campaign (especially if compared with the contemporary case of Nazi Germany), the Italian travel writings on Japan of this period demonstrate a strategic use of racism that is consistent with any twentieth-century nationalist ideology. In fact, as George Mosse argues, racist slogans serve a nationalist ideology by

---

portarono alcuni cuscini e li lasciarono soli" (Comisso, 2002: 1044). The following part is added in *Amori d'Oriente* to make explicit Lorenzo's request and introduce the designated geisha who will spend the night with him: "Tentò qualche carezza alle due geishe, ma queste gli fecero capire che non erano lì per l'amore. Pertanto dal ballatoio apparve sorridente un'altra geisha, meno montanara e con i capelli tagliati all'europea. Era una delle belle del villaggio che veniva a farsi vedere dal forestiero" (Comisso, 2002: 1044).

defining the roots of the nation for the people, while marking differences from other nations.[17] The "Other" to be used as a foil to unite citizens under the Fascist banner is usually an internal one (the Jews, the Marxists, the Masons, etc.), but, in the case of Mussolini, a lack of a racial policies based on biological differences made the enemy profile, both internal and external, more ephemeral and opaque in nature.

Ruth Ben-Ghiat focuses attention on culture's role in Fascism as a useful device for consensus building and promoting its foreign policy: "Culture was also assigned a key role in the regime's projects for international expansion. Italy's formidable cultural patrimony made fascists acutely aware of the role aesthetic prestige could play in the arrogation of international influence. A regenerated Italian culture would advertise national creative genius throughout the world, much as it had during the Renaissance" (Ben-Ghiat, 2001: 6). A comparison with the Italian Renaissance is particularly appropriate in expressing the Fascist agenda of diffusing a collective ideal of Italian supremacy in civilization, culture, spiritual life and ethical values. In this respect Japan, with its growing power, was a potential opponent to be feared.

An example of this cultural campaign against the "wicked Japs" is Clemente Ferraris's *Al di là del Paese di Butterfly* (1928) ["Beyond the country of Butterfly"]. As the title suggests, Ferraris's journey to Japan aimed to debunk widespread opinion about Japanese heroic virtues and gracious beauty:

> [Ho deciso di] fare un viaggio in quel Giappone dove gli uomini (specie dopo la loro vittoria sulla Russia) ci vengono dipinti come tanti eroi, anzi come tanti mezzi quintali di virtù fatta carne, e le donne come tante geishe che nel famoso e festoso yoshivara prodigano le loro grazie tra languori e suoni di chamisen nelle loro mille gabbie lucenti di lacca. (Ferraris, 1928: 3)

> [(I decided to) take a trip to Japan where men (especially after their victory over Russia) are described as heroes, indeed like many fifty

---

17 See George L. Mosse, 1999, *The Fascist Revolution: Toward a General Theory of Fascism* (New York: Howard Fertig): 55–68. Barbara Spackman notices that prior to the late 1930s, Mussolini was substantially indifferent to the idea of "race purity" (see Spackman, 1996: 153). The relevance of the discourse of race to Fascist practices is still the object of debate: see Patrick G. Zander, 2016, *The Rise of Fascism: History, Documents, and Key Questions* (Santa Barbara, CA: Crossroads in World History): 186–95.

quintals of virtue made flesh, and women are described like geishas who in the famous festive yoshivara lavish their graces between languor and chamisen sounds, while staying in their thousand shiny lacquer cages.]

With this passage at the beginning of the book, Ferraris sets the parodic tone of his description. On one hand he maliciously observes that the well-known Japanese "virtue" is carried out by men who weigh roughly one hundred pounds ("mezzi quintali di virtù fatta carne"); on the other hand, he shows no respect whatsoever for the artistic image of the geisha, who is compared with a prostitute living in a cage. As we continue reading, Ferraris's intentions become more and more explicit: "Questo preambolo per dire che io non sono troppo entusiasta di questo popolo giapponese, che in Europa, ci viene dipinto come l'incarnazione della virtù, con le sue relative uggiose conseguenze" (66) [This is a preamble to say that I am not too enthusiastic about this Japanese people, who in Europe, are portrayed as the incarnation of virtue, with its relative annoying consequences].

An influential fascist voice in Japan was that of the journalist and novelist Arnaldo Cipolla (1877–1938), whose popular writings (journals, novels and reports) contributed to molding the representation of faraway lands, including colonial territories in Africa, to a large Italian audience. Cipolla worked as a reporter for some of the most important national dailies, such as *Corriere della Sera*, *La Stampa*, *Il Messaggero* and *Il popolo d'Italia*. His allegiance to the Fascist regime manifested in a form of intellectual effort to create a nationalistic type of Orientalist archive of knowledge about Asian countries – based on the "territorial either/or" theory of identity – in the same fashion as other European powers. In the preface of *Per la Siberia, in Cina e Giappone* (1924) ["Through Siberia, in China and Japan"), the editors stress that one of the highlights of the book is a redesigned map of Italy's geopolitical interests. Indeed, Cipolla demonstrated that "l'Estremo Oriente era pur sempre a tre settimane di distanza da noi e non ad una lontananza chimerica" (Cipolla, 1924: *Prefazione degli editori*) [The Far East was still three weeks away, which is not a chimerical distance]. Cipolla is explicit in his goal of working at the service of Italy's imperialistic ambitions, by contributing to an awareness of the Italian presence in the world, in competition with France, England, China and Germany. Cipolla's work was the beginning of a process that aimed to expand Italian's territorial views:

l'Italia è la sola Grande Potenza che consideri ancora la Cina ed il Giappone come paesi fuori dalla sua ordinaria osservazione ed attività; il solo grande popolo che abbia sull'Estremo Oriente delle idee imprecise e sorpassate. Dinanzi alla imponente bibliografia moderna inglese, francese e tedesca sulla Cina e sul Giappone, noi italiani non abbiamo, si può dire, nulla da contrapporre e si possono contare sulle dita di una sola mano gli scrittori italiani che, in questo ultimo quarto di secolo, vennero da queste parti con lo scopo preciso di studiarle e volgarizzarne la vita e gli aspetti. (Cipolla, 1924: 388)

[Italy is the only Great Power that still considers China and Japan as countries out of its ordinary observation and activity; the only great people with inaccurate and outdated ideas on the Far East. Compared to the imposing modern English, French and German bibliography on China and Japan, we Italians, it is fair to say, don't have anything to counteract, in fact there are only a few Italian writers who, in this last quarter of a century, came here with the precise purpose of studying them and explaining their life and other aspects.]

The expansion of the Italian government's geopolitical interests came hand by hand with the racist claims of Western superiority. By gaining the advantage point of seeing the "Other," Cipolla is adamant in comparing the Asian people in terms of difference and inferiority with the Europeans. While in Japan, Cipolla is consistent in rejecting any argument put forth by the locals that suggested similarities between Italians and Japanese. He is irritated when he is presented with the possibility of recognizing a physical resemblance between the two peoples, who are "lontane come lontana è la distanza che li separa" (Cipolla, 1924: 276) [distant, as remote is the distance that separates them]. He is equally dismissive in accepting a comparison of artistic quality ("il culto artistico giapponese è ristretto, limitato all'interno di una camera, alla forma di un oggetto, al disegno" (278) [Japanese artistic worship is restricted, limited within a room, to the shape of an object, to the design], or of the architectural design of cities ("Le città giapponesi – tolti alcuni edifici di Kioto, di Nara, di Nikko – sono sinceramente brutte" (278) [Honestly the Japanese cities – except for some buildings in Kyoto, Nara, Nikko – are ugly]. The attitude toward the visited country is partially in contrast with the tendency to elevate the Italian presence abroad. He explains that "la lingua e la letteratura italiana hanno in Giappone un certo culto. Nella Scuola imperiale di lingue estere vi sono due corsi di lingua italiana, uno diurno e l'altro serale, con una sessantina di allievi tenuti dal professor Pastorelli" (280) [Italian language and literature have a certain cult following in Japan. At the imperial school of foreign languages there are two Italian language courses, one during the day and the other in the evening, with about sixty students taught by Professor Pastorelli]. "Esiste una grande passione per lo studio di Dante. – 'Vogliamo studiare l'italiano per imparare a conoscere Dante' – dicono i giovani giapponesi" (280) [There is a great passion for Dante's study. – "We want to study Italian to learn about Dante" – say the young Japanese]. Yet, Cipolla concludes, the reciprocal interests that the two countries are demonstrating toward each other in the recent years cannot override the structural foreignness of the Japanese; in fact, "nessun soggiorno qui, per quanto lungo, e nessun studio riusciranno mai a rivelarci il segreto di queste terre" (337) [no visit here, however long, and no study will ever reveal the secret of these lands].

In 1931, as the "Manchurian Incident" brought worldwide attention to Japan's expansionism in Asia, Cipolla published his account of his Asian journey in *Nel Giappone dei grattacieli: viaggio da Tokio a Dehli* ["In skyscrapers' Japan, journey from Tokyo to Delhi"]. As in the previous publication Cipolla described Japan as an unfamiliar place, ultimately unfathomable and out of reach, yet the most recent expansionist policy changes the nature of the discourse:

È probabile che l'esperimento mancese inclini il Giappone a rinunciare definitivamente a ogni idea di conquista territoriale in Cina preferendo invece la penetrazione economica. Ma c'è lo spirito d'espansione militare che volere o no è ancora acuto in Giappone, il quale unito alle difficoltà del sovrappopolamento nelle isole che potrebbe sommergere le tendenze pacifiste dei governi responsabili. In altre parole esiste da queste parti e nei riguardi del Giappone un problema del tutto analogo a quello italiano ed è anche per questo che la sua volgarizzazione ci interessa. (Cipolla, 1931: 10)

[It is probable that the Manchurian experiment will bring Japan to renounce definitively any idea of territorial conquest in China, preferring instead economic penetration. But there is the spirit of military expansion that, willy-nilly, it is still acute in Japan, which, in addition to the difficulties of overpopulation in the islands, could overwhelm the pacifist tendencies of responsible governments. In other words, there is a problem here with regard to Japan that is completely analogous to the Italian one, and this is also why we are interested in understanding it.]

By looking at Japan from the Italian standpoint, Cipolla manages to accomplish a double goal. First, while keeping the focus on the Asian Empire he ends up legitimating Italy's imperialistic ambitions by connecting them with the problem of population growth. Also, the parallel with Japanese expansionism in Asia implicitly exalts the Italian army in regard to its potential for achieving the outstanding victories of its Asian peers. Cipolla's renewed interest in Japan is explained by the process of "fascistization" that the Asian country was undertaking following the Manchurian Incident. As Reto Hofmann points out, the 1930s saw a wider interpretation of the word "fascism": "In a shift from an earlier discourse that identified fascism with Italy, Japanese intellectuals, politicians, and bureaucrats now associated it with a world trend" (Hofmann, 2015: 64). While Japanese lawmakers and commentators were debating about the possibility of adapting the Italian fascist ideology to the specific core values and policy of Japan, Cipolla seizes the opportunity to create a narrative about Italy's ideological dominion in the Far East.

The following pages foster the idea that the political and cultural presence of Italy was intended to play a major role in East Asia, sometimes at the cost of placing Japan in the background. The section of the book dedicated to the institutional presence of Italian ambassadors and consuls in the territory points in the direction of Italy's political prestige and international authority, as it is acknowledged by one of the most powerful nations in the world: "Il Console Gasco è talmente conosciuto, apprezzato ed amato in Estremo Oriente e in Italia che non gli farò il torto di tentare di tesserne l'ennesimo elogio" (Cipolla, 1931: 30) [The Consul Gasco is so well known, appreciated and loved in the Far East and in Italy that I will not do him the wrong of trying to weave yet another eulogy]. A long interview with Alfonso Gasco, the Italian consul in Kyoto at the time, is an opportunity to celebrate Italian achievements in Japan. During the interview Cipolla praises the popularity of Italian subjects in the current Japanese theater: "l'Italia è oggi di grande attualità al Giappone. Fra l'altro vi sono tre Compagnie drammatiche giapponesi che non fanno che rappresentare soggetti italiani di creazione puramente nipponica" (30) [Italy is today very relevant to Japan. Among other things there are three Japanese drama companies that do nothing but represent Italian subjects of purely Japanese creation]. On the other hand, the consul responds by stressing the growing interestest toward the Italian language:

> Il corso di lingua e lettere italiane che tengo a Kioto è diventato dall'ultimo agosto obbligatorio ed è frequentato da una folla di studenti

che, dico il vero, mi seguono con appassionante interesse. Abbiamo anche il prof. Arundel Del Re, laureato ad Oxford, che insegna italiano e inglese a Formosa e all'Accademia delle Lingue a Tokio il Prof. Pastorelli occupa, seguitissimo e da molti anni, la cattedra d'italiano. Possiamo dire che la nostra lingua è conosciuta in Giappone come il francese ed è da notarsi che i francesi fanno qui una attivissima propaganda alle cose loro. Però come influenza culturale e straniera, primeggia sovrana l'America, che ha conquistato il popolo soprattutto con il cinematografo. (Cipolla, 1931: 31)

[The Italian language and literature course that I hold in Kyoto has become mandatory since last August and is attended by a crowd of students who, I tell the truth, follow me with exciting interest. We also have the prof. Arundel Del Re, a graduate of Oxford, who teaches Italian and English at Formosa and at the Academy of Languages in Tokyo, Prof. Pastorelli has been very closely involved with the chair of Italian for many years. We can say that our language is known in Japan as much as French, in spite of the fact that the French make here an active propaganda of their own things. But as a cultural and foreign influence, America is the sovereign power, which has conquered the people above all with the cinema.]

Not only could the Italian language live up to the competition with more influential languages like French (because of France's colonial presence in Indochina), but Italian literature was also very popular: "Per quel che ci riguarda, gli autori italiani meglio conosciuti in Giappone sono D'Annunzio, Croce, Gentile e Papini. Per parlare dei vivi. Si sono fatte in questi ultimi tempi ottime traduzioni in giapponese dei 'Sepolcri' di Foscolo e Dante è più che mai in onore" (31)[18] [As far as we are concerned, the best known Italian authors in Japan are D'Annunzio, Croce, Gentile and Papini. To talk

---

18   It is not surprising to find works of the popular philosopher Benedetto Croce on the list of Italian best-sellers, and this observation can be extended to Dante Alighieri as well. The presence of Ugo Foscolo next to well known Fascist authors is less obvious. Of course, Japanese right-wing/nationalist beliefs in the 1930s and their patriotic ideals exerted a strong influence and can help to explain the reason behind this selection. Foscolo's patriotic sonnet "A Zacinto," mourning for the unreachable homeland, can be manipulated and adapted into nationalist discourse. The mythological origin of Foscolo's homeland Zante in particular can be compared to the myth of the divine origins of the imperial family, which became popular during the Meiji restoration.

about the living. In recent times there have been excellent translations into Japanese of the "Sepolcri" by Foscolo, while Dante is appreciated more than ever].

After glorifying Italian's cultural success and prestige in the Far East, the interview finally reaches the crucial point – the political impact of Benito Mussolini on Japanese public opinion:

> La semplice verità è che Benito Mussolini gode in Giappone di una popolarità che nessun grande uomo occidentale si è mai sognato di avere. E la popolarità è di quelle che non seguono il capriccio della moda o sono limitate ad una categoria più o meno larga di persone, ma va dalla Casa Imperiale ai poveri contadini che rimestano il fango delle risaie. Il Giappone vede in Mussolini non solo l'uomo d'eccezione che ha portato l'Italia all'altezza di Nazione paragonabile in potenza e prestigio al Giappone, ma l'eroe, segnato dalla divinità, simile agli eroi che hanno personificato i periodi salienti della sua storia favolosa. In altre parole il Duce d'Italia corrisponde perfettamente alla concezione immutabile del "buscido" dello spirito, per il quale le Nazioni progrediscono e si affermano soltanto attraverso determinate personalità di essenza sovrumana. Ecco perché i biografi più notevoli del Duce hanno trovato in Giappone i lettori più numerosi ed appassionati. Oggi il Giappone vede in ogni Italiano un allievo di Mussolini e come tale lo stima e lo onora. (Cipolla, 1931: 31)

> [The simple truth is that Benito Mussolini enjoys in Japan a popularity that no great Western man has ever dreamed of having. And it is a type of popularity that it is temporary or limited to a more or less large category of people, but it extends from the Imperial House to the poor farmers who stir the mud of the rice fields. Japan sees in Mussolini not only an exceptional man who brought Italy to the height of a nation comparable in power and prestige to Japan, but a hero, marked by divinity, similar to the heroes who personified the salient periods of its fabulous history. In other words, the Duce of Italy corresponds perfectly to the immutable conception of the "bushido" spirit, for which nations progress and are affirmed only through certain personalities gifted with superhuman essence. This is why the most remarkable biographers of the Duce have found in Japan the most numerous and passionate readers. Today, Japan sees in every Italian a student of Mussolini and as such he esteems and honors him.]

The point that Cipolla is making goes far beyond the political goal of assuring the popularity of the Italian dictator abroad, or making the case for Italy as an international superpower equal to Japan.[19] The rhetoric of the discourse applies a secondary connotation to the traditional image of Mussolini, who is now viewed as a "totalitarian" leader standing as a symbol of "unity" for the nation (Spackman, 1996: 155), a role similar to the one that members of the imperial family play in Japan. The persona of Mussolini is "exported" to East Asia and molded to fit the image of a Japanese royal family member; as a consequence, his figure is raised to the level of a potential leader even for the Japanese. In the eyes of his Asian estimators, Mussolini is a hero chosen by a god ("l'eroe, segnato dalla divinità, simile agli eroi che hanno personificato i periodi salienti della sua [giapponese] storia favolosa" [the divine hero, similar to the heroes who personified the salient periods of Japanese fabulous story]). He also embodies the spirit of an authentic samurai whose code of honor is expressed by the word *bushido* (the way of the warrior): "Il Duce d'Italia corrisponde perfettamente alla concezione immutabile del 'buscido' dello spirito" [the Duce of Italy corresponds perfectly to the immutable conception of the "bushido" spirit].

Cipolla describes Mussolini's persona in a kimono style, as a charismatic Japanese figure who inspires the opposition front against the Soviet "red peril":

> Il primo maggio del 1923 è celebrato frammezzo manifestazioni d'una violenza ignorata sino allora al Giappone. I fascisti giapponesi marciano per le vie di Tokio portando il ritratto di Mussolini in testa dei loro battaglieri cortei e proclamano che i malanni vengono dall'accoglienza cordiale fatta negli ambienti governativi ai rappresentanti dei Soviet e che tutto sarebbe rientrato nell'ordine se essi avessero lasciato per sempre il territorio nipponico. Da parte loro i sovversivi hanno già stabilito un "Comitato centrale rivoluzionario" con un giornale, "Bandiera rossa," in relazione con Mosca. (Cipolla, 1931: 123)

---

19 The popularity of Mussolini in Japan (as well as in the rest of the world in the 1920s and 1930s) is documented by Reto Hofmann in the chapter entitled "The Mussolini Boom, 1928–1931" in his book *The Fascist Effect* (2015: 38–62). However, Hofmann's chapter helps to recognize the shortcomings included in Cipolla's narrative of Mussolini being celebrated as hero in Japan. In fact, public opinion, writers, intellectuals and journalist in Japan were all but united under this positive view of the *Duce*. Liberals and right-wing commentators alike were often critical of Mussolini, as they feared Japan could be exposed to a foreign ideology that would clash with the *kokutai* ("Japanese polity") ideology.

[The anniversary of May 1, 1923 is celebrated among manifestations of violence ignored in Japan until then. The Japanese fascists march through the streets of Tokyo carrying the portrait of Mussolini at the head of their combative processions and proclaim that the problems come from the cordial reception in government circles to the representatives of the Soviets and that everything would be returned if they had left the Japanese territory forever. For their part, the subversives have already established a "revolutionary central committee" together with a newspaper, "Red Flag," in connection with Moscow.]

May 1, 1923 is a symbolic date, recalling the demonstrations in London's Hyde Park in support of withdrawing Japanese troops from the island of Sakhalin, whose territory was divided between Japanese and Russian administrations. Nationalist manifestations in Japan exploited the Duce's portrait ("il ritratto di Mussolini") for the purpose of anti-Soviet propaganda. Cipolla succeeds in presenting Mussolini as a symbol of the traditional Japanese spirit to the extent of describing young intellectuals using his portrait to remind the elected Japanese government of those values.

In *Nel Giappone dei grattacieli* (1931) Cipolla perpetuates an Orientalist representation of Japan, using the vantage point of the observer as a means to overshadow the people who are the object of his observation. Unlike his previous 1924 book, Cipolla here does not portray the Japanese in a negative fashion, emphasizing their radical alterity and uniqueness; on the contrary, he prefers to stress similarities between the two nations, as almost envisioning a future military alliance. In this sense Cipolla sets the tone for the pro-Japan propaganda that followed the Anti-Comintern Pact in 1936, which is the subject of the following pages.

5. Brother in Arms

Nel giorno in cui l'antica amicizia dei nostri due paesi trova definitiva consacrazione sui campi di battaglia, il mio pensiero si rivolge all'eroico popolo giapponese in armi. L'alba dell'ordine è già spuntata su tutti i continenti e il popolo italiano è, con lo spirito e con le armi, vicino ai camerati nipponici nell'incrollabile volontà di vittoria che unisce l'Italia, la Germania e il Giappone. (Mussolini, 1960: 250)

[On the day when the ancient friendship of our two countries finds definitive consecration on the battlefields, my thoughts turn to the heroic Japanese people in arms. The dawn of order has already arrived on all the continents and the Italian people are, in spirit and with arms, close to the Japanese comrades in the unshakable desire for victory that unites Italy, Germany and Japan.]

A few days after the Japanese raid on Pearl Harbor (December 7, 1941), Benito Mussolini wrote this telegram to Prime Minister Hideki Tōjō, guaranteeing that Italy would respect the Axis Pact with Germany and Japan (1940) and stating his decision to join the war. Suddenly the Japanese were being addressed in the same way as any Italian Fascist, as "camerati" (comrades). In addition to the adoption of Fascist jargon, the reference to a generic long-standing history of friendship ("l'antica amicizia dei nostri due paesi") was used to hide the absolute lack of political relations between the two countries.

In the previous sections we observed how Italian writers in the 1920s from various perspectives and different fashions (even those not were not affiliated with the regime) adopted a nationalistic view to belittle and disparage the rise of the Japanese Empire, portraying its inhabitants as inferiors. We noted that this diffused ideology was fueled by Mussolini's belief in the rise of Italy as an international power, whose uniqueness could only be marked through a discourse aimed at emphasize other countries' differences and inferiority.

After Mussolini's decision to align with Japan, a different narrative was needed in order to explain to the Italian people the alleged Fascist foundations of Japanese society and the reason for this atypical brotherhood. This is the reason behind Mario Appelius's urgency to travel to Japan and write about his impressions:

Il volume m'era dettato dal desiderio di contribuire a far conoscere al popolo italiano un elemento così importante del mondo moderno come è il Giappone. Il Fascismo ha buttato l'Italia nell'aringo delle grandi lotte internazionali prima che l'opinione pubblica si fosse preparata a guardare il mondo con un occhio da conquistatore. Il Duce non poteva aspettare. Il mondo andava in fretta e l'Italia aveva camminato troppo piano durante il Risorgimento. Lo studio della geografia mondiale, della storia mondiale, dell'economia mondiale, della politica mondiale è ancora appannaggio, in Italia di troppe poche persone. Bisogna che la nazione intera entri in questo vasto ordine di idee. (Appelius, 1941: 15)

[The volume was inspired by the desire to introduce the Italian people to such an important element of the modern world as Japan. Fascism has thrown Italy into the mainstream of the great international struggles before public opinion was prepared to look at the world with a conquering eye. The Duce could not wait. The world was going fast and Italy had walked too slowly during the Risorgimento. The study of world geography, of world history, of the world economy, of world politics is still a prerogative, in Italy, of too few people. The whole nation must enter this vast array of ideas.]

In spite of what Appelius writes here, Italians were obviously acquainted with Japan, at least since earlier in the twentieth century. It was part of the Fascist strategy to present Japan as a congenial ally that, because of the previous government's historically limited scope and ambitions, the Italians had never had the chance to discover. In order to introduce Japan as the ideal political partner that was so similar to us, it was necessary to reset all the data accumulated in Italian memory about this anomalous land full of ladies of weak morals and effeminate or irrational men. The date of this book's printing was October 1941, a turning point for the representation of Japan. The successful military campaigns in the Pacific of this period galvanized the Italian ally and an extensive collection of propaganda began to be released from this moment on, designed for soldiers on the front line and civilians as well.

6. Inside the Propaganda

The uneasy task of the regime's propaganda during the 1940s was to prove Mussolini's above statements about the long-standing historical relationship between Italy and Japan, as well as the many similarities between the two nations. The Italian government devised a series of strategies to promote friendship with the Asian ally, including the foundation of a "Società Amici del Giappone" in Rome (Society of the Friends of Japan) and its equivalent in Tokyo "Itaria No Tomo No Kai" (Society of the Friends of Italy). The Society played an active role in supporting the introduction of Japanese culture in Italy by opening offices in different Italian cities with the task of offering Japanese language courses, as well as conferences, art exhibitions and plays.[20]

From January 1941 to August 1943 a monthly journal entitled *Yamato* gathered some of the most influential scholars of Asia, including the ambassador to Japan (1933–40) Giacinto Auriti (1883–1969), the ethnologist of Asia, Giuseppe Tucci (1894–1984) and the Japanologist Pietro Silvio Rivetta (1886–1952). While the journal published translations of modern and contemporary Japanese authors (Akutagawa Ryûnosuke [1892–1927], Sakae Tsuboi [1897–1967], Ueda Akinari [1734–1809], Takeda Rintarô [1904–46]) the demagogical character of the editorial project often prevailed in distorting the historical events, by presenting a triumphal image of the Japanese campaign in the Pacific until the end of World War II.[21]

The difficulty of this task prompted the publication of a long series of brief documents booklets, leaflets and journals that will be briefly outlined here. This material was meant to have an impact on the larger public by providing short and easy-to-approach readings.

In a booklet titled *Vincere* (1940) ["To win"], Mario Appelius attributed the historical distance between Italy and Japan to the Anglo-Saxon influence in Europe:

> V'erano molti ostacoli di lontananza, di diversità razziale, di vecchi modi di pensare che separavano Roma e Berlino da Tokio. L'influenza anglo-nordamericana aveva creato una barriera artificiale tra l'Occidente e l'Oriente. Il genio del Duce intuì che bisognava scavalcare risolutamente quegli ingombri artificiali ed avvicinare decisamente le due capitali europee alla lontana capitale asiatica ove pulsava il forte cuore di un popolo giovane, valoroso e capace il quale come l'italiano e come il germanico cercava il suo posto al sole e ne era impedito dall'egoismo anglosassone. (Appelius, 1940: 12)

---

20   See Rosaria Beviglia, 1966, "La letteratura giapponese in Italia: parte 1 (1871–1950)," *Il Giappone*, 6: 7–26.

21   See, for instance, the article "Amore del popolo giapponese per la pace" by Andō Yosirō, 1942, published in *Yamato* II, 3: 69–71, a few months after the Japanese invasion of the Philippines and Thailand and the attack on Pearl Harbor. After discussing the historical value of peace in Japanese culture the author concludes: "Si dice che i Giapponesi siano un popolo bellicoso essi non amano affatto la guerra. L'amore per la pace, appoggiato sull'amore per la vita, è ardente nel cuore di ogni Giapponese che adesso sta combattendo coraggiosamente con i suoi Alleati per costruire un ordine nuovo e giusto nel mondo" (Andō Yosirō, 1942: 71).

[There were many obstacles of distance, racial diversity, old ways of thinking that separated Rome and Berlin from Tokyo. The Anglo-American influence had created an artificial barrier between the West and the East. The genius of the Duce sensed that it was necessary to step over the artificial dimensions resolutely and bring the two European capitals to the distant Asian capital, where pulsed the strong heart of a young, valiant and capable people, who, like the Italians and the Germans, sought their place in the sun and was prevented by Anglo-Saxon egoism.]

In the same year the anonymous writer of a 1942 booklet entitled *Il Giappone e le sue forze armate* ["Japan and its armed forces"] tried to outline an inconsistent historical framework in an attempt to justify Mussolini's far-fetched connections between Japan and Italy:

Le molte analogie che si riscontrano tra l'Italia e il Giappone, non solo per la configurazione geografica dei territori e per la somiglianza del clima, ma anche per lo spirito e per molti caratteri comuni ai due popoli, hanno favorito rapporti di comprensione, di simpatia e di amicizia, che si sono sempre rafforzati, nonostante la lontananza geografica tra i due Paesi.

Già nel 1585, tre Principi Giapponesi, sotto gli auspici del Missionario Padre Alessandro Valignano, di Chieti, vennero a Roma e visitarono il Papa Gregorio XIII. (*Il Giappone e le sue forze armate*, 1942: 2)

[The many similarities that are found between Italy and Japan, not only for the geographical configuration of the territories and for the similarity of the climate, but also for the spirit and for many other characteristics, have fostered relations of understanding, sympathy and friendship, which have always been strengthened, despite the geographical distance between the two countries.

As early as 1585, three Japanese Princes, under the auspices of the Missionary Father Alessandro Valignano of Chieti, came to Rome and visited Pope Gregory XIII.]

While an exceptional historical encounter at the Vatican is celebrated, no mention is made of the violent extirpation of the Christian missions in Japan, or the fact that no relations existed between the two countries until at least the end of the Edo period.

In his attempt to drastically overturn the image of Japan in Italian public opinion, Mussolini tried to involve influential and reliable writers.

In the 1940s Luigi Barzini Sr. who, as we saw in the previous chapter, in his younger years sparked sympathy in Italy for the Japanese soldiers with his dispatches, was the right profile for the purpose of boosting the propaganda effort. Although he never owned a Fascist party card (*la tessera fascista*), he was one of the signatories of the *Manifesto degli intellettuali fascisti* (1925) and wrote for the Fascist newspaper *Il popolo d'Italia*, covering the news from the Spanish Civil War (1936) and the Russian invasion (1942).[22] In 1942 he wrote a booklet in support of fascist propaganda titled *Perché il Giappone vince* ("Why Japan is winning"). His portrait of the Asian ally is extremely positive:

> La scomparsa del sistema feudale, invece di far sparire i nobili, ha nobilitato l'intera Nazione. Ogni giapponese che va sotto le armi si sente elevato, si considera un samurai, e si comporta come un samurai. L'educazione rigida e severa della nobiltà è divenuta educazione di popolo. La lealtà, il coraggio, l'impassibilità, il senso dell'onore, lo spirito di sacrificio, sono le doti di ogni uomo. (Barzini, 1942: 6)

> [The disappearance of the feudal system, instead of making the nobles disappear, has ennobled the whole nation. Every Japanese who goes under arms feels uplifted, considers himself a samurai, and behaves like a samurai. The rigid and severe education of nobility has become a popular education. Loyalty, courage, impassivity, the sense of honor, the spirit of sacrifice, are the qualities of every man.]

Only a few years earlier these same characteristics of obedience, willingness to sacrifice oneself for the sake of the emperor, and a rigorous education were valid elements making the case for Japan as an inhuman nation and for comparing the Japanese people to a multitude of "monkeys" or "ants." During the period of the Axis alliance those characteristics became positive qualities. Barzini's attempts to rehabilitate the Japanese image also include the effort to eradicate the well-known opinion about the silliness of the Japanese smile and facial expression, as noted in Ercole Patti's *Un lungo viaggio lontano*:

---

22 According to Ludina Barzini, Luigi Barzini's granddaughter and author of a biography of the Barzini's family, Luigi Barzini collaborated with the Fascist regime only for the sake of his children: Barzini, 2010, *I Barzini: Tre generazioni di giornalisti, una storia del Novecento* (Milan: Mondadori): 254.

E il Giappone è perciò un paese di volti sorridenti e inespressivi, dall'aria un po' atona e stupita, e di cuori eroici.

Chi non ha vissuto a lungo in mezzo a questa gente scambia facilmente l'impassibilità per incomprensione. La parola prudente e reticente, che trattiene il pensiero invece di rivelarlo, è presa per un segno di tardezza mentale. La cortesia rituale, deferente, con i suoi sorrisi insignificanti e i suoi inchini, è ritenuta indice di umiltà e sottomissione. Perciò i giapponesi non hanno mai goduto, in genere, nel mondo bianco, una reputazione adeguata alla realtà. (Patti, 1975: 6)

[And Japan is therefore a country of smiling and inexpressive faces – which have a meaningless and amazed appearance – as well as heroic hearts.

Those who have not lived in the midst of these people easily confuse impassivity for misunderstanding. The cautious and reticent speaking attitude, which prefers to hold on to a thought instead of revealing it, is taken for a sign of mental tardiness. Ritual courtesy, deferential, with its insignificant smiles and its bows, is considered an index of humility and submission. Therefore, the Japanese have never generally enjoyed a fair reputation, among white people.]

Barzini was also determined to prove the adopted Western idea about the lack of glamour in Japanese men to be evil and slanderous:

Vi è poi l'aggravante della piccola statura e di una fisionomia asiatica che non corrisponde sempre al concetto europeo della bellezza; e il comune uomo caucasico che, ritenendosi al gradino più alto della scala umana, è propenso a ritenere inferiori tutti i popoli che non gli somigliano, è tentato di mettere i giapponesi al posto di quelli che gli somigliano meno. Gli è più simpatico il cinese, perché più alto. Nel comune linguaggio americano la parola "monkey" (scimmia) si accoppia spesso alla parola "Jap" (giapponese in dispregiativo). (Barzini, 1942: 6)

[Then there is the aggravating circumstance of the small size and of an Asian physiognomy that does not always correspond to the European concept of beauty; and the common Caucasian man who, considering himself on the highest step of the human scale, is inclined to deem all peoples who do not resemble him inferior, and is tempted to put the Japanese in place of those who resemble him less. He is more sympathetic toward the Chinese, because they are taller. In the common American language the word "monkey" often goes along with the word "Jap" (derogative for "Japanese").]

In this atypical use of orientalist arguments by a fascist author in defense of his Asian ally, it is remarkable how the racial theories of the *Manifesto della razza* (1938) ["Manifesto of the race"] were entirely overlooked. As non-descendants of the Aryan race, Japanese men and women should have been deemed inferior as the Jews were. In contrast, racist allegations against the Japanese were attributed only to Anglo-American propaganda, despite the fact that perceptions of the Japanese as subhuman or evolutionarily inferior were recurrent in the Italian account of Japan prior to the military alliance.

In fact, during the period of the Alliance, intellectual Fascists were called to solve the conundrum of how to consider the Japanese on the same level of dignity as the Italians. It was clear that the same level of bombastic and preposterous historical readings aimed at presenting Italians as belonging to a race of Roman-Aryan descent – in order to appeal the Nazi ally – would not suffice for this goal. A solution was eventually put forth by the biweekly journal *La difesa della razza*, which, for six years, between 1938 and 1943, supported fascist, racist and anti-Semitic policies by focusing entirely on the issue of race. The director Telesio Interlandi (1894–1965) was actively involved in promoting a racial biological discourse, in line with both the recent publication of the *Manifesto della razza* (published in *Il giornale d'Italia* on July 14, 1938) ["The race manifesto"] and the Nazi German theories of racial superiority. However, the journal also hosted articles that insisted less on a German-style discussion of race and biology, and more on the Italian elaboration of racial discourse, which was predicated upon a spiritual and cultural ascendancy from Roman civilization. While promoters of the biological approach were anxious to steer away from any racial theory that considered Italians as belonging to the Latin/Mediterranean race, those who insisted in the affiliation between the ancient Romans and modern-day Italians insisted on the distinct aspects of the Italian race.

If because of the alliance with Hitler's Germany, Italian racists attempted to develop racial theories that would conform the Italian ethnic characteristics to the Aryan model, the logic behind acceptance of the Japanese race required the Japanese to appear less Asian and more European. The argument that was made to underpin the exceptionality of the Japanese race conjured up a combination of biological and spiritual racial theories. In a 1940 article published on *La difesa della razza*, Armando Tosti did not hesitate to dismiss the association, popular until then, of the Japanese with the "yellow peril" in order to put forth, unabashedly, the idea of Japanese being as white as the Europeans: "I Giapponesi per il loro aspetto, per la loro mentalità, per le loro istituzioni, per le loro costumanze, non hanno in sé nulla di mongolico, ma sono 'bianchi' come gli Europei" [The Japanese for their appearance, for their mentality, for their institutions, for their customs, do not have anything in Mongolian, but are "white" like the Europeans]. The attempt at "whitening" the Japanese race was not an original approach in itself, but was in fact based on the conclusions of the American pastor and writer on Japan, William Elliot Griffis, who is explicitly mentioned as a source in Armando Tosti's article *Razza giapponese* ["The Japanese race"].[23] Griffis's effort was to concentrate attention on the Ainu population, who represented a component of the Japanese's complex ethnic origins, rather than on the Mongol people. In contrast with previous research that considered the Ainu a Slavic race, Griffis insisted on their white aspect and on the Aryan origins of their language. By contending that the Ainu represented the original stock from which the Japanese race had derived, Griffis (together with other writers such as the missionary Arthur May Knapp and *Outlook* correspondent George Kennan) vainly tried to influence US immigration policy by making the case for the Japanese people as a neglected white race that should be eligible for citizenship. Ironically, however, the US Congress's ban on Japanese immigrants, occurring a few years later, brought an end to Griffis's argument on the North American continent, but instead paved the way for his theories to be resumed in the context of the Italian racial debate. Indeed, the opinion of an American pastor of the Reformed and Congregational churches became the basis for justifying the racial discourse underpinning the Italo-Japanese alliance, and for counteracting American racial stereotypes against the Japanese.

The biological thesis was complemented by more cultural and spiritual arguments that were used, perhaps, to provide a more solid case than the one

---

23 Armando Tosti, 1940, "Razza giapponese," *La difesa della razza*, 1: 21–25. For a similar approach to the Japanese race see Eugenio De Aldisio, 1940, "La razza giapponese," *La difesa della razza*, 7: 30–33 and Vlora Alessandro Kemal, 1942, "La razza giapponese," *La difesa della razza*, 22: 4–7 continued in *La difesa della razza*, 23: 7–11. On Griffis's theories of Japanese as a white race see Joseph M. Henning, 2007, "White Mongols? The war and American discourses on race and religion" in *The Impact of the Russo-Japanese War*, edited by Rotem Kowner (London and New York: Routledge): 153–66.

focused on the Aryan origins of the Japanese. This second line of argument emphasized a list of virtues that "fit" the portrait of the ideal fascist. In the October 1942 issue of *La difesa della razza*, Alessandro Kemal Vlora published an article listing the affinities of culture and habitus that established a spiritual community of the Italian and Japanese people ("La comunanza spirituale [...] del popolo italiano e giapponese," Pisanty, 2006: 185). The article described how Japanese share with Italians an endless devotion to the homeland, from which they draw inspiration for a life of sacrifice, discipline, courage and benevolent respect toward other fellow patriots. After this article, *La difesa della razza* abandoned the subject altogether: the negative turn of the Japanese campaigns in the Pacific War, as well as the progressive complication of the Italo-Japanese relationship, must have suggested to the editorial board a strategy of concentrating the racist discourse on the African colonies and the persecution of the Jews.

Yet Mussolini's Social Republic continued to exercise a pro-Japanese propaganda, despite the damaged relations between the two countries as a result of Italy's signing of the armistice with the Allies on September 8, 1943, therefore breaking the pact with Germany and Japan. An example of propaganda in this period is a booklet titled *Sogno delle Hawaii* ("Dreams of Hawaii"), which was printed and distributed in Italy at the end of 1944 when it was becoming obvious that Japan was losing ground in the Pacific battles (see Figure 2). This document contains an accurate list of Anglo-American losses of both ships and airplanes during the Pacific War since the battle of Pearl Harbor.[24] Of course, in contrast to the report on this booklet, the reality was quite different. For instance, as evidence of Japanese military success this document mentions the Formosa Air Battle of October 12–16, 1944, when in fact the Japanese losses at the end of this battle were three times as high as the American ones. The cover illustration shows someone relaxing on an exotic beach in the foreground, while in the background a huge sunrise emerges from the sea and a paper with musical notes is superimposed over the image. The propaganda in this image is based on a dual interpretation of

---

24 "Ora sappiamo perché gli angloamericani tentano di passare sotto silenzio le perdite subite sui fronti dell'Asia Orientale. Le cifre, che precedono, parlano un linguaggio oltremodo eloquente e fanno apparire in una luce ben strana le smargiassate di Churchill e di Roosevelt, che vaneggiavano di 'debellare le scimmie con un'offensiva di proporzioni mai viste.' Il crudele risveglio che attende questi signori dai loro rosei 'sogni dei mari del sud', è dimostrato dal risultato delle battaglie navali del 12 ottobre 1944" (*Sogno delle Hawaii*, 1944: 4).

Fig. 2 Cover of a propaganda brochure circulated in Italy at the end of 1944 (Image by courtesy of the Department of Special Collections, Memorial Library, University of Wisconsin-Madison)

a system of signifiers. At first reading they express an idea of "exoticism": the palm tree, the island, the sun, the bather, the phrase "the dream of Hawaii." But, as Roland Barthes would say, "None of this information is innocent" (Barthes, 1982: 30): war propaganda uses evocative exotic images to fulfill its purpose. A political signification is disseminated in the way that these signifiers are assembled. In this sense the sun on the horizon stands as a metaphor of the upcoming victory of the Empire of the Rising Sun in the Pacific War. The name of the island, "Hawaii," reminds the reader of the Japanese victory at Pearl Harbor. The "dream of Hawaii" therefore stands for the dream of a colonial empire that Italy, as a member of the Axis Pact, is on the verge of being a part of. The successful effect of the message relies on signifiers employed by mass tourism agencies to advertise their exotic journeys: information about military operations overlaps with the message about Hawaii as a paradise for a relaxing vacation. The use of these exotic signifiers to convey a political message has the advantage of locating the content of the message at an indefinite distance: the distance that separates any exotic location from the civil world of tourist consumers. At a time when Italians were coping with the idea that the war was irreversibly lost, exoticism was a useful source for delivering false information by locating it in a space and a time completely apart from the present.

7. Making Sense of Japan to Average Italians

As we have seen, the Axis alliance generated an intense cross-cultural exchange between nations that had historically very little in common. Japan was no longer the distant and unapproachable superpower admired by Italian nationalists at the dawn of the twentieth century, but in the Italian collective representation this land became much closer and more familiar. Was this just an illusion created by war propaganda? Or did the encounter between these two countries in fact generate, at times, a sense of mutual understanding and intercultural communication? Overall, the operation of aggrandizing the Japanese–Italian alliance was the result of fascist propaganda at its worst, and an opportunity to deepen the knowledge and import of Japanese culture in Italy at its best.

At the apex of these official efforts to fill the cultural and historical gap between the two countries, there was a diplomatic visit to Japan by an official delegation of the Italian regime in 1938. The one-month journey, from the main cities in Japan to Manchuria, was followed by a large cohort of media and local supporters. While in Japan, the Italian delegation shot a documentary for the "Istituto LUCE" to be seen in Italy, they promoted the image of the "Duce" in Japan by screening a documentary titled *Mussolini visto da vicino* ["A Mussolini close-up"].[25] A key member of this Fascist delegation was the writer and journalist Pietro Silvio Rivetta, whose deep knowledge of the Japanese language and culture helped him play the role of mediator during the visit.

Rivetta (who went by the penname Toddi) was born in Rome in 1886, where he also died in 1952. He lived in Japan working as a diplomat at the Italian embassy in Tokyo from 1910 for three years and again in 1926, and he taught Japanese language at the *Regio Istituto Universitario Orientale* in Naples. As an eclectic and polyglot writer with occasional forays into cinema and radio journalism, Rivetta devoted himself, among other interests, to the promotion of Japanese language and culture in Italy by publishing manuals of grammar, newspaper and magazine articles about the linguistic curiosities of the Asian language, as well as essays on several aspects of Japanese culture and art.

His major work on Japan was published in 1941 under the title *Il paese dell'eroica felicità* ["The Country of the Heroic Happiness"], which was intended to introduce the Italian reader to everyday life in Japan.[26] As a book written by an intellectual who colluded with the Fascist regime with the intention of "selling" the deal of the military alliance to the Italian public, there is no doubt that this publication falls under the category of regime propaganda. Japanese officials, for instance, are photographed on the battlefield while they perform a tea ceremony, while no mention is made of the war crimes and other atrocities committed by the same soldiers during the Second Sino-Japanese war (from 1937 to 1945). In the same tone are observations related to the fondness of the Japanese for the fascist ideology of the totalitarian state, the cult of the motherland and of its undisputable leader. Japanese authorities are even praised for suppressing jazz concerts and nightclubs as sign of their efforts to push back Anglo-American influence and reestablish traditional forms of entertainment.

---

25 See Daniela Calamanca, 2016, *Bianco e nero: L'Istituto Nazionale Luce e l'immaginario del fascismo (1924–1940)* (Bologna: Bononia University Press): 239–76.

26 Rivetta is the author of a Japanese grammar: *Nihongo no tebichi: avviamento facile alla difficile lingua nipponica* (Milan: Hoepli, 1943). Among other contributions to Japanese culture, Rivetta introduced the Japanese fairytales in Italy by editing a personal translation in the volume entitled *Momotarō: fiabe giapponesi come sono narrate ai bimbi in Giappone* (Milan: Hoepli, 1940).

Nonetheless, it would be limited to dismiss Rivetta's painstaking effort to import and translate Japanese culture in Italy solely as a reflection of the regime's ideology; for it is also important to stress the role of Rivetta as mediator of culture, and to challenge the notion that casts the Asian "Other" as impenetrable and, ultimately, incomprehensible to a Western citizen. Three points in support of this thesis will be presented. First, Rivetta's book exposes the fallacious nature of translation to a large audience; second, the transnational project of this book moves in parallel with its political message; finally, the strength of Rivetta's portrait of Japan is demonstrated by the fact that it outlived Fascism and in certain aspects foresaw the post-war revival of Japanese society.

Il paese dell'eroica felicità combines a complex look at Japanese culture and language with a choice of topics that is meant to attract the curiosity and interest of an ordinary reader. This introduction to the Japanese society is not addressed to small circles of academic scholars, but is geared toward the larger public of magazine readers, who were Rivetta's privileged audience throughout his entire career as journalist, film director and radio commentator. His rather didactic approach to the subject matter is enriched by frequent translations of Japanese words that help readers grasp basic knowledge of the target language while at the same time becoming aware of the miscommunication inherent in the process of translating languages and cultures. The sequence of chapters in the book does not focus on essential aspects of Japanese history and society; in fact, the macro-history of the country is barely sketched in favor of a selection of topics oriented to debunk misconceptions and misunderstandings that are popular among Italians. Rivetta calls for a reconsideration of what Westerners consider odd norms of behavior, such as: leaving shoes outside the house; kneeling down on a *tatami*, instead of sitting on a comfortable chair; granting special importance not to gifts per se, but to the paper in which they have been wrapped; also, the supposedly frigid nature of the Japanese people, compared to the allegedly warmer and more sensitive Europeans. Rivetta challenges these assumptions on the grounds that they are merely expressions of Western Orientalism that do not cross linguistic and cultural boundaries.

What makes his account different from others is his confidence in mastering the language and his familiarity with the country. By situating himself in between two languages he warns the non-specialized reader of the inevitable impasse comprised in the act of translating. For instance, in explaining why the Japanese choose an apparently more uncomfortable way of sitting around the table by genuflecting instead of using chairs, the author guides the reader through the difficulties of translating the Japanese verb that is used to describe this action: "Non è facile tradurre in italiano una tipica espressione nipponica nella quale interviene il verbo *suwaru*, quel medesimo che serve ad esprimere la posa abituale del giapponese assiso: 'dokyô ga suwaru' significa 'diventar coraggioso,' 'aver sangue freddo.' È mai possibile immaginare un simbolico e personificato coraggio adagiato mollemente su una poltrona o su una sedia a sdraio?" (Rivetta, 1941: 6) [It is not easy to translate into Italian a typical Japanese expression in which the verb *suwaru* intervenes, the same one used to express the usual pose of the Japanese assisi: "dokyô ga suwaru" means "to become courageous," "to have cold blood." Is it possible to imagine a symbolic and personified courage lying softly on a chair or on a deckchair?]. The author points out that the more tense pose required by this way of sitting helps the Japanese to continue to be aware of her/his own body, in contrast with the Western act of sitting, in which the body is passively abandoned in the chair. This specific custom is a direct consequence of the different meaning of the verb *suwaru* within the Japanese linguistic system. This particular signifier assumes a specific connotation that expresses the act of sitting in an active and performative way, which does not exist in the Italian lexicon. By signaling the difficulty of translation, Rivetta exposes the reader to the semantic differences that are encoded in the two languages, while highlighting the rationale and consistency of Japanese behavior. Penetrating the linguistic code is the key to avoiding the *cliché* of deeming Japanese people mysterious and irrational.

The Italian reader is also invited to revisit the superficiality inherent in the description of the Japanese "animal-like nature," popular in the 1930s, to embrace a eulogy of a people who belong to a very distinguished place in the progress of human civilization. Pledging to work against the previous shallow and disparaging reports of the East Asian country, Rivetta describes the deep humanity and sensibility of Japanese people, their compassion for "Others" including animals, and their positive attitude to life.

While warning the common reader of the fallacious nature of translating cultures, Rivetta suggests a seamless continuity of values between Fascist Italy and its distant ally: in his view, the two countries share an ingrained sense of discipline, a preference for a political autarchy, respect for ancient traditions, and a rejection of individualism in favor of full devotion to a totalitarian state.

As part of his strategy to reach less educated readers, images and drawings play a key role in this book. The wide display of images is an example of how the Fascist regime exploited visual media to help Italians become more familiar with the distant ally by showing a seamless ideological continuity. However, in the case of Rivetta, propaganda is only one aspect that explains the deployment of images: on a different level this material is instrumental to the educational goal of the book. Photographs are alternated with drawings that help illustrate aspects of Japanese language and culture for a wide audience. A reproduction of the cover of a Japanese magazine, for instance, is meant to exemplify the alternation of characters Hiragana, Katakana and Kanjii in contemporary Japan. This didactic use of images participated in the marketing of this book as an effective "intro manual" of Japanese culture and society for non-specialists, while carrying a clear political message aimed at promoting the Japanese–Italian partnership.

As I have suggested, Silvio Rivetta's tireless effort to get Italians acquainted with Japan reaches far beyond the Fascist propaganda, and indeed it can even be seen to anticipate the discussion of certain aspects of East Asian society that would become objects of interest during the post-World War II Japanese economic revival. First of all, Rivetta introduces the notion of a Japan that imitates the West only in its exterior forms, like science and technology, while maintaining a peculiar, purely Japanese pattern of modernity. This idea is not new in itself, as the Meiji leaders organized the restoration of the country based on the principle of the *wakon-yōsai* ("Japanese spirit and Western technology"), but what is new is the idea – later developed by Fosco Maraini – of a Japanese tradition that can live up to the challenges of modernity: "La tradizione nipponica trova conferma nella modernità: nella essenziale sostanza della modernità" (Rivetta, 1941: 18) [The Japanese tradition finds confirmation in modernity: in the essential substance of modernity]. Japan's fast pace of modernization maintains an anti-Western outlook, oriented mainly at refusing an Anglo-American ideological influence. According to this view, Japan does not need to adopt materialistic philosophies, or a Western-style system of values and religions; for the Japanese spirit already contains the features necessary to be projected into the modern era. In line with the lowbrow tone of the book, Rivetta offers some curious examples in this regard. He notices that the European scientific results on the dangers of bacteria lead the Japanese to consider irrational the Western tradition of wearing shoes inside the home without carefully sanitizing the domestic space, as they normally do in Japan. He also intends to debunk the opinion that women's rights are less important in comparison to Italy: in both cases women play a subservient role to men, with the difference that in Japan women are in charge of the finances of the family. Also, he notices that in Japanese mythology there is a cult of the Goddess Amaretasu Ōmikami, and that the literary canon showcases famous women poets such as Murasaki Shikibu (author of the *Tale of the Genji*) and Sei Shōnagon (author of *The Pillow Book*). It was not by chance that this argument against the coerced status of the Japanese woman would be put forth by Fosco Maraini in the 1970s to demonstrate the modernity of the Japanese household (see ch. 3, pp. 140–51).

Rivetta's *Il paese dell'eroica felicità* is both an example of fascist propaganda and a testimony of a time when, because of the political ties between the two countries, a relational orientalism (see Introduction, pp. 4–5) between Japan and Italy took place. The demise of Fascism at the end of World War II and the role of the United States, in both Japan and Europe, in rebuilding states as democracies disconnected from their nationalistic past, help explain why these transnational exchanges came to an end and were, ultimately, neglected. Nevertheless, Rivetta's lifetime commitment to move the Italian public beyond a strictly Orientalist view of Japan preceded the advent of the Axis alliance and continued later, as a form of legacy that a writer such as Fosco Maraini would successfully take up. While his educational project reached its apex during the war, it stands as a demonstration that fascist propaganda built on an existing network of exchanges between Italy and Japan, continued to operate notwithstanding the restrictions of the media and the acquiescence of intellectuals.

8. A Transnational Story in the Age of Nationalisms

If Rivetta was able to walk a fine line between the service paid to the regime and independent interest in building cultural bridges between Italy and Japan, the period of the Tripartite Pact presented cases, like Fosco Maraini, of Italians living in Japan who were not committed to any form of pro-Axis propaganda. A lesser known example is the life of Arundel Del Re (1892–1974), who immigrated to Japan in the 1920s, but remained aloof from the politic of the Italian regime and connected to a transnational network of people and countries. What makes his case relevant today is the fact that Del Re carried out a quest for a more complex cultural identity during the time of Italian Fascism and Japanese nationalism when homogeneous and clear-cut identities rooted in one country were the object of intense state-driven propaganda.

Del Re was born in 1892 in Florence, Italy, of an Irish poet and an Italian military officer. He grew up in Tuscany at a time when Anglophone artists and writers, from Gordon Craig to Harold Monro, chose Italy as muse to inspire their artistic creations. As he writes himself in autobiographical notes, Arundel describes Tuscany during his teenage years as a transnational space contaminated by his dual Anglo-Italian roots.[27] Arundel lived in Tuscany until his college years, before moving to England in 1920 where he worked for the poet and editor Harold Monro in the Poetry Bookshop, an experience that introduced him to poets such as Ezra Pound and William Butler Yeats. Between 1920 and 1927 he was lecturer in Italian at Oxford and London Universities. In 1927 Del Re, with his English wife Joan, made the most adventurous decision of his life by accepting a position as English professor at Tokyo Imperial University, where he taught both English and Italian literature. At the end of this period, in 1930, he moved to Taiwan (at the time Formosa), where he became Professor of English and Latin language and literature at Taihoku Imperial University until 1943. When the alliance between Italy and Japan fell apart, Del Re refused to swear allegiance to Mussolini's Social Republic and, for this reason, he was arrested with his family and interned, probably in Tokyo, for two years. After the war he was able to reinvent himself by offering his experience in the field of education in Japan at the service of the American Occupation Forces, where he was employed by the chief of the Civil Information and Education Sector about all matters pertaining to the educational reorganization of Japan between 1945 and 1951. When the American occupation forces left Japan in 1951, Del Re moved to Nagoya to become chair of the English Department at Nanzan Catholic University. In 1954 he moved from Japan to Sydney for medical reasons and from there, in 1958, to Wellington New Zealand where he was a lecturer in English and Italian at Victoria University until 1967. In Sydney Del Re was founding member of the Oriental Society of Australia, while in Wellington he was founding member of the Japan Society of New Zealand. In parallel with Japanese culture, Del Re was fully involved in promoting Italian culture as well – in fact he organized the exhibition for the Michelangelo centenary at Centre Gallery in Wellington in 1964 and a year later he was involved in organizing an exhibition to celebrate the Birth of Dante at the National Art Gallery. As result of this commitment to

---

27 In "Georgian Reminiscences" he writes that "Florence, when I was a boy in my teens, had its regular colony of English writers, artists and art critics, most of whom owned villas or rented flats in the city and came regularly every year in the autumn or spring to work or to enjoy themselves" (Arundel Del Re, 1932, "Georgian Reminiscences," *Studies in English Literature* (Tokyo, XII): 322).

multiple countries, Del Re received a gold medal for his services to Italy and a special order from the Emperor of Japan. In the last few years of his life, Del Re returned to Australia, to finally settle in Melbourne with his family until his death in 1974.

During his nomadic life across nations and continents, Del Re never contemplated a permanent return to his birthplace, yet Italy, among the countries in which he lived, was the one that he remained most committed to, not only by promoting its cultural heritage, but also by collaborating with its institutions. During World War I, he publicly defended the right of Italy to enter the war and he became private secretary to the military attaché in the Italian embassy in London, where he worked from 1916 to 1919. In his twenty-seven years in Japan Del Re did not endorse the Fascist government, but he nonetheless helped Italian institutions with cultural expertise and logistical support. For instance, in Taiwan he was appointed as Honorary Consular Agent, a position that he held until 1943, and while in Tokyo he acted as personal secretary of the Italian ambassador Pompeo Aloisi with the goal of organizing the 1930 exhibition of Japanese art in Rome. In other words, his migrant trajectory was characterized by a progressive forward movement, but without neglecting his origins.

In an article published on his departure from Japan, Arundel looks back over the war years and the period straight after the liberation, using words that help explain the reason for his decision to stay in Japan:

> Never did I experience so intensively the strength of that community feeling that knit together spontaneously those of us who had watched Tokyo in flames and remembered the wailing of sirens and those evil-looking fish flying overheard and the deadly swish of the fire bombs. Nor am I likely ever to forget the scenes I witnessed after the nightmare was over when people slowly returned to consciousness, wandering in search of familiar landmarks and happy memories through this strange city – a wilderness of rubble and solitary chimney stacks dotted here and there with small oases, miraculously forgotten, of trees and greenery sprawling endlessly over hill and valley. [...] But most impressive of all was the sudden meeting with old friends and students mysteriously stepping like ghosts out of the past; the renewal of old friendships and the forging of new and stronger links and with it a clearer insight into the significance of the Japanese past not as something dead to be dug up and embalmed by scholars, but as perennial fountain of life and creative force. (Del Re, 1954: 611)

Del Re envisioned collaboration with the American occupation troops in Japan as an opportunity to act effectively in rebuilding the relationship between Japan and the West. At least, this is what Del Re wrote in the pages of the Japanese journal *The Rising Generation*, when he had relocated with his family in Sydney. However, the documents in possession of the National Library of Australia reveal how controversial this decision was and how increasingly uncomfortable his stay in Japan became after the war. The most significant moment of this experience was the "Memorandum" (1950–51) that he wrote for the education section of the American occupation forces about the risk of transferring Western values to the Japanese education plan. This document contradicts the positive attitude and the possibility of integration to which Del Re alludes in his article, written as a farewell to Japan. In writing to the American Chief of Education, Del Re lays out the problem of collaboration in essentialist terms: in his own words there exists an "essential dividing line between ourselves [Westerners] and the Japanese which constitutes perhaps the greatest obstacle to a deep spiritual communion."[28] There is no doubt that Del Re's overriding concern was to work through the differences in order to promote "cooperation," yet the logic of his discourse betrays a classic Orientalist approach predicated upon patronizing assumptions. In fact, he observes, "to those who have come into close contact with the Japanese it will have become apparent that their actions and way of thinking are mainly determined by [...] emotion rather than thought."[29] The key-words here are to "come into close contact": Del Re explains that a phenomenon that must be factored in when attempting to understand the Japanese is the fatal influence that the country has on its own people. In fact he says: "the more one becomes conditioned to Japan the more one becomes conscious of the predominance of the sensory [sic] and emotional rather than intellectual elements in individual and social life, controlled and directed in accordance with the traditional patterns expressive of its naturalistic culture."[30] While Del Re acknowledges that Japanese people are not intrinsically irrational because they live according to values and mores rooted in their tradition, he fails to see the inherent racism of his discourse based on a subjective notion of reason and morality, beyond which only the territory of irrationality can unfold. His rational approach fails

---

28   Arundel Del Re, 1950–51, "Memo from Mr. Del Re: 'Educational Reorientation in the Post-Treaty Period,'" *Papers of Arundel Del Re*, National Library of Australia, MS 1879/2/11.
29   NLA MS 1879/2/11.
30   NLA MS 1879/2/11.

to account for the rationality of the "Other," and thus limits the possibility of common understanding. If the dividing line between "us" and "them" is conceived as a sense of belonging to a nation (with its one race, language, and history), the consequence is that the coexistence of the foreigner with the "Other" in a foreign land becomes increasingly problematic and harmful in the long term. Between the lines of the Memorandum it is possible to read the sense of discomfort due to a lack of empathy and inter-subjective understanding that Del Re must have experienced in Japan. He recalls the phenomenon he observed of Japanese living abroad and speaking English fluently as becoming completely different individuals once they came back to their country. In his own words he indicates that: "However Westernized and un-Japanese they may have seemed until that moment, they become in some subtle way, different persons. Meet them again at parties or on the university campus a short time afterwards and – in spite of their Savile Row tailor and command of colloquial English – you felt that a kind of barrier had grown up between you and them."[31] Del Re had to reckon with the limits of his transnational identity, which was the trademark of his success as international scholar. It is certainly true that the failure is partially due to the fact that he had never learned Japanese in his twenty-seven years spent in the host country. In this sense the "Memorandum" is perhaps the cultural and historical rationalization of a barrier that was subjective and personal. In any case, the American Lieutenant Colonel Donald Nugent, who had a PhD in Far Eastern History from Stanford University, received the "Memorandum" and, while he appreciated and shared Del Re's observations, he also suggested keeping it secret as the content could have offended the locals.[32] As a Japanese scholar himself, Nugent understood

---

31   NLA MS 1879/2/11.

32   In a document in response to Del Re's "Memorandum," Nugent writes: "Please inform Mr. Del Re that I have read and re-read his memorandum. I consider it perhaps the most-thought provoking analysis of the subject which has been made by anyone in the headquarters. [...] Because of certain statements in the memorandum which might offend Japanese sensibilities, I am asking Mr. Rockefeller not to publish the memorandum, but to use it as a basis for discussion in his over-all program to stimulate 'voluntary' cultural cooperation between Japan and the West" (Donald R. Nugent in response to "Memo from Mr. Del Re, 'Educational Reorientation in the Post-Treaty Period'": NLA MS 1879/1/1). A few months later, Del Re published an article titled "Notes on Japanese and Western Cultural Attitudes": *Academia*, 1953, 4: 1–11. In this article he repeats some of the points stated in the "Memorandum" but he treats the subject as an academic one, leaving aside his personal feelings about being excluded in Japan as they are present in the "Memorandum." However, he is quite negative about the possibility of understanding between Japanese and European cultures: "One explanation

that the *Memorandum*, while born out of an attempt at finding new avenues for an intercultural dialog, could be interpreted as an indictment against the Japanese for being isolationist and hostile toward cultural hybridization.

However, Japan is not the dead end of Del Re's transnational journey: his failure to negotiate his own identity with the Japanese "Other" did not result in the counter movement of tracing back his steps toward the "sameness" of his country of origins, whether that might be Italy or England. His decision to live in Anglophone nations, between Australia and New Zealand, is a choice obviously determined to favor his cultural integration; nevertheless, it is also derived from the desire to follow the transnational geography of migration, that is, a space populated by individuals like him, whose stories reveal far-reaching ties and allegiances to other countries around the world. While apparently finding refuge in the English speaking world, Del Re was in search of an in-between space where cultural traditions met and new forms of mutual understanding were required. In other words, his move indicates not an effacement of his inclination toward intercultural exchange, but rather a recalibration of it, toward a reinstatement of the distance between the "Self" and the "Other," that is a necessary space for cultural dialog to happen. In a letter to his former colleague in Japan, Arthur Loomis, on July 3, 1967, when he was about to leave Wellington to relocate in Melbourne, Del Re looks back at his time in New Zealand and comments on how such a country has represented the middle ground that allowed him to negotiate his multiple identities: "I think the peacefulness of New Zealand – a country that physically and climatically often recalls Japan – has served to establish a kind of critical equilibrium between West and East – and between Romance and Germanic cultural reactions and emotions."[33] The new country became an imaginary space where East and West are reconciled in the mind of the author, as Del Re's own Italian and English cultural heritages being equally represented.

---

for the failure to achieve reciprocal and adequate communication comparable to the effort expended, may be that, so far, no common meeting ground has been found other than of an empirical nature nor, what seems of even greater consequence, an agreed set of values to replace elusive and unreliable preferences and prejudices" (5). Among the papers of the collection I found the reaction of Del Re's Japanese friend Tatsunosuke Ueda, which is quite different from Nugent's response. In fact he writes that the article appears to him like "the roar of a lion disarmed of […] of his teeth." Then, he finished by teasing Del Re, saying: "Excuse my usual candor, for what I want to say is 'Spruce up, my dear Sensei, and blossom again, you worthy son of Florence!' and certainly not 'The glory and greatness that *were* del Re Sensei'" (NLA MS 1879/1/3).
33   NLA MS 1879/1/3.

Transnationalism normally implies a movement between home and abroad, but in the case of Arundel Del Re, the places of origin (Italy and England) as well as the elsewhere place (Japan, New Zealand, Australia) are equally blurred and the link between local and global is compromised by interferences and experiences of displacement. By locating his transnational story during the time of Japan's rising nationalism and its alliance with Fascist Italy, Del Re complicates the picture that portrays Italians residing in the Far East as representative of the regime and its political ideology. His post-war trajectory of migration to New Zealand and Australia inscribes his biography within a community of cosmopolitan citizens whose sense of belonging and heterogeneous ties are transient and far-reaching.

9. An Invitation to a More Complex Look

The approach to the writers summoned up in this chapter (among many possible others) questions the monolithic interpretations, often taken for granted, of fascist Orientalism, based on hierarchical distinctions between the Italian "I" and the Oriental "Other." On the one hand, anti-fascist intellectuals, such as Comisso and Patti, resorted to the rhetoric of fascist virility in order to describe an effeminate and irrational Japan. On the other, from the far-fetched pro-Japanese propaganda of the Axis alliance period, authors like Rivetta and Del Re emerged as distinct voices engaged in more or less successful attempts to bridge cultural differences. The landscape of fascist Orientalists comprehends not only the intellectuals in full-blooded service to the regime's foreign policy (like Arnaldo Cipolla or Mario Appelius), but also more complex individualities who negotiate their affiliation, or distance, from the regime while pursuing idiosyncratic plans to introduce Japanese culture to the Italian peninsula.

In 1930 Silvio Rivetta published the book *La pittura moderna giapponese* ["Modern Japanese painting"] on the occasion of the exhibition of Japanese art in Rome at Il Palazzo delle Esposizioni, in which Arundel Del Re himself was involved. Both Rivetta and Del Re seized the opportunity given by the historical convergence of political interests between Italy and Japan to update Italian knowledge of Japanese art. The exhibition, entitled "Mostra d'arte giapponese: Roma, Aprile-maggio 1930" ["Exhibition of Japanese art: Rome, April–May 1930"], introduced Italians to the Nihonga style of painting, showcasing a group of painters more allegedly faithful to traditional Japanese aesthetics. For the first time in Europe an exhibition of Japanese art was

Fig. 3   Interior of the Japan exhibition in Rome
(*L'Illustrazione Italiana* VII, 18 (May 4, 1930), 767)

hosted inside a recreated typical Japanese tea house, making the overall experience for the visitor more pedagogical and attractive, especially to the large audience of non-experts.

Indeed, one of the exhibition's explicit goals was to reach a wider audience, as well as to capture the attention of the national and international press. Beyond the aberrations of the political propaganda,[34] Italians during the fascist *ventennio* received unprecedented exposure to a Far Eastern country,

---

34   This Japanese-style of painting developed during the Meiji Restoration in response to demand from Western artists and experts who wished to preserve the "traditional" Japanese art from the contamination of European oil painting and other pictorial forms. Such choice seems to reflect the regime's predilection for clear-cut identities that demark differences between "us" and "them," while showing the Fascist potential to reach out far-away cultures. On the day of the inauguration the nationalist painter Yokoyama Taikan (1868–1958) presented the exhibition: see Yokoyama Taikan, 1930, *Esposizione d'arte giapponese: Roma, Aprile Maggio 1930* (VIII Rome: S.A. Poligr). The main sponsor of the event was the Baron Ōkura Kihachirō of the Okura Financial Group. Mussolini was invited to the inauguration together with the King of Italy, Victor Emmanuel III. For more information about the exhibition, see Pilar Araguás, "La obra. La pittura moderna giapponese (1930) de Pietro Silvio Rivetta," *Ecos de Asia*, 23 (2016): 14–17.

which represented an element of continuity between this period and the post-war success of Japanese literature in translation, as we shall see in the next chapter.

Works Cited

Andō, Yosirō. 1942. "Amore del popolo giapponese per la pace." *Yamato* II, 3: 69–71.
Appelius, Mario. 1940. "Vincere." Rome: Editrice La Vittoria.
—. 1941. *Cannoni e ciliegi in fiore*. Milan: Mondadori.
Barthes, Roland. 1982. *Empire of Signes*. Translated by Richard Howard. New York: Hill and Wang.
Barzini, Ludina. 2010. *I Barzini: Tre generazioni di giornalisti, una storia del Novecento*. Milan: Mondadori.
Barzini, Luigi Sr. 1942. *Perché il Giappone vince: i nipponici sono esatti, cronometrici e formali*. Rome: Novissima.
Ben-Ghiat, Ruth. 2001. *Fascist Modernities*. Berkeley: University of California Press.
—. 2015. *Italian Fascism's Empire Cinema*. Bloomington: Indiana University Press.
Benvenuti, Giuliana. 2008. *Il viaggiatore come autore: L'India nella letteratura italiana del Novecento*. Bologna: Il Mulino.
Burdett, Charles. 2007. *Journey through Fascism: Italian Travel Writing between the Wars*. New York and Oxford: Berghahn Books.
Cipolla, Arnaldo. 1924. *Per la Siberia in Cina e Giappone: racconto di viaggio*. Turin: Paravia.
—. 1931. *Nel Giappone dei grattacieli: viaggio da Tokio a Delhi*. Turin: Paravia.
Comisso, Giovanni. 1958. *Donne gentili*. Milan: Longanesi.
—. 2002 [1949]. "Amori d'Oriente." In *Opere*, edited by Rolando Damiani and Nico Naldini, 967–1090. Milan: Mondadori.
Cronin, Michael. 2000. *Across the Lines: Travel, Language, Translation*. Cork, Ireland: Cork University Press.
Del Re, Arundel. 1932. "Georgian Reminiscences." *Studies in English Literature*. Tokyo, XII.
—. 1950–51. "Memo from Mr. Del Re: 'Educational Reorientation in the Post-Treaty Period.'" *Papers of Arundel Del Re*, National Library of Australia, MS 1879/2/11.
—. 1953. "Notes on Japanese and Western Cultural Attitudes", *Academia*, 1953, 4: 1–11.
—. 1954. "On Leaving Japan." *The Rising Generation*, Tokyo, Vol. C (12).

Dollimore, Jonathan. 1991. *Sexual Dissidence: Augustine to Wilde, Freud to Foucault.* Oxford: Clarendon Press; New York: Oxford University Press.
Duncan, Derek. 2002. "Travel and Autobiography: Giovanni Comisso's Memories of the War." In *Cultural Encounters: European Travel Writings in the 1930s,* edited by Charles Burdett and Derek Duncan, 49–63. New York and Oxford: Berghahn Books.
—. 2006. *Reading and Writing Italian Homosexuality: A Case of Possible Difference.* Aldershot, UK and Burlington, VT: Ashgate.
Ferraris, Clemente. 1928. *Al di là del Paese di Butterfly: impressioni di viaggio in India, Cina, Giappone, Manciuria.* Florence: Bemporad.
Hinsch, Bret. 1990. *Passions of the Cut Sleeve: The Male Homosexual Tradition in China.* Berkeley: University of California Press.
Hofmann, Reto. 2015. *The Fascist Effect: Japan and Italy, 1915–1952.* Ithaca, NY: Cornell University Press.
Il Giappone e le sue forze armate. 1942. Rome: Stato Maggiore R. Esercito, Ufficio Propaganda.
Mussolini, Benito. 1960. *Opera omnia di Benito Mussolini,* vols xxix–xxx, edited by Edoardo and Duilio Susmel, Florence: La Fenice.
Patti, Ercole. 1975. *Un lungo viaggio lontano.* Milan: Bompiani.
Pellegrino, Angelo. 1985. *Verso Oriente: Viaggi e letteratura degli scrittori italiani nei paesi orientali (1912–1982).* Rome: Istituto dell'enciclopedia Treccani.
Pisanty, Valentina. 2006. *La difesa della razza. Antologia 1938–1943.* Milan: Bompiani.
Rivetta, Pietro Silvio. 1941. *Il paese dell'eroica felicità, usi e costumi giapponesi.* Milan: Hoepli.
Said, Edward W. 1978. *Orientalism.* New York: Pantheon Books.
Schwab, Gabriele. 2012. *Imaginary Ethnographies: Literature, Culture, and Subjectivity.* New York: Columbia University Press.
Sogno delle Hawaii. 1944. [Anonymous and without editorial information.]
Spackman, Barbara. 1996. *Fascist Virilities: Rhetoric, Ideology and Social Fantasy in Italy.* Minneapolis and London: University of Minnesota Press.

CHAPTER THREE

Little Italy, Big Japan: Patterns of Continuity and Displacement among Italian Writers in Japan

> Comment peut-on s'empêcher de sombrer dans le bon-sens, sinon en s'exilant de son pays, sa langue, son sexe, son identité?
>
> (Julia Kristeva, *Un nouveau type d'intellectuel: le dissident*)

1. Tradition and Modernity

The post-war period of reconstruction was for Italy and Japan a time to rethink the concept of democracy and its effective application as both countries had experienced the failure of sovereign power in the face of nationalism. Intellectuals from both countries were aware that the path toward becoming late-developing modern industrial nations included the creation of functional democratic systems. In Japan the solution was also the problem, as many interpreters considered the US-imposed constitution as an artificial attempt to force a Western political template onto an Eastern nation.[1] Therefore, the experiment was destined to fail. Maruyama Masao's assessment of the Japanese political and historical catastrophe included a radical critique of the Meiji state for introducing an East–West paradigm. This paradigm preserved a Japanese cultural ethos (represented by the central authority of the emperor) while simultaneously imposing Western materialism on the other (represented by the opening to Western technology and science). For

---

1 The Japanese constitution forced the emperor to lose his divine prerogatives to become a "symbol of the State and of the unity of the people."

Maruyama, the formation of an autonomous approach – one that did not require the imposition of Western materialism – was the only way to create a functioning democracy.

In Italy the immediate solution to its dysfunctional political system was also received with skepticism. The June 1946 referendum between a monarchy and a republic saw a slim majority vote in favor of republicanism, a sign that the desire for radical change was tenuous. Even though the effort of the 1947 Constituent Assembly to craft the text of the Italian constitution represented a rare moment of political cohesion among the parties (mainly the left, the Catholics and the Liberals), the subsequent years were tainted by reciprocal accusations of Italian dependence on the US government, the Vatican and the Soviet Union.

If, in the historical context of the Cold War, Italy and Japan were unable to create democratic governments that were independent of foreign influence, they did succeed in abolishing premodern forces that had facilitated the emergence of past authoritarian regimes. Forces that could potentially hinder the formation of a democracy were manifest in the link between tradition, national identity and nationalism, with narratives of tradition employed to tell a magnificent national origin story and project future expansion. In post-war Japan, pressures from above called for preservation of the *kokutai* ("the national polity"). Yet those pressures were met with a critical response; the retention of the emperor role as representative of the polity "were but pitiful bleats compared to the surge of 'progressive' opinion demanding a spiritual and social revolution (namely, democracy). As the Tokyo War Crimes Trials reminded them daily, 'tradition' was relegated to a negative, shameful past" (Kersten, 1996: 113). In Italy the rise of nationalism was complicit in the creation of a national identity based in Roman history and entrusted with the mission of restoring the downfallen Empire. In sum, the post-war years were dedicated to the extirpation of what Gaetano Salvemini called "the Roman-Imperial cancer," with its "dreams of impossible supremacies" that impeded democracy from flourishing (Samuels, 2003: 181).

In this chapter I examine the post-war years and reconstruction, which involved rapid economic growth in both Italy and Japan, to consider how such loaded terms as "tradition" and "modernity" were employed in both countries as they sought to reinvent new democratic societies and break with totalitarian states. For three decades after World War II, Western intellectuals presented a remarkable aspect of Japanese reconstruction: the nation with the highest economic growth rate was also a society in which traditional values of the medieval age (for example, respect for the divinity of the emperor and the structure of personal relations) were still very much alive. In the 1960s, anthropologists, sociologists, and philosophers (such as Chie Nakane, Robert N. Bellah, and Maruyama Masao) debated the nature of the intensive Japanese recovery by highlighting the paradox of a society that was rapidly embracing modernization, democracy, and a capitalist economy while simultaneously holding on to many features of its traditional structure. As I show, the paradox of Japan's structural change and continuity with its past was of special interest to Italian observers whose nation embraced a similar set of problems at the dawn of the Italian Republic's founding. During the 1950s and 1960s, twentieth-century Italy experienced similar economic development followed by an intense phenomenon of migration from the south to the cities driving the north's "economic miracle." The consequence of this rapid growth was unprecedented social and cultural transformation resulting in a perceived break from the past and change in the national identity. For Italians who traveled to Japan during these years to try to observe and account for its rapid modernization, comparing the Japanese example with the historical circumstances that Italy was experiencing was inevitable. As the Italian model of evolution was predicated on a rupture, or break from tradition, and thus displacement, the Japanese model of societal evolution, as I contend, played a central role in the writings of Italians traveling to Japan during the post-World War II period.

Of course, Japan experienced, perhaps on a larger scale, rapid change in the society brought by massive industrialization during the years of its "economic miracle." Notably, the intense industrialization drastically remodeled the cityscapes, exposing an increasingly overcrowded urban population to the culture shock caused by the erosion of the rural landscape and increasing levels of pollution. In this regard, Yukio Mishima's spectacular suicide in 1970 represents the most vehement protest against post-war Japan's turn toward materialism and capitalism, driven by Western influence. As Edwin Reischauer maintains, the narrative of continuity between past and present in post-war Japan is commonly held by foreign travelers: "Despite [...] the rapid changes that have swept Japan, foreign observers have commonly sought to find in some single trait or tightly knit group of traits as an open sesame that would explain everything in Japan as it is today and was in the past" (Reischauer, 1977: 124). As we will see, what distinguishes Italian narratives from this general foreign gaze is the projection of anxieties related to a disrupted national history on to the all-encompassing explanations about Japanese society.

2. Three Encounters with Japan

When approaching how different cultures and civilizations relate, one must consider diversity in terms of not only national identity but also the biases and subjectivities of observers.

Their awareness of a different society depends on several factors, such as the amount of time spent in the visited country, their general awareness of its history and culture, and their knowledge of the language. For this reason, three Italian authors were selected for this chapter, as they vary in terms of these factors. Fosco Maraini (1912–2004), Alberto Moravia (1907–90) and Goffredo Parise (1929–86) all visited Japan between the 1950s and the 1980s, a period when Japan captured the world's attention for its accelerated modernization and economic growth. These writers all address the theme of modernity in relation to tradition. Despite their differences in terms of the time spent in Japan and their familiarity with its cultural norms, all arrive at a similar conclusion: rapid changes in Japanese society have not displaced the traditional structure of the society, relations among individuals or its set of rules. What distinguishes the assessments of the three authors is how Italy's post-war path, as a point of comparison, figures in their conclusions. As I show, the less observers know about Japan (the less time they spend within its territory and among its peoples), the higher the probability that they will be engaged in a comparison with their own country. Encountering a new culture has the immediate effect of enhancing and intensifying awareness of the observer's national identity and of stimulating his/her reaction by emphasizing the differences.

To demonstrate the inverse relationship between time spent in Japan and making comparisons with Italy's post-war development, I analyze the works of Maraini, Moravia and Parise in the order that corresponds to their different degrees of knowledge of Japanese culture and their inclination to compare it with Italy. For each author, the encounter with Japan results in an experience of infatuation that is different from the typical reaction of travelers in an exotic land. Behind their wonder a shadow is cast, that of the Italian Republic and its uncertain path toward the acquisition of a clear new identity.

3. The Defense of Otherness: Fosco Maraini and Japan

Fosco Maraini was a writer, photographer, mountaineer, traveler, ethnologist, and an Italian intellectual whose acquaintance with Japan was deep and consistent over the course of his lifetime. Maraini first traveled to Japan in 1938 at the age of twenty-four to study the Ainu people on the island of Hokkaido. Five years later, following Italy's signing the armistice with the Allies on September 8, its coalition with Japan fell apart. Subsequently Maraini, his wife Topazia, and their three children, were imprisoned in a Japanese POW camp. Maraini could have avoided captivity if he had agreed to swear loyalty to Mussolini's republic in the north of Italy, but he remained committed to his democratic values. As a desperate protest against officials' inhumane treatment of inmates, Maraini lopped off his finger with a hatchet. The dramatic gesture of a self-inflicted wound was aimed at gaining the camp supervisors' respect by showing familiarity with a Japanese code of honor, which draws on the yakuza's code of ethics. The family was finally released in 1945 when the American troops took control and Maraini decided to go back to his home country. He subsequently returned to Japan, living there between 1953 and 1956, during which period he collected sources for his book about Japan, *Ore Giapponesi* (1957, the English translation was published in 1960 with the title *Meeting with Japan*). He again took up residence in Japan from 1963 to 1972, during which time he divorced Topazia and married his second wife, a Japanese woman named Mieko Namiki, in 1970.

In 1971, Kodansha International published Maraini's book *Japan: Patterns of Continuity*. Originally published in English, the book immediately became a best-seller, with thousands of copies sold. Along with the superb quality of the photographs, the book's success must be attributed to the popularity of the subject – the relation between continuity and change in Japanese society. The rapid pace of modernization undertaken by Japan after the humiliation it suffered during World War II intrigued readers, fascinated with the country's emergence as one of the strongest economic powers in the world. Part of the fascination with Japan's "economic miracle" was the image of the country as traditional and mysterious, the "only complex society with a Bronze Age monarchy, where the emperor until recently was believed to be the lineal descendant of the sun goddess and, in some sense, himself divine" (Bellah, 2003: 184). The international community of anthropologists and sociologists who turned their attention to Japan was interested in the nature of this change: that is, in how Japanese society remained unaffected by structural change. How could one explain the coexistence of unchanging structural features of Japanese society and the process of transformation?

As Maraini mentions at the beginning of his book, dichotomizing tradition and change is common in the literature: "Similar views [the dichotomist views], usually less explicitly stated, can be found in most writings on Japan, from the papers of economists to the articles of foreign correspondents or the books of missionaries" (8). Such a perspective is too simple, was the conclusion Maraini drew after his many years of visiting and residing in Japan. As he notes, "The author feels inclined towards different conclusions. Thirty years of loving acquaintance with Japan, its people, its language and culture, have been a progressive discovery of unity and continuity underlying all superficial conclusion and change" (8). Maraini points out that while the typical visitor to Japan is impressed by the contrast of ancient elements existing side by side with all the elements of a modern industrial superpower, there exists a unity and continuity rather than contradiction.

In the fourth and last chapter of *Patterns of Continuity*, "The Future of the Past," Maraini further elaborates his point by insisting upon Japan's independence and autonomy, denying that Japan's success in the modern world is due to its full acceptance of Western (mainly American) ideology, political thought and ethics. In Japan, he writes, change has the distinction of adopting Western technology (modernization) rather than its way of thinking or lifestyle (Westernization).[2] As a consequence, "Japan's success must be explained in human terms and, one must add, predominantly in Japanese terms" (Maraini, 1971: 183). The essence of Maraini's argument is that over the centuries, Japanese civilization developed an ideal environment for the emergence of a modern society. He identifies five main factors that explain the difference between Japan and the West. First, "in the case of Japan [compared to Europe], a series of historical circumstances and some extremely lucky coincidences place its civilization in a most favorable position as regards the scientific mutation" (185). According to Maraini, Japanese society has the advantage of lacking the negative historical forces that have arguably impeded the rise of modern progress in Europe. In particular, he refers to the Christian bias toward the scientific revolution in medieval and

---

2   In 2001 a new edition of *Le ore giapponesi* (*Meeting with Japan*) was released. Maraini added a new introduction in which he confirms the same view illustrated in *Patterns*: "Venendo adesso al Giappone, potremo affermare ch'esso è altamente, splendidamente modernizzato, assai più modernizzato di noi per molti aspetti, ma poco, pochissimo, occidentalizzato. Numerosi e continui malintesi tra stranieri e giapponesi hanno luogo proprio perché, visitando l'arcipelago e notando tanti segni di somiglianza con l'Occidente nel vestire, nella casa, nel mangiare, nel lavoro, nei giochi, nelle abitudini più comuni della giornata e della notte, il viaggiatore conclude: ma allora sono come noi! Niente affatto, sono diversissimi: in molte cose meglio di noi, in altre peggio, però sempre diversissimi. Regola basilare dunque: non si scambi modernizzazione per occidentalizzazione": Maraini, 2001: 19.

early modern Europe as compared to the alleged religious tolerance of the Japanese: "Japan, therefore, appeared on the modern scene with a mental outlook particularly adapted to accept in full the essence of the Western scientific cultural mutation and of its dependent technological revolution, leaving behind all the antagonistic and retarding elements that were, and still are, so deep a part of Western civilization" (187).

A second aspect of Japanese people's attitude toward modernization is the love of nature, which is mostly considered divine. This adoration of nature facilitates a scientific approach to its study:

> In this attitude to nature and to life, I think one can appreciate an extraordinarily favorable background to the acceptance and understanding not merely of the methods and application of science but of its very spirit. Men and women who for thousands of years have approached nature in trepidation and wonder and who have been inspired by it to extraordinary heights of artistic and poetic feeling are now admirably prepared to face this same nature in a framework of pure rationality. [...] Such ideas may seem obvious today. It should be noted, however, that this attitude, achieved in the West by bitter victories over stake and proscription, springs in Japan from the most ancient frontiers of the collective mind, from myth, proverb, and folksong. (Maraini, 1971: 189)

This love of nature is conducive to another similarity between Japanese traditional values and the essence of modern times. In this regard Maraini observes that in Japan, "Transcendence and contemplation are out; immanent values and action are in" (189). Subsequently, Maraini considers Japanese society to be pragmatic and achievement oriented. A successful career is well rewarded on all sides; there is no contradiction between the spiritual sphere of life and the more interior needs of the soul.

A third aspect is the relationship between the individual and the society. Japanese culture eschews individualism and prioritizes the individual as embedded in a social network, which seems to meet the demands of modern life. As Maraini points out, "The modern age stresses communal life: ours are times of groups, crowds, collaboration, and social integration" (191).

Maraini's fourth reason considers Japanese ethical values, as they are not entirely rooted in religious beliefs. Thus, the process of secularization underway in the West did not affect Japanese society: "The development of Japanese ethics has taken place predominantly under the auspices of secular philosophy, especially of Confucianism, and only to a limited extent under religion" (192).

Finally, Maraini discusses the popular perception of Japan as a male-dominated society and counters this image with his discussion of women and household economies. As he observes, women serve as guardians of domestic finances, a dynamic consistent with the ongoing evolution of the heterosexual family roles and power distribution within households: "One may say, however, that modern Japanese women [...] have seized with spirited eagerness most of the opportunities offered to them. There are few countries in the world where the average husband hands over the entire monthly paypacket to his wife. The wife then takes care of household expenses, perhaps saves some, and doles out small sums for her husband's personal pleasures" (194).

The overall picture provided by Maraini presents an image of Japan as an ideal country for modernization, one that still faces negative influences from the West, mostly due to the supposedly detrimental effects of a religious legacy over society.

While Maraini claims his three decades of visiting or living in Japan engendered his skepticism toward dichotomizing tradition and change, a review of his sources helps us better understand what is omitted from his line of argument as well as outlining his idiosyncratic views within the contentious debate related to Japan and modernity between American and Japanese scholars. The author tries to downplay his subjective cultural representation by claiming the status of a neutral observer when he states, "We are not expressing judgments; we are merely observing a cultural scene that has certain definite characteristics – the modern world" (191). As I argue, Maraini's views reflect an understanding of modernity informed by an uneasy relationship with his native country.

Indeed, "modernity and Japan" was the basis of a long, complex and multifarious debate in which the positions at stake reflected the different ideological premises of those involved, and result in failing to find common ground on the very definition of "modernization." At the core of the problem was the framing of the discussion about the relation between tradition and modernity within the opposite poles of East and West. At the 1960 Conference on Modernity, in Hakone, Japan, Japanese intellectuals challenged their US counterparts on their assumption of modernity as a value-free concept to narrate the process of industrialization. With the negative example of the Meiji revolution in mind, Japanese intellectuals were wary of a framework of modernization that assessed a country's progress against a Western template as this would have legitimized the equating of modernization with Westernization. Relatedly, Japanese intellectuals were also suspicious of the assertion that the maintenance of traditions represents resistance to modernization. Maruyama Masao, among others, pursued the task of shifting the conversation from an essentialist debate grounded in binary logic (East/West, spirit/matter, etc.), in which Japan was painted as inferior. For Maruyama, a better approach focused on autonomy, both for Japan and for the individual citizen considered as a member of an "open" society.

It is within this context and with this emphasis on autonomy that Maraini's remarks about Japan and modernity are made. His idea of tradition reflects positions gaining traction at the beginning of the 1960s; scholars such as "Ward, Schwartz and Reischauer agreed that 'traditional' cultural and religious mores may in some cases actually assist the modernization process" (Kersten, 1996: 112).[3] Maraini takes this line of reasoning to extremes, by claiming that Japan's religious tradition paved the way for the country's modernization.[4]

One of the first proponents of the idea of continuity between traditional and modern Japan was the Japanese anthropologist Nakane Chie (1926–) in her book *Japanese Society* (1970), published in English one year before

---

3   The hypothesis that Maraini is responding to ideas about Japan and modernity circulating during the 1960s is demonstrated by the fact that in the first edition of *Meeting with Japan* (New York: Viking Press, 1960), Maraini outlines five characteristics that help to explain Japan's success in the world, which are radically different from the five characteristics that he puts forth in *Japan, Patterns of Continuity*. In Maraini's words: "Summing up the experience of many years in Japan, I should say that there are at least five important characteristics which throw light on their success in the world" (Maraini, 1960: 71). The characteristics are: "the sense of communion with nature," "the extraordinary manual skill," "the traditional specialization of classes," their frugal and Spartan habits" (73) and "the lack of outstanding personalities." These pages would be suppressed in future editions of *Meeting with Japan*.

4   Maraini repeats the same line of argument in "Japan, the Essential Modernizer," an essay included in the 1988 volume edited by Sue Henry and Jean-Pierre Lehmann, *Themes and Theories in Modern Japanese History: Essays in Memory of Richard Storry* (London and Atlantic Highlands, NJ: Athlone Press), which hosts a variety of essays by relevant Japanese and American scholars. In this way Maraini opens his thesis to comparison with other similar propositions: in particular, his essay is located next to Maruyama Masao's theory of "*Basso ostinato*" (Masao Maruyama, 1988, "The Structure of 'Matsurigoto': The 'Basso Ostinato' of Japanese Political Life," in Henry and Lehmann, 1988), which is also based on the premise that Japan has changed "not in spite of, but precisely because of, some basic continuous factors that underlie the Japanese experience" (27).

Patterns of Continuity. At that time a Japanese self-interpretation was quite rare and Nakane's book became one of the best-known examples of *nihonjinron* (discourse about the Japanese), with more than one million copies sold in her country and about thirty different translations published.[5] *Nihonjinron*'s discourse aims at demonstrating Japan's distinct cultural features and its uniqueness in the world. The core of Maraini's position is the same as that articulated by Chie Nakane in the following quotation:

> Some of the distinguishing aspects of Japanese society that I treat in this book are not exactly new to Japanese and Western observers and may be familiar from discussions in previous writings on Japan. However, my *interpretations* are different and the way in which I *synthetize* these aspects is new. Most of the sociological studies of contemporary Japan have been concerned primarily with its changing aspects, pointing to the "traditional" and "modern" elements as representing different or opposing qualities. [...] The proponents of such views are interested either in uprooting feudal elements or in discovering and noting modern elements that are comparable to those of the West. *The fabric of Japanese society has thus been made to appear to be torn into pieces of two kinds. But in fact it remains as one aspect (not element) of the same social body that also has "modern" features.* (Nakane, 1970: viii–ix, emphasis added)

Piecing together previous propositions on the subject, Nakane foreshadows Maraini's idea of a pattern of continuity between traditional and modern Japan. Whereas Maraini is comparatively oblivious to the shortcomings of the Japanese economic revolution, Nakane examines both positive and negative aspects of modern Japanese society. By reading Nakanes's book we learn more about what Maraini does not disclose regarding his praise for Japan's achievements in "high-level education, in ambition, organization, group solidarity, in a pragmatic approach to problems both large and small" (Maraini, 1971: 212). According to Nakane, the key to understanding Japanese society is the principle of vertical human relations. The typical Japanese group model is formed by an inverted "V." The superior member, located at the apex, establishes a link with two subordinated groups, located in the two branches. The only possible human relation is vertical and, ideally, each subordinate branch is not aware of the other's existence.

---

5 Nakane Chie is also famous for being one of the few women of her generation to become a professor at a major university, the University of Tokyo.

Any horizontal collaboration among lower ranks is prevented by superior hegemony. The result is that each individual is identified with a group (usually a group of co-workers) to the extent that individual identity overlaps with the group's identity. According to the vertical principle, individual freedom is undermined because what counts is the tie of the individual to one group (Nakane, 1970: 57). Maraini joins Nakane in celebrating the modernity and efficiency of a society based on group affiliation but, unlike his Japanese counterpart, he avoids acknowledging the cost in terms of individual freedom that this model implies. "It is interesting to observe that the traditional system, manifested in a group organization," Nakane posits, "has generated both the major driving force toward a high degree of industrialization and the negative brake that hinders the development of individual autonomy" (Nakane, 1970: 120). When Maraini emphasizes Japanese group solidarity, he refers to the traditional household system and the great solidarity among members, but he disregards the realm of hostility and ruthless competition among heterogeneous groups within society. As Nakane observes, "the entire society is a sort of aggregation of numerous and independent competing groups that by themselves can make no links with each other: they lack a sociological framework which to build up a completed and integrated society" (102). Another potential shortcoming that Nakane points out is the absence of mobility for workers among different companies: "The prohibition on mobility in the Japanese system promotes inefficiency" (107).

Even though Maraini does not deny the subjugation of the Japanese woman in contemporary society, he believes that the rising modern women's rights movement is consistent with Japanese history, in which women often occupy a privileged position in the social ranking. Although quoting Nakane in this regard, Maraini remains unconcerned with the different pattern of gender relations that Nakane lays out: instead of the rising independence of Japanese women, she observes that "Japanese wives adopt the role of mother rather than wife to their husbands; this is the traditional pattern, little affected by post-war change" (128). Excluded from any social activities and neglected by husbands more concerned with their careers, Japanese wives direct their attention to their children; even the husband–wife relationship comes to resemble a parent–child relationship.

Maraini's idealized portrait of Japan is partly due to the contingent historical context in which Japan was a rising superpower. The 1970s were the beginning of Japan's economic boom, which had clear effects on society. The enthusiastic prediction that the twenty-first century would be the "Japanese century"[6] is manifested throughout his book. Nakane's book on the same subject leads to a different conclusion. As a native-born Japanese woman, Chie Nakane presents an optimistic interpretation of her country but does not spare it from criticism. Maraini's case is just the opposite: he makes Japan his elected country and haven from the Western world. What is missing here is a point of reference for this interpretation: Maraini depicts a bright image of Japan in contrast to a generic "Western society" left behind on the path of modernization. It is likely that the accusation of backwardness and decadence has much more to do with Italy than with a generic "Western society." Behind this label one recognizes the dissatisfaction of an Italian intellectual with his country and the path that Italy undertook after World War II. At the end of the war Italy and Japan were both defeated countries in need of reconstruction. But while Japan was able to achieve unexpected growth, Italy's economic development and social change failed to transform the country into an independent and leading nation, as promised by Mussolini.

It appears that Maraini's conclusion is partly derived from the influence of the Christian church in Western societies.[7] According to him, Japan stands as an example of a non-Christian country, as Confucian ethics and Buddhist spirituality are the main spiritual influences. In short, Japan culture shows little interest in the Christian linkage between ethics and the idea of the divine revelation. Yet for sociologist Robert Bellah, "Christianity has had a perennial appeal in modern Japan," especially because it "made more explicit the transcendental implications of Confucianism and demanded an ultimate loyalty to Christ rather than the emperor or the state" (Bellah, 2003: 202). These fissures in Maraini's line of argument are directly connected to his

---

6   In this regard see Herman Kahn, 1970, *The Emerging Japanese Superstate* (New York: Prentice-Hall).
7   For a detailed reconstruction of the role played by the Christian Democrat party in shaping the image of Italy see Emilio Gentile, 2009, *La Grande Italia: The Myth of the Nation in the Twentieth Century*, translated by Suzanne Dingee and Jennifer Pudney (Madison: University of Wisconsin Press): "The way the Christian Democrats officiated at the 'Italy '61' celebrations [Italians' celebrations of the centennial of its unification] seemed to consecrate, with the pope's blessing, both the Catholic leadership of the national state and the reappropriation of the nation by the Catholics, who returned it to the Church's folds. The governing party was leading the country toward modernity under the emblem of Christ, moderating conservatism and progress, conciliating modernization and Christian tradition. At the same time, the Jubilee celebrations allowed the Christian Democrats to claim they were the legitimate winners of the competition with the communist party for the monopoly of the national myth" (344).

ideological position and reveal his subjective stance in the debate on Japan and modernity.

In a 1973 book interviewing foreigners living in Japan, Maraini was asked to describe how living in Japan had affected him. His answer points heavily toward the pervasive influence of the Catholic Church in Italy: "I grew up in a prevalently Catholic country," he says, "religion in Italy is part of the landscape, like cypresses and olive trees." Then he says,

> Japan was a shock. It woke me up. Here was an highly civilized country which had reached maturity and splendor along other paths, owing practically nothing to the spiritual forces which had become such fetishes in the West: classical learning, Christianity, the Reformation (or the Counter-Reformation, according to longitudes and latitudes). Here were also, all around, examples of moral coherence, of righteousness, of spiritual maturity, often more numerous and more striking that anything I had seen before. (Maraini, 1973: 11–12)

Japan's attraction for Maraini, then, is rooted in his ambivalence toward the influence of Christianity in the West and his own upbringing, resulting in a representation of Japan as a country that was completely devoid of Christian spirituality and ethics. We can also consider how Maraini promotes this dichotomization between a Christian West and a non-Christian Japan at a time that the Vatican's influence in Italy's public sphere was being reinforced by a government coalition led by the "Christian Democratic Party." Maraini's depiction of Japan as a country untainted by Western cultural and spiritual influences is one of the major pitfalls of his main argument about Japan being a modernized country without being Westernized. To support his thesis, Maraini posits a simplistic definition of modernization as a phenomenon limited to the "impact of science and technology" (Maraini, 1988: 45). In this way, he is able to sidestep the contentious debate of this period,[8] between an historically progressive view, according to which

---

8 The interpretation of modernity as a Western intrusion in the spheres of Japanese daily life (consumerism), perception of time (ceaseless change and rapid transformation), polity (democracy), aesthetics, philosophy and spirituality (materialism, fragmented view of life, etc.) was at the center of the conference titled "Overcoming Modernity" launched by a group of Japanese scholars, artists, writers and thinkers who met in Tokyo in July 1942. Presenting the invasive and foreign nature of modernization as a fact, unlike Maraini, they focused on how to "overcome" this negative force toward the reestablishment of an authentic Japanese spirit. "The import meant accepting a culture driven

Japan was entering the capitalist stage only to comply with the expectations and interests of its US ally, and a view of Japan as timeless, which depicts culture as the site of perpetual repetition of traditional elements unable to explain Japanese dynamism or exceptionalism. By considering modernity an inevitable outcome of history, rather than a powerful ideology, Maraini's position was aligned with that of some US scholars, but with an important distinction. He did not subscribe to the predominantly American narrative that associated the instrumental rationality of the market with the positive values of Western democracy, nor did he consider a democratic society as a natural return to normalcy for Japan after the anomaly of the nationalist period.[9] While intellectuals such as US ambassador Reischauer and Robert Bellah drew a comparison between the Japanese tradition – which combined the structural elements containing the shock of the rapid modernization process – with the Christian values wrought in the American tradition – assumed instrumental to the US's own modernization – Maraini had something different in mind. Rather than seeking in Japan a narcissistic reflection of his own country, on the contrary, he conceptualized Japan as an essential "Other," in order to leave behind the bitter reminder of the disappointing outcome of Italian post-war reconstruction.[10]

---

by 'progress' and the ceaseless differentiation and specialization within the spheres of knowledge [...] The immediate consequence of this 'progressive specialization of knowledge' and the loss of connection was the elimination of cultural 'wholeness' and its unifying principle": Harry D. Harootunian, 2000, *Overcome by Modernity History, Culture, and Community in Interwar Japan* (Princeton: Princeton University Press): 36. For the members of the conference it was clear that modernization was nothing more than a mode of exercising hegemony on behalf of the United States: "by the time of the symposium met and took stock of the preceding two decades, the everydayness of the masses and their culture of consumption were bonded to the idea of Americanism, which represented, for the participants, the condensed sign under which Japanese culture was now collapsing into valueless mediocrity, shallowness, and triviality. All the ills that had poisoned Japan were found in Americanism, which, for most, was the model of modernity that had to be overcome" (Harootunian, 2000: 49).

9   On attempts made to forge an image of Japan that could satisfy American interests and expectations, see Harry D. Harootunian, 1993, America's Japan/Japan's Japan," in *Japan in the World*, edited by Masao Miyoshi and Harry D. Harootunian (Durham and London: Duke University Press).

10   The way that Maraini depicts his Japanese "dreamland" shows an implicit disappointment in the lack of significant change in Italian society. This bitter and implicit side of Maraini's conclusion, this perception of decline of a sense of the nation, was common among Italian intellectuals during the period considered, as the journalist Domenico Bartoli sharply observes: "We are not capable of being the kind of state or

This climate of disillusionment among Italian intellectuals – of whom Maraini is a representative – deeply affects his representation of Japan; it constitutes a social imaginary of Western modernity that propels Italian intellectuals like him to travel toward alternative worlds.

4. Moravia and the Japanese Crowd

Moravia went to Japan three times, as a reporter for the Italian magazine *L'Espresso* and the newspaper *Corriere della Sera*, and as an intellectual invited by Japanese cultural institutes. In 1957 Moravia accepted an invitation to participate in the PEN Club Congress in Tokyo, with Stephen Spender (1909–95), Angus Wilson (1945–2005), John Steinbeck (1902–68) and John Dos Passos (1896–1970), among others.[11] Ten years later he returned to Japan with his new wife Dacia Maraini (1936–), and together they traveled to China and Korea as well. In 1982 Moravia was sent by *L'Espresso* to Hiroshima, where he wrote articles on the atomic bomb. As Moravia said in an interview, "The first time, the encounter with Japan, not always pleasant, was totally new for me. The second time, I met many writers and intellectuals, including Yukio Mishima, and I had the opportunity to understand Japanese life more profoundly; on the other hand, the Japanese experience became mixed with those of China and Korea. Finally, the third time I also visited the Japanese provinces. I went as far as the island of Hokkaido, and in particular, after visiting Hiroshima, I decided to devote myself to the antiatomic campaign" (Moravia-Elkann, 2000: 282).

Unlike other Italians who had previously traveled to Japan, Moravia was known in Japan as a writer, thanks to the translations of two of his novels, both in 1951: *Agostino* and *La romana* ("The Woman of Rome"), originally published

---

nation that we are, or were, as civilization or culture. This incapacity exasperates particularly the intellectuals, active minorities and those who should be the ruling class, and turns everybody toward extreme pessimism or evasion, which almost always ends up in cynical indifference as soon as the first moments of fury have passed" (Gentile, 2009: 354).

11 In 1957 Moravia was invited to the PEN Club as replacement of Ignazio Silone, who was ill at the time, and decided to turn the invitation down. Apparently, one of the reasons that convinced Moravia to set out for this journey was financial, as his earnings from the author's rights (about 620.000 yen) could not be spent outside Japan. *The Woman in Rome* was Moravia's most popular novel in Japan with more than 30,000 copies sold. See de Ceccatty, 2010, *Alberto Moravia* (Paris: Flammarion): 341–42.

in 1944 and 1947, respectively. During his 1967 trip he was welcomed as an international writer by virtue of the Japanese translations of *La mascherata* ("The Fancy Dress Party") and *Il conformista* ("The Conformist"), which added to the popularity of novels such as *Gli indifferenti* ("The Time of Indifference") and *Il disprezzo* ("The Contempt"), which were now republished in a second edition (Ciapparoni La Rocca, 1998: 67). When he first visited Japan, Moravia was not knowledgeable about Japanese literature and culture, as he had just started to read Jun'ichirō Tanizaki and was acquainted with the works of Ruth Benedict and Lafcadio Hearn. On this initial trip, his companion was the American scholar of Japanese film Donald Richie, who helped Moravia, along with Angus Wilson and Stephen Spender, to see Japan off the beaten tracks.[12] During his second trip, Moravia took the opportunity to meet some of the authors who most influenced his writing at the time, such as Yukio Mishima, or to see Japan through the eyes of Yasunari Kawabata and Tanizaki, who were translated into Italian in the 1960s (Beviglia, 1967: 159).

Between the first and the second journey, Moravia observed the rise of the Japanese "economic miracle," and, along with Fosco Maraini, drew attention to the particular phenomenon of tradition and modernity coexisting in post-war Japan. Unlike Maraini, who emphasizes the continuity between past and present in the Land of the Rising Sun, Moravia considers these two elements to be independent and juxtaposed. The European Industrial Revolution is considered an achievement of humanistic culture and technical change engendered by European thought. On the other hand, Moravia considers the Japanese Industrial Revolution to be a consequence of opening the country to the rest of the world; it is a revolution based on imitating European technical

---

12 In his published journals of his life in Japan, Donald Richie mocks Moravia's overexcited attitude toward Japanese women, in pursuit of whom Moravia does not hesitate to ask Richie to visit night clubs, such as the Queen Night Club, and to use him as interpreter while he attempts to flirt with them. After being forced to leave Tokyo and its sexy night life, Moravia grudgingly followed the rest of the group to Mount Koya. Here he became irritated by the seemingly masculine ambiance and he protested to his trio of gay friends: "*Agh*, so easy for you! So fortunate homosexuals. Your run down beach, you find simple fisher lad, you come back radiant. But, *agh*, we heterosexuals. The hope, the failure. So difficult": Donald Richie, 2005, *The Japan Journals, 1947–2004*, edited by Leza Lowitz (Berkley, CA: Stone Bridge Press): 96). Richie also completed the clumsy portrait of Moravia in Japan by turning into comedy the description of the episode during which the group of friends accompanied Moravia to the doctor, who gave him an enema. Behind Moravia's disquiet there was the crisis of his marriage with Elsa Morante, which eventually ended up in a separation few years later. This depressive mood sets the stage for the writing of *La noia* ("The Boredom"), 1960.

progress without absorbing the philosophical culture that, according to the trajectory of the European Industrial Revolution, nourished such progress. In the end, post-war Japan reveals a unique overlapping of the feudal structure of society and modern technology:

> Le Nazioni asiatiche non sono affatto inferiori a quelle europee; ma hanno tradizioni religiose e culturali che, a differenza di quelle europee, non portano necessariamente alla rivoluzione industriale; di modo che questa, più che la continuazione di età precedenti, come in Europa, è in Asia il volontaristico e innaturale innesto di un fatto straniero sopra un ceppo nazionale.
>
> Il dramma è dunque questo: capacità di sviluppo pari a quello dei paesi europei; tradizioni religiose e culturali diverse da quelle che in Europa precedettero e prepararono il progresso scientifico. Questo è il dramma soprattutto del Giappone da un secolo e mezzo a questa parte; ed esso è al centro non soltanto della vita sociale di questo Paese ma anche delle coscienze individuali. Ad esso si deve da un lato l'incredibile, meteorica trasformazione del Paese in grande potenza industriale; dall'altro, attraverso il continuo, ostinato sforzo di assimilazione, la immobilità mimetica e l'ibridismo di molta parte della vita culturale. (*Corriere della Sera*, October 1, 1957, in Moravia, 1994: 790)

[The nations of Asia are not in the least inferior to those of Europe but they have religious and cultural traditions that, unlike those of Europe, don't necessarily lead to industrial revolution; which is for Asia a voluntary and unnatural grafting of a foreign idea onto the traditional foundation of the nation rather than, as in Europe, the continuation of previous epochs.

The drama is therefore this: capacity for development equals that of European countries; religious and cultural traditions differ from those that preceded and prepared for scientific progress in Europe. For a century and a half this has been Japan's particular drama, and it not only occupies the center of the country's social life but also individual consciousness. One owes to it on one hand the incredible, meteoric national transformation of the country into a great industrial power; on the other hand, through the continual, obstinate force of assimilation, the mimetic immobility and hybridism of many sectors of cultural life.]

Moravia not only denies the existence of a "Japanese way of modernization," but he goes as far as to suggest that the country's cultural and spiritual traditions thwart its scientific progress. He concludes that the Japanese technological revolution is nothing other than Western penetration in a culturally unfamiliar territory. Japan's transformation as an economic power is, according to Moravia, the result of US influence and the imposition of a new capitalistic ethos on to an old and perishing culture. De Ceccatty observes, "Il va de soi que pour Moravia une seule attitude est possible face aux autres cultures: humanisme et universalisme. [...] Il est certain que l'économie, l'industrialisation et la mécanisation unifieront le degré d'évolution des nations" (de Ceccatty, 2010: 344–45) [For Moravia there is only one possible attitude when confronted with other cultures: humanism and universalism. [...] He is certain that the economy, industrialization and mechanization will unify the degree of evolution of nations]. Indeed, Moravia's initial commentary about Japanese society glosses over the ethnic and racial differences so as to focus on historical and philosophical categories recognizable to a European audience. Ultimately, Moravia insists upon including his view of Japan within his critical discourse on the alienating effects of neocapitalism on a global scale.

Alienation, a concept borrowed from Marx, is a cornerstone of Moravia's perspective, which is evident in how he authors many protagonists in his novels (for example, *Gli Indifferenti* ["Time of indifference"], 1929 and *La noia* ["The boredom"], 1960). Moravia's essay *L'uomo come fine* (1964) ["Man as an end"] goes deeper to explain how such concepts as "neocapitalism," "alienation," and "antihumanism" operate in the present world:

> Sarebbe *interessante* vedere perché, con apparente contraddizione, l'antiumanesimo oggi coincida con le vittorie del neocapitalismo. [...] Sarebbe difficile trovare nel mondo moderno la robusta fiducia, la sanguigna pienezza, il ricco temperamento che furono propri all'umanesimo ai suoi albori. L'uomo del neocapitalismo con tutti i suoi frigoriferi, i suoi supermarket, le sue automobili utilitarie, i suoi missili e i suoi set televisivi è tanto esangue, sfiduciato, devitalizzato e nevrotico da giustificare coloro che vorrebbero accettarne lo scadimento quasi fosse un fatto positivo e ridurlo a oggetto tra gli oggetti. Purtroppo però l'uomo del neocapitalismo non riesce a dimenticare la propria natura dopo tutto umana. Il suo antiumanesimo per questo non riesce ad essere positivo. Sotto apparenze scintillanti e astratte, si celano, a ben guardare, la noia, il disgusto, l'impotenza e l'irrealtà. (Moravia, 1964: 6)

> [It would be interesting to ask why, despite the apparent contradiction, today's antihumanism coincides with the victorious achievements of

neocapitalism [...] In the modern world it would be hard to find the solid confidence, the full-bloodedness and the richness of temperament that were the hallmarks of humanism at its dawn. The man of the neocapitalist age, with his refrigerators, his supermarkets, his mass-produced cars, his missiles and his televisions sets, is so bloodless, insecure, devitalized and neurotic that he provides every justification for those ready and anxious to accept his decline as positive fact, and reduce him to the position of an object among other objects. And so his antihumanism falls short of real conviction. Beneath the bright, abstract appearance, we find – if we look carefully – boredom, disgust, impotence and unreality.] (Moravia, 1965: 9–10)

All three concepts – neocapitalism, alienation, and antihumanism – are, in Moravia's view, applicable to Japan. The Japanese "economic miracle," then, is only an example of a new capitalistic phenomenon with all its negative consequences in terms of alienation. Taken together, Japanese modernization is not, according to Moravia, a result of an alternative humanism or an Asian scientific revolution but rather the avant-garde of antihumanist ethos still lingering in Europe. Consider how Moravia describes the Japanese path to modernization:

Finché durava nella cultura europea il retaggio dell'umanesimo cristiano e rinascimentale, il Giappone poteva veramente definirsi come il vaso di coccio tra i vasi di ferro. Ma la crisi, o meglio la liquidazione di questo retaggio negli anni recenti hanno fatto fare al Giappone un salto qualitativo che lo ha allineato alla pari con le grandi Nazioni occidentali in cui si è verificata la rivoluzione industriale con le note conseguenze dell'avvento delle masse e della produzione in serie. Il Giappone si trova perfettamente a suo agio, come le sue tradizioni, in un mondo in cui l'individuo scompare sommerso dalla massa, in cui il fatto economico appiattisce ogni rapporto e l'angoscia esistenziale nega la realtà. (*Corriere della Sera*, October 6, 1957, in Moravia, 1994: 796)

[As long as the legacy of Christian and Renaissance Humanism endured in European culture, Japan was able to indeed define itself the clay pot among pots of iron. But the crisis, or better the liquidation of this legacy in recent years has allowed for Japan a qualitative leap that aligned it equally with the big nations of the West, which brought about the industrial revolution with the noted consequences of the rise of the masses and mass production. Japan finds itself perfectly at ease, like her traditions, in a world where the individual disappears submerged by the mass, where the economic situation flattens every relationship and existential anxiety negates reality.]

In his effort to provide a critical perspective of neocapitalism, Moravia avoids addressing substantial differences between Japan and the West, and thus draws naïve conclusions about the presumed "absence d'historicité, l'absence de subjectivité, l'absence d'individualisme, l'absence de religion" [absence of historicity, subjectivity, individualism, religion] (de Ceccatty, 2010: 345) in Japanese society. While Moravia stresses that Japan is not inferior to the West, his attempt to describe contemporary Japan as part of this neocapitalist crisis implies a negative connotation of Japanese tradition and culture as incapable of producing an alternative, modern form of humanism. In Moravia's assessment, it seems that Japanese culture simply imitates its European counterpart: "L'assimilazione a dosi massicce, forzata e affrettata, della cultura occidentale che da un secolo circa ha luogo in Giappone, ha finito quasi per produrre in questo Paese uno stato d'animo schizofrenico, diviso tra l'ingorda e indiscriminata avidità di tutto ciò che è straniero e un conservatorismo e tradizionalismo altrettanto eccessivi" [The massive doses, forced and swift, of Western cultural assimilation that took place in Japan for almost a century ended up almost producing in this country a state of schizophrenia, divided between the greedy and indiscriminate avidity of all that is foreign and a conservatism and traditionalism just as excessive] (*Corriere della Sera*, November 10, 1957, in Moravia, 1994: 830).

At this point it is worth asking how Moravia justifies his idea of Japanese culture as an empty container suitable for every kind of Western intrusion without the country offering any resistance. It is interesting to investigate how Moravia explains this passive and conservative attitude of Japanese civilization. In one article Moravia uses the image of a paper sheet ("un foglio di carta") to depict the allegedly one-dimensional Japanese culture:

Se [Il Giappone] fosse un oggetto qualsiasi, che oggetto sarebbe?
   La risposta potrebbe anche essere questa: un foglio di carta, uno di quei pesanti fogli di carta che incorniciati di bambù verde o di acero bianco o di ciliegio rosso, ornati di qualche disegno impressionistico di paesaggio o di qualche ideogramma calligrafico, fungono da pareti nelle case giapponesi. In altri termini, l'impressione che si riporta al Giappone, non solo per quanto riguarda gli aspetti fisici ma anche quelli psicologici e

culturali, è quella di un mondo che abbia le dimensioni del foglio di carta: lunghezza a larghezza ma non spessore e profondità o volume. (*Corriere della Sera,* October 6, 1957, in Moravia, 1994: 792)

["If [Japan] were any object, what object would it be?" The answer might also be thus: a sheet of paper, one of those heavy sheets of paper bordered with green bamboo or white maple or red cherry, ornamented with some impressionistic landscape design or some calligraphied ideogram, functioning as walls in Japanese houses. In other words, the impression that one brings back from Japan, not only regarding physical aspects but also psychological and cultural, is that of a world that has the dimensions of a sheet of paper: length and width but no thickness, depth or volume.]

The source of Moravia's sharp judgment of contemporary Japanese society is *The Pillow Book of Sei Shōnagon* (1929), one of the first English translations of a diary of observations and remarks recorded by the court lady Sei Shōnagon during the 990s in Heian Japan (794–1185). The translator of the book is Arthur Waley (1889–1966), an English Orientalist, a member of the Bloomsbury Group (to which Moravia had the chance to be introduced during his 1931 stay in London), and famous primarily for his English translation of the masterpiece of Japanese literature, *The Tale of Genji*. In his introduction, Waley uses the precious sources gathered from *The Pillow Book* as well as from *The Tale of Genji* to give a portrait of Japanese society and the spirit of the tenth century. The final result is an image of Japan during the Heian period as a refined civilization with a heightened sensibility for literature and aesthetic forms in general.

Waley then attempts a bizarre (from a historical perspective) comparison between this ancient aesthetic world and twentieth-century England (or the Western world in general). He argues that what distinguishes "them from us" is a lack of historical awareness: unlike contemporary Western societies, tenth-century Japanese people were completely oblivious of and indifferent to their country's history. Their only concern was the present: "It is indeed our intense curiosity about the past that most sharply distinguishes us from the ancient Japanese. Here every educated person is interested in some form or another of history" (Waley and Shōnagon, 1929: 10). After disqualifying Sei Shōnagon's culture by stressing its "absence of intellectual background" (12), Waley finally uses the image of the paper page that Moravia recalls: "It is this insecurity that gives to the Heian period that oddly evasive and, as it were, two-dimensional quality, its figures and appurtenances all sometimes seeming to us to be cut out of thin, transparent paper" (12). It must also be noted that although his translations were influential between the 1920s and the 1960s, Waley never set foot in Japan. His knowledge of Japan was based on his acquaintance with the collection of Oriental Prints and Manuscripts in the British Museum, where he was appointed as assistant keeper. He always "maintained a profound textual attitude toward his subject" (De Gruchy, 2003: 165), and his image of Japan "bought into and sanctioned the one-sided feminine or aesthetic view of Japan" (De Gruchy, 2003: 164), in line with Bloomsbury's aesthetic sensibility and antagonism toward morally constituted authority.

Despite having visited Japan several times, Moravia's representation of Japan as a one-sided and aestheticist society relies on Waley's Orientalist portrait. What really matters is his attempt to ignore chronology by overlapping the Japanese civilization of the tenth century with that of the present time. Borrowing Waley's characterization of medieval Japan, Moravia effaces historical and cultural differences between Western and Eastern modernization. In this way he oversimplifies the approach to modern Japan for Italian magazine readers by resorting to a Marxist criticism of capitalism.

This is evident in Moravia's article on the crowd in Japan ("La folla in Giappone," November 10, 1957). At the very beginning of the article Moravia highlights the conflict between modernity and tradition in contemporary Japan through the contrasting images of Kyoto and Osaka: "Kioto è l'antica capitale, città bellissima ma addormentata nelle memorie dei suoi antichi monumenti; Osaka, invece, è la Manchester del Giappone: brutta, attiva, piena di traffici, con fabbriche, empori, sedi di società commerciali e industriali e via dicendo" (825) [Kyoto is the old capital, a beautiful city but asleep in the memory of its ancient monuments; Osaka, intead, is the Manchester of Japan: ugly, active, full of traffic, with factories, department stores, commercial and industrial social centers and so on]. While Kyoto is the symbol of an embalmed cult of the past, Osaka embodies the spirit of the rootless new Asian capitalism, a counterpart to the analog Western phenomenon. Once Moravia has established the distance between past and present in Japan, he can now focus on the similarity between Western and Eastern modernization. In doing so he chooses to set the narration of the Japanese crowd in the space of a train, a typical example of a "nonspace," neither Western nor Eastern, the perfect setting in which all geographical and cultural differences are abolished: "Questi treni sono dunque luoghi molto adatti per osservare la folla giapponese" (825) [These trains are therefore places very suited to observing the Japanese crowds]. The next step is to delete all differences in terms of social class, emphasizing the bourgeoisie character of the Japanese crowd: "Direi che la folla giapponese ha un aspetto piccolo-borghese anche quando è composta di operai" (827) [I would say that the Japanese crowds have a petty-bourgeois aspect even when they are comprised of workers]. After removing all geographical differences (Osaka as Manchester), spatial differences (train as neutral space), and social differences (the universal image of the bourgeoisie), Moravia can apply to the Japanese world the ideological message of the "moral crisis of the middle class." Like his other stories in which the protagonist is Italian middle class, even the Japanese bourgeoisie is affected by boredom: "Infatti la noia è una delle malattie di questo paese" (829) [Indeed, boredom is one of the diseases of this country]. The final step is a universal, metaphysical definition of boredom within which all the anthropological distance between Europe and Asia is elided: "Ma si tratta probabilmente di una noia di tipo cosmico o esistenziale: originata, mi sembra, dal divario bovaristico tra gli ideali che sono talvolta istericamente magnanimi (si pensi alla morale eroica del samurai per tanti decenni insegnata nelle scuole) e la modesta realtà. Ogni volta che l'ideale fallisce cozzando contro la realtà, il giapponese può ricadere in fondo alla noia, cioè ad una svalutazione massiccia della propria esistenza e di quella altrui" (830) [But one is probably dealing with a cosmic or existential ennui: originating, it seems to me, from the bovaristic gap between ideals that are so hysterically noble (one thinks of the heroic spirit of the samurai taught in schools for decades) and modest reality. Each time that the ideal fails clashing against reality, the individual might fall back to the depths of ennui, that is, to a massive undervaluing of their own existence and that of others]. Here we are no longer in Japan but in the realm of a universalistic view of contemporary history as characterized by alienation. This definition of boredom is the same as that for Dino, the protagonist of the novel *La noia* [Boredom], which Moravia published only a few years later (1960): "Per molti la noia è il contrario del divertimento; potrei dire, anzi, addirittura, che per certi aspetti essa rassomiglia al divertimento in quanto, appunto, provoca distrazione e dimenticanza, sia pure di un genere molto particolare. La noia, per me, è propriamente una specie di insufficienza o inadeguatezza o scarsità della realtà" (Moravia, 1960: 7) [For many people, boredom is the opposite of amusement; I might even go so far as to say that in certain of its aspects it actually resembles amusement inasmuch as it gives rise to distraction and forgetfulness, even if of a very special type. Boredom to me consists in a kind of insufficiency, or inadequacy, or lack of reality (Moravia, 1999: 5)]. At this point the process of modern Japan's assimilation into Western society is completed.

In conclusion, if Moravia conceived of Japan's modernization as a result of Western influence and the erosion of national culture, he also indicated that this was not a strictly unilateral process, since Japan influences aspects of Western culture. In the article *Il Giappone al posto dello "Zen" ha scelto la religione dei grattacieli* ["Instead of Zen Japan has chosen the skyscrapers' religion"], Moravia recalls his interview with a Buddhist bonze in Kamakura temple, one of the most important Zen shrines of the country. He mentions his surprised reaction when, in a vain attempt to direct the conversation to topics related to Zen thought, he realized that the bonze successfully kept the conversation on a superficial level and on topics unrelated to Zen and spirituality. In Moravia's view, the bonze's pragmatic and materialistic attitude is an unequivocal sign of the intrusion of the so-called "American way of life" into the core of Zen tradition. At the same time, Moravia refers to an encounter, in the same convent, with a young American student of Zen. The American student seemed to have much more interest in Zen practice than the Japanese bonze. This student, in Moravia's view, represents the cultural appropriation of Eastern traditions by Americans who are eager to find a valid alternative to their consumer society. Moravia's conclusion is that "Giappone e Stati uniti sono come due vasi comunicanti: dal vaso giapponese è passato nel vaso americano lo *zen*, l'arte, la decorazione, il gusto nipponico; dal vaso americano in quello giapponese, in una misura addirittura eccessiva, molta *american way of life*. Quale dei due paesi abbia guadagnato è difficile dire" (Moravia, 1994: 1249) [Japan and the United States are like two communicating vessels: from the Japanese vessel Zen, art, decoration, and Nipponic gusto pass into the American vessel; from the American to the Japanese the American way of life in an almost excessive measure. It is difficult to say which of these two countries gains more]. In the contemporary world, Zen Buddhism is what makes Japan an influential partner among capitalist societies and it represents a critical cultural element that complements the predominant American culture. Japan's ability to infiltrate Western ideas with Eastern spirituality prompts Moravia to reflect on the passive role that Italy holds in this regard. Despite its chauvinism toward Japanese culture, Moravia's depiction of Japan as providing a solution to the spiritual crisis of the West is related to his negative characterization of post-war Italy. Moravia analogizes the authoritarian power that the United States wields in the Orient and a glorious image of premodern Italy:

> Il rapporto con l'Oriente, durante il Medioevo, non fu per l'Italia gran che diverso da quello che oggi gli Stati Uniti hanno con il Giappone

e in genere con l'Asia orientale: guerre, interventi, scambi culturali, commerci, viaggi, eccetera. Il risultato di tutto questo si può vedere a Venezia, a Ravenna, in Sicilia, a Siena, e un po' dappertutto. Allora gli italiani sapevano appropriarsi idée e modi di sensibilità dell'Oriente vicino o lontano, col quale l'Italia aveva rapporti diretti. (*Corriere della Sera*, November 4, 1967, in Moravia, 1994: 1268)

[The relationship with the East during the Middle Ages was for Italy not much different than what the United States has with Japan and with East Asia in general today: wars, interventions, cultural exchanges, commerce, travel, et cetera. The result of all this can be seen in Venice, in Ravenna, in Sicily, in Siena, and a bit everywhere. At that time the Italians knew how to appropriate ideas and philosophical sensibilities of the near and Far East, with whom Italy had direct relationships.]

Moravia's nostalgic recollection of Italy, as a country that was able to receive and integrate cultural contributions from the East with the disappointing portrait of Italy during the 1960s results in a frustrated diagnosis of the country's cultural and political inertia.

L'Italia è un paese completamente e limitatamente occidentale; anche quelli che adottano dall'esterno la moda *beat*, ignorano che gran parte di quella moda risale allo *zen*. Non si può chiamare tutto ciò provincialismo, si farebbe torto alla provincia. Bisogna purtroppo dire che si tratta di una mancanza di inquietudine esistenziale, cioè di una mancanza di quello che comunemente ma forse non impropriamente viene chiamato idealismo.
    L'Italia è oggi il paese meno inquieto che ci sia in Occidente. Essa è ancora immersa nel *boom* o esplosione del benessere. La grande polemica americana contro la civiltà del consumo o meglio contro il fatto che il consumo possa diventare il fondamento di una civiltà, polemica che trae la maggior parte dei suoi argomenti dallo *zen*, è ancora da venire. (*Corriere della Sera*, November 4, 1967, in Moravia, 1994: 1268)

[Italy is a country completely and narrowly Western; even those that adopt the foreign beat style ignore that a big part of that style comes from Zen. One cannot call this provincialism; that would be an insult to the province. It is unfortunately necessary to say that one is dealing with a lack of existential restlessness, that is, a lack of what is communally but perhaps not improperly called idealism. Today Italy is a nation less restless than those of the East. It is still immersed in the boom or the explosion of affluence. The great American debate against a civilization of consumption or better against the fact that consumption might become the foundation of a civilization, a debate that pulls a significant part of its argument from Zen, is still to come.]

"Existential restlessness" for Moravia is a positive attribute employed in his novel *La Romana* (1947) ["The woman of Rome"] to express the main character's ability to survive the dire conditions of war and poverty. "In my novel [Moravia says during an interview *à propos* of *The Woman of Rome*], the bitter ideas of Sartre and Heidegger were overthrown and took a positive aspect which is very close to the morality of survival that is very ancient in Italy" (Moravia, 1979: 32). The novel's other main character is an idealist official who becomes disillusioned upon having betrayed his colleagues to fascist authorities during an interrogation. If Italy, in Moravia's view, seems to have lost the strength to survive foreign domination, as metaphorically represented by the protagonist of *The Woman in Rome*, its current moral status is close to the disillusioned official, beyond the façade of economic security that the country was then experiencing.

For Moravia, a primary reason for this stagnant scenario is the all-encompassing influence of the Roman Catholic Church in a country where the political success of the Christian Democrat party raised questions about the boundaries between the Vatican and the Parliament. According to Moravia, this conflict can be detected at the beginning of Italian unification: "The unity of Italy, as Goldoni says in his comedy *Il bugiardo*, is a 'witty invention.' After its unification, Italy has remained disunited and, what's worse, with a capital that isn't a capital, but the main city of the Lazio region. If anything, it's the capital of the Church" (Moravia and Elkann, 2000: 238). As he concludes, the problem of Italy's lack of criticism of society is rooted in the fundamental lack of national spirit due to never fully accomplishing political unification.

5. The Utopia of Otherness

In his experience as a journalist around the world (the United States, Chile, China, Cambodia, Vietnam, and Laos), Goffredo Parise came to Japan in his later years. The opportunity to visit this new country by official invitation was extended by the Italian ambassador to Japan, Boris Biancheri, in 1980. *L'eleganza è frigida* is Parise's fictional account of this journey through the eyes of Marco, an autobiographical character whose name is derived from the famous travel writer Marco Polo.[13] The title is borrowed from the Japanese poet Saitō Ryokuu (1868–1904). It refers to the absence of passion as the ethical norm that rules social life in Japan, in contrast to the sensual and passionate realm of art in which the hidden feelings of the Japanese are expressed.[14] In the preface of the Italian edition of Kawabata's *House of the Sleeping Beauties*, Parise deploys the same idea by portraying Kawabata's personality:

> [Kawabata] doveva essere un uomo di estrema sensualità. Il segreto della sua fine di suicida, con il gas, si dice per amore sfortunato o comunque disperato per una servetta, sta appunto nella sua sensualità. Se si osserva il suo ritratto, il suo volto di diavoletto o di pipistrello, si direbbe l'opposto, si direbbe una persona gelida e secca come uno stecco di cedro. Ma è proprio quell'apparenza, in parte diabolica in parte animale a rivelarci la sua sensualità potente e tragica. (Parise, 1989: vol. 2, 1458)

> [[Kawabata] must have been a man of extreme sensuality. The secret of his suicidal end, by using the gas, is said for unfortunate or, in any case, desperate love for a maid, is precisely in its sensuality. If you look at his portrait, his face of a devil or a bat, one would say the opposite, one would say that he is a person cold and dry as a stick of cedar. But it is precisely that appearance, partly diabolical and partly animal, that reveals to us his powerful and tragic sensuality.]

---

13 Parise visited Japan between September and October 1980 and published his reports in the newspaper *Corriere della Sera* between January 1981 and February 1982. *L'eleganza è frigida* (Milan: Mondadori, 1982) is Parise's fictional story derived from his articles on Japan.
14 Parise learned about this poem through the English edition of Jun'ichirō Tanizaki's *In Praise of Shadows*. In fact, by translating Ryokuu's line with "The elegance is frigid" the English version represents the closest translation of Parise's title. Italo Calvino's book review of *In Praise of Shadow* (Italian edition) observes the imperfection of the Italian translation: "Ma la casa giapponese, dalla 'spoglia eleganza,' non ha nulla di molle né di tiepido. Un'aurea massima che egli cita (da Saito Ryoku, scrittore del secolo scorso) suona: 'Le refinement est chose froide.' (Qui preferisco la traduzione francese a quella italiana: 'l'eleganza è fredda')": Italo Calvino, 1995, *Saggi: 1945–1985*, Vol. 1, edited by Mario Berenghi (Milan: Mondadori-Meridiani): 1447. For Parise's personal interpretation of Ryokuu's line see Vito Santoro, 2009, *L'odore della vita: Studi su Goffredo Parise* (Macerata: Quodlibet): 111–12.

Parise's novel is not for Italian readers seeking to remain oblivious to their own country by consuming a representation of an exotic land and unique people. Italy is by all means present on every page of the novel, to such an extent that Parise succeeds in performing a representation of Italy while focusing on Japan. In this sense, Japan serves as a standpoint for examining Italy. The reason that Parise writes about Japan in order to talk about Italy can be detected within this framework: in the representational interplay between the two countries, Japan is the dreamland by which he emphasizes the negative aspects of Italian society, which is often referred to in the narration as the country of the politic ("il paese della Politica"). By using the expression "dreamed land," I underscore the fictional space that Japan takes up in the narration, that is, a certain degree of unreality of the representation that the narrator makes explicit for the reader by using the narrative expedient of the dream. It is not by chance that the whole account of Japan begins and ends with the protagonist's dream. After his arrival at Tokyo's airport, Marco enjoys a placid and restful night:

> La notte parve estremamente silenziosa a Marco, che dormì di un sonno al tempo stesso felice e lontano, simile a quelli delle convalescenze o della salvezza. Questa era infatti la speranza di Marco nel lasciare il paese della Politica, sconvolto per millenni da furti, ricatti e assassinii, e questo il nuovo stato d'animo che lo accompagnò per tutto il tempo del suo soggiorno in Giappone. (1060)

> [The night seemed extremely silent to Marco, who slept a sleep that was both happy and distant, similar to those of convalescence or salvation. This was in fact Marco's hope in leaving the country of politics, upset for millennia by thefts, blackmail and murder, and this was the new mood that accompanied him throughout his stay in Japan.]

And at the conclusion of the book:

> Come trafitto da questi [tre artisti] nel profondo, Marco pencolante di sonno andò a letto e dormì per l'ultima notte in Giappone. Ancora in sogno gli apparve la signorina Momoko Tokugawa, quasi a riassumere quelle ultime emozioni e per la prima volta mostrò i bei denti in un sorriso di invito. (1178)

> [As pierced by these [three artists] deep inside, Marco, as he was feeling tired, went to bed and slept for the last night in Japan. Miss Momoko

Tokugawa appeared again in his dream, as if to summarize his last emotions, and for the first time she showed her beautiful teeth in an inviting smile.]

By diminishing his own country with such sarcastic comments (such as "il paese della Politica"), Parise marks an overwhelming distance in terms of history, ethics, and politics, between Italy and Japan.

It is necessary to explain the historical reasons for Parise's juxtaposition. The 1980s was a fragile period in the making of Italian democracy. In 1978 Prime Minister Aldo Moro was kidnapped and murdered by a militant communist group known as the Red Brigades (*Brigate rosse*). At the beginning of the decade the vice-director of the Marghera's Petrolchimico was assassinated, and just few days later the director of an important chemical industry (ICMESA) was shot and killed in Monza. In February Vittorio Bachelet, vice-president of the Superior Council of the Magistrates and former president of the Roman Catholic association *Azione cattolica*, was killed in Rome. In August a bomb killed eighty-five people at the railway station in Bologna (Belpoliti, 2010: 278).[15]

---

15 For a deeper understanding of the definition of Italy as the land of the Politic, it is worth noticing that in 1978 Parise published in *Il Corriere della Sera* a short story entitled "Politica," which focuses on the topics of Italian corruption and injustice in Italian society. As Marco Belpoliti observes: "Nell'ottobre del 1978 [Parise] pubblica sul 'Corriere' un nuovo racconto. S'intitola *Politica* e non entrerà mai a far parte del *Sillabario n. 2*. La storia è quella di Giuseppe Fracasso, che nell'ottobre del 1945 ha un nuovo insegnante di italiano, latino, greco e storia. È il professor Tonolo, 'un grosso e sporco uomo dell'Ottocento' che conosce molto bene la sua materia, ma che ha una evidente ed eccessiva passione, il vino. Giuseppe capisce che quella è la strada giusta per conquistarsi le simpatie dell'insegnante: ogni settimana porta in classe un fiasco di vino da cui Tonolo comincia ad attingere. I pessimi risultati scolastici di Giuseppe migliorano. Nel contempo egli coltiva i suoi compagni di classe con piccoli regali, e non si dimentica neppure dei bidelli. Alla fine dell'anno ottiene la promozione. Un unico compagno di classe contesta il risultato ottenuto; è il primo della classe, un orfano. Gli altri ragazzi lo riprendono: 'Erano forse affari suoi? E poi, lui era stato promosso, con tutti otto e nove, che cosa gliene importava se Fracasso, così allegro, così simpatico, di cui tutti, nessuno escluso avevano mangiato i panini, anche lui era stato promosso?' Il racconto riguarda ovviamente il tema della corruzione e allude alla situazione della società italiana a cui, due anni dopo, lo stesso Calvino dedicherà sul 'Corriere' *L'apologo sull'onestà nel paese dei corrotti*, che si conclude con l'immagine di una società rovesciata, in cui gli onesti sono una piccola minoranza, una contro società, rispetto alla società dei corrotti": Belpoliti, 2010, *L'occhio di Calvino* (Turin: Einaudi): 272.

On the other hand, in the late 1970s Japan achieved the status of the world's second largest economy. Several publications by US scholars focused on giving Japan – the United States' best ally in the Far East and a strategic partner during the Cold War – a positive interpretation of its success, which required not mentioning the price that Japan had to pay to achieve its goals (social conflict and dissent, labor exploitation, political corruption, ecological battles). The Japanese were depicted as close allies in terms of the path toward democracy. Specifically, they were described as hardworking people who obeyed easily: "Harmony and consensus prevailed, and strife was a foreign thing, for the Japanese were a modest people given to compromise in all matters" (Smith, 1997: 19). A well-known example of this idealization of Japan is Ezra Vogel's *Japan as Number One*, published in 1979. Japan is praised as being a "modern democratic nation with a free enterprise system" (4). What is interesting is that Japan is used as the basis of comparison for examining the shortcomings of the US economy, politics, and society. Vogel proposes that the United States can learn a lesson from Japan; for the first time an Eastern nation models a modern, capitalistic society for the benefit of Western countries. Japan can teach the United States how to gain a democratic consensus, organize a meritocratic system, and establish a flexible bureaucracy, an efficient educational process, and a superior economy based on planning, organization and effort. In his attempt to gather all of the possible lessons to be learned from the "Japanese miracle," Vogel creates an image of a modern society that can hardly be applied to Japan. Like Maraini, the contradictions that Vogel prefers to overlook are too numerous.

In Vogel's case, the depiction of Japan as a realm of social order, harmony, respect for hierarchy, and unity of purpose conceals a reality of violence and exploitation, especially regarding labor politics: "There were tales of what Koiso called 'coercive labor,' full of intimidating managers, corrupt union officials, executive suicides, *karoshi* incidents, 'service overtime' scams, vindictive personnel departments, and employees banished to various Siberias for being too independent of mind" (Smith, 1997: 131).

Parise's image of Japan ultimately stems from the same set of cultural representations; it is affected by the Japanese success stories. Moreover, Parise applies a conceptual schema consistent with Vogel's, in which Japan represents the cornerstone from which his own country is criticized. In fact, beyond the rhetoric of the "lesson to learn," Vogel's *nihonjinron* (discourse on Japan) is rather a practice of self-criticism and disillusion.

In Parise's work, Japan as a mirror of Italy has specific traits other than the typical juxtaposition of a society nourished by spiritual and aesthetical values versus Western materialism. He praises Japan for reasons that must be located in what he perceives as missing in the Italian society of the late 1970s. First, there is the longing for a sense of patriotism, or for moral values based on patriotism:

> Infine parve a Marco che il carattere fondamentale del popolo giapponese fosse l'orgoglio nazionale o la superbia individuale che per un giapponese è la stessa cosa anche se nel paese della Politica questo sembrerebbe un controsenso. Ma il paese della Politica è il paese della Politica e dell'affermazione individuale e non quello dell'orgoglio nazionale. Ma il paese della Politica, si sa, tanto è geniale, più di ogni altro geniale nella politica, cioè nella mediazione, la trattazione, lo scambio delle merci, tanto è ignorante e sordo nella Morale di cui però si riempie la bocca. Al contrario Marco ebbe l'impressione che la "questione morale" insieme a quella estetica fosse patrimonio del Giappone più di molti altri paesi e continuamente vedeva intersecarsi, nel comportamento dei suoi abitanti, le due questioni, estetica e morale. (Parise, 1989, vol. 2: 1078)

> [Finally, it seemed to Marco that the fundamental character of the Japanese people was national pride, or individual pride, which for a Japanese is the same thing, even if in the country of Politics this would seem a contradiction. But the country of Politics is the country of Politics and individual affirmation and not of national pride. But the country of Politics, it is well known, is as ingenious, more than a genius in fact, in political matters such as arbitration, negotiation, and the exchange of goods, as it is ignorant and deaf in Moral matters even when its mouth is full of moralizing. On the contrary, Marco had the impression that the "moral question," along with the aesthetic one, was the heritage of Japan more than many other countries and continually saw the two questions, aesthetic and moral, intersect in the behavior of its inhabitants.]

The idea of patriotism has nothing to do with the dream of the Italian Empire or the nationalist belief in possessing a superior civilization, by which Mussolini built political consensus. What is missing in Italy according to Parise's analysis, is a form of patriotism generated by awareness of an artistic tradition, such as treasures of art, which should stir up among Italians a feeling of national solidarity oriented to preserving and extending the richness of an inherited cultural tradition. Instead, Parise argues, in Japan an aesthetic tradition had been kept alive by people who apply aesthetic knowledge in decorating their houses, as well as in urban space.[16]

In Italy, however, a sense of obliviousness to the past predominates. Italians, he argues, are like foreign citizens in their own country because they have no interest whatsoever in achieving an aesthetic education. This conclusion can be reached when reading *L'eleganza è frigida*, but it becomes explicit when we read Parise's views in some of the articles he wrote as columnist of the *Corriere della Sera*, from January 1974 to mid-1975. Here, for instance, is his opinion on the relation between the Italians and the nation in which they live:

> Inoltre, questo è il concetto fondamentale della mia risposta, l'Italia non vuole più essere l'Italia. Gli Italiani (parlo della grandissima maggioranza) non vogliono più essere italiani. Se ne fregano dei monumenti, dei musei, di San Pietro, della Chiesa cattolica, dei Palazzi Pitti e Uffizi; ci mandano i loro figli con la scuola, ma se ne fregano e se ne fregheranno i loro figli quando sarà il momento. (Parise, 1998: 187)

> [Moreover, this is the fundamental concept of my answer, Italy no longer wants to be Italy. The Italians (I speak of the vast majority) do not want to be Italians anymore. They do not care about monuments, museums, San Pietro, the Catholic Church, the Pitti Palace and the Uffizi; they send their children to school, but they do not care and their children will not care either when the time comes.]

---

16 See, for example, Marco's remarks in front of a small theater in Tokyo: "Poiché di quegli alberelli erano piene tutte le strade dell'immensa città di Tokyo pensò che certamente era necessario un esercito di giardinieri per fare quel lavoro. Cartesio agì immediatamente nella successione dei pensieri di Marco: altri informatori giunti da quel paese gli avevano detto che il Giappone era quasi interamente meccanizzato quando non robotizzato, la prova era l'enorme quantità di minuscoli calcolatori, televisori, radio e via dicendo che giungevano dal Giappone in tutto l'altro emisfero, quasi a rappresentarlo. Ma quello che aveva sotto gli occhi era un lavoro interamente fatto a mano. [...] Eppure avrebbero potuto essere fatti a macchina. [...] Era un lavoro che si era sempre fatto a mano, che per tradizione esigeva di essere fatto a mano. Ma perché? La sola risposta che Cartesio seppe suggerire a Marco fu questa: per ragioni estetiche. Cioè per ragioni che dovevano rispettare al tempo stesso la tradizione, la materia dell'albero, che era vegetale, l'armonia tra materia e materia [...] e l'apporto creativo dell'uomo. Era insomma quanto bastava per fare di quel lavoro di avvolgimento e di quell'asola un'opera d'arte. E infatti Marco provò di fronte a quella cordicella e a quell'asola la stessa emozione che si prova davanti a un'opera d'arte" (1094).

In answering a letter from a reader of the newspaper, Parise is even more explicit in emphasizing this sense of a dichotomy between Italy's present and the reality until thirty years ago, when a humanistic culture was still actively present in the society:

> Del resto questa dissociazione, questa frattura così sentita dai ragazzi a scuola, è la frattura stessa dell'Italia. Da una parte le immagini e le testimonianze di un vecchissimo passato (l'Italia monumentale, storica e agricola), dall'altra una *no man's land* senza storia: l'Italia della speculazione edilizia, delle piccole e grandi industrie, delle autostrade all'Americana, dei motel, degli snack. Non siamo in America, dove non c'è cultura umanistica che affonda nel passato, e dove il paesaggio e la realtà giornaliera coincidono perfettamente con la cultura Americana. Questa frattura italiana è per il momento insanabile nonostante il velocissimo processo di integrazione in corso. (97–98)

> [After all, this dissociation, this fracture that the students feel at school, is the same fracture of Italy. On the one hand the images and the testimonies of a very old past (monumental, historical and agricultural Italy), on the other a no man's land without history: the Italy of building speculation, of small and big industries, of American-style highways, motels, snacks. We are not in America, where there is no humanist culture that sinks into the past, and where the landscape and the daily reality coincide perfectly with American culture. This Italian fracture is, for the time being, incurable despite the very fast integration process under way.]

Here we again find the same perception of a discontinuity between the present and a certain way of being Italian that belongs to the past as already observed in Maraini's and Moravia's writings. It is not a coincidence that Parise is fascinated by the continuity between new and old Japan, as Maraini was. See, for instance, the following passage:

> [In Giappone] luoghi e uomini si erano per così dire "adattati" all'ordine centrale e la sostituzione del castello nella fabbrica, del palazzo imperiale o feudale nei capannoni produttivi non doveva aver procurato nessun danno nel loro animo praticamente uguale, cioè obbediente e gerarchico, nell'uno e nell'altro caso. (Parise, 1989, vol. 2: 1083)

[In Japan places and men had so to speak "adapted" to the central order and the replacement of the castle in the factory, of the imperial or feudal palace in the productive sheds had not caused any harm in their mind, which is practically the same, that is obedient and hierarchical, in either case.]

Again, the conclusion is reached that Japan's rapid industrialization is nothing but the consequences of a strong work ethic and discipline rooted in the traditional structure of the society. According to Parise, such familiarity with modern mass production safeguards the Japanese worker from being affected by the alienation emphasized by Moravia (see the previous paragraph); indeed, Japan does not fit Marx's description of the alienated worker in capitalistic societies. In fact, mass production in Japan is not the mechanical repetition of a process in which the worker as individual is an alienated part, but is rather the perpetuation of a routine based in the Japanese craft tradition:

Marco fu colpito dal fatto che l'artista era giunto a scolpire sul legno anche un Budda al giorno, così gli dissero le guide e non poté fare a meno, una volta di più, di considerare che nulla in Giappone era cambiato dai tempi feudali dove non esisteva la produzione in serie: si vede che anche a quei tempi la spinta alla produzione in serie e in qualche modo all'esportazione era non soltanto *in nuce* ma *de facto*. (1087)

[Marco was struck by the fact that the artist had also carved a Buddha a day in wood, so the guides told him, and could not help but consider once again that nothing in Japan had changed since feudal times when mass production did not exist: we can see that even at that time the push for mass production and in some way for export was not only *in nuce* but *de facto*.]

The final image of Japan as a mirror of Italy is represented by idealizing an equal society, in which the harmonic division of responsibilities among social classes is achieved despite – or rather because of – the absence of ideologies. The social justice hoped for in Italy's future was already a reality in Japan:

Quei giapponesi, con i loro gradi morali, con i loro "inferiori-superiori" senza alcuna fede né ideologia erano già arrivati a quel dopo dove gli uomini non sono affatto tutti uguali ma ognuno ha il posto che gli spetta.

Di questo e di niente altro era fatto "il dopo," quel dopo che nel linguaggio del suo paese viene chiamato "progresso" e che egli sapeva invece ottenuto con il ricatto dell'invidia di classe, a quanto pareva inesistente nel paese dove si trovava. (1084)

[Those Japanese, with their moral ranks, with their "inferior-superiors" without any faith or ideology, had already arrived at that future where men are not all the same, but everyone has their rightful place. This was the fabric of "the future," that future that in the language of his country is called "progress," which was, in fact, obtained – as he thought – through a mechanism of class envy, apparently non-existent in the country where he was.]

This representation is nothing but the mirror image of the situation in Italy during the "economic miracle" (the so-called *boom economico*), as perceived by Parise in the novel *Il padrone* (1965) (translated as *The Boss*, 1966), which describes the labor dynamics inside a factory in Milan. The protagonist and narrator is a twenty-year-old man who moves to Milan from a small town and begins work in a factory. His enthusiasm and expectations of a better life are soon crushed by the hideous exploitation and selfishness of his boss, whose inhumane behavior causes distress and the end of the protagonist's dreams. The protagonist even agrees to marry a woman because his boss's wife wants him to. The boss's personality is characterized by individualism and a language oriented to promoting his egotistic morality. Here is how he responds to his workers when they complain about his tyrannical behavior:

"Sono il padrone, il padrone, il padrone...! Sono stufo di essere il servo dei miei dipendenti, sono stufo di aver a che fare coi furbi, con le volpi, con i ricci, con le donnole della ditta. Non ne posso più, vi caccio via tutti... il vostro comportamento fa schifo, io vi pago ed esigo rispetto. Non è per i soldi, io me ne frego dei soldi, potrei benissimo farne a meno, è il fatto morale che conta. E tutto ciò è immorale, immorale, immorale, avete capito? Purtroppo Dio non c'è per fulminarvi, ma lo farò io se necessario, avete capito?
  Avete capito? Avete capito?" (Parise, 1989, Vol. I: 877)

[I'm the boss, the boss, the boss! ... I'm tired of being the servant of my employees, I'm tired of dealing with smart alecks, with foxes, badgers, with the weasels of the firm. I can't take any more of it; I'm going to throw you all out ... your behavior's disgusting. I pay you and I demand respect. It's not because of the money. I don't give a damn about the money, I could perfectly well do without it. It's the moral aspect that counts. And all this is immoral, immoral, immoral, do you understand? Unfortunately, there's no God to strike you dead with a thunderbolt, but I'll do it myself if necessary, you understand?

You understand? You understand?] [Parise, 1966: 45]

Unlike Japan, Italy at the end of the 1970s was a country in which ideologies were the source of terrorism rather than social equality. This was the inheritance of the so-called "Years of Lead," the European period of sociopolitical turmoil marked by left- and right-wing terrorism, which lasted in Italy from the late 1960s to the early 1980s. The typical Italian attitude, according to Parise, was like that of the factory's owner to his workers in *Il padrone*: social violence was constantly legitimized in the name of morality (with an evident reference to Enrico Berlinguer's famous speech "The moral question," *La questione morale*, in November 1980). The hypocrisy of the rhetorical appeal to morality, dominant in public as well as private speech, was part of a broader problem related to an absence of patriotic morality: more than a hundred years after political unification, Italy was still an individualistic society with no awareness of its glorious aesthetic heritage. Parise's images of Japan as a mirror of Italy derive from these perceptions of a rhetorical, individualistic, and unpatriotic country.

Morality and aesthetic sensitivity in Japan were intertwined and kept alive by the awareness of an ancient civilization.[17] In contrast, Parise's perception of immorality and patriotic indifference at home are the consequence of a historical gap in the making of Italy as a nation. Parise detects in the rise of post-war Italy, the foundation of the Italian Republic, the moment of breakdown in a perceived image of a country radically different in every respect:

[Non] ricordo più l'Italia di venti-trent'anni fa. E la colpa non è mia, ma della 'forza delle cose' (la storia) che ha mutato profondamente il volto

---

17   Parise makes another interesting observation on Japanese patriotism by commenting on the heroic suicide of the Japanese writer Yukio Mishima: "Essendo nato e cresciuto nel paese della Politica Marco giudicava pazzo colui che si era suicidato in quel modo, e proprio entro il ministero della difesa, per protestare contro il governo, l'amico Chigusa gli disse invece che la sua memoria era molto rispettata in Giappone perché mostrava comunque un'azione di massimo onore nei confronti del proprio paese" (1070).

del nostro Paese. Non ricordo e non voglio ricordare, per molte ragioni, conscie e subconscie. Prima fra tutte perché l'Italia di trent'anni fa è lontana, lontanissima, in tutti i suoi aspetti, politici, culturali, linguistici, fonici, agricoli, non soltanto paesaggistici. (Parise, 1998: 186)[18]

[I no longer remember the Italy of twenty or thirty years ago. And it is not my fault, but the fault of the"force of things" (history), because it has profoundly changed the face of our country. I do not remember and I do not want to remember, for many conscious and subconscious reasons. First of all because the Italy of thirty years ago is far, far away, in all its aspects, political, cultural, linguistic, phonic, agricultural, not just landscaping ones.]

Let us now turn our attention to how Parise utilizes the concept of race in this book, given how fascist notions of race were still present in Italian society, despite the post-war debate on the subject.

6. On Race and Culture: A Dialog between Parise and Calvino

L'eleganza è frigida is much more than an account of a journey to an imaginary country, a utopian land, by which Parise presents a stern judgment on the social, cultural, and political context of Italy. The boundaries between Japan and Italy that Parise delineates include not only culture and religion, but also the idea of race. Parise depicts the Japanese as racially distinct and demarcates racial boundaries by assuming a link between presumed biological differences and behavior. The protagonist Marco explicitly notes those differences with the expression, "A Marco parve di cogliere in quegli sguardi del resto molto belli, e solo per fulminei istanti, la coscienza di una profonda diversità non soltanto culturale ma razziale" (1064) [Marco seemed to grasp in those looks, very beautiful after all, and only for lightning-fast moments, the awareness of a profound diversity that is not only cultural but racial]. Here is Parise's outline of Japanese racial identity:

Abituato a generalizzare, perché riteneva che geografia, clima, razza e cultura di un Paese fossero culla e patrimonio comune ai suoi abitanti,

---

18 Parise's article was published in *Corriere della Sera*, February 16, 1975.

Marco provò a definire il carattere base dei giapponesi: si trattava di persone innanzitutto timide e infantili, curiose, paurose, estremamente attente e molto più emotive di tutti gli altri abitanti del mondo.

Con ogni persona che incontrava Marco stabiliva dei piccoli test per fare la prova e mai ne fu contraddetto; confuso qualche volta perché alcuni giapponesi avevano così fortemente assorbito abitudini e modi di pensare (e di parlare) occidentali che le caratteristiche fondamentali e indigene erano andate quasi perdute, anche se mai fino in fondo; ma generalmente Marco fu confermato nella sua idea coltivata del resto già da molto tempo, che non soltanto esistono le razze ma esistono appunto geografie, climi e culture che ne conservano la purezza e l'autenticità. I giapponesi erano inoltre quelli che Marco era uso definire "razza pura" in vari sensi e direzioni: sia nella conservazione delle strutture fisiche comuni, delle abitudini culturali e delle forme in cui esse si mostravano; e questo era dovuto innanzitutto all'assenza quasi totale di incroci con altre razze, come per esempio avveniva nella razza europea e mediterranea; inoltre erano puri perché la loro cultura, come aveva perfezionato e purificato la cultura cinese, così aveva purificato il proprio corpo e la propria mente tenendoli lontani dalle contaminazioni per molti secoli. (1077–78)

[Being used to generalizing, because he believed that geography, climate, race, culture of a country were the cradle and common heritage of its inhabitants, Marco tried to define the basic character of the Japanese: they were first of all shy and childish, curious, scary, extremely attentive and much more emotional than all the other inhabitants of the world. With every person he met, he set up small tests to prove his point and, in fact, he was never contradicted; sometimes he was confused because some Japanese had so strongly absorbed Western habits and ways of thinking (and speaking) that the fundamental and indigenous characteristics had been almost lost, even if never to the end; but generally Marco was confirmed in his own cultivated idea of long-standing that not only do races exist, but that moreover they are kept pristine and authentic by the geographical, climatic and cultural environments in which are embedded. The Japanese stood as an example of what Marco considered a "pure race" with various meanings and aspects: like the preservation of common physical structures, as well as the forms through which those physical structures are shaped. Such a pure race depends on the lack of racial crossover, unlike for instance what happened with the European and Mediterranean races; moreover, the Japanese were more pristine because their own culture, while it brought the Chinese culture to a higher level of perfection and purity, had also purified their own body and mind, by keeping both of them away from contamination for many years.]

Parise's discourse on race and culture relies on nationalistic theories of "pure race" and a "Japanese spirit" that emerged in the context of post-restoration Japan. In an attempt to lay the foundations for a national consciousness, the new Meiji state set up a propaganda campaign to spread a sense of homogeneity and community throughout a heterogeneous population (Weiner, 2009: 1). The Meiji restoration aimed to impose a sense of the nation as an extended family in which the emperor played the role of both the semidivine father to the national community and the head of state (Weiner, 1994: 19). This homogeneous community or family is forged by national characteristics that are the result of a shared genetic base: the definition of *Yamato minzoku* (Japanese race) regarded culture as embedded in the blood relationship of a group of people.

Parise's concept of "pure race" is borrowed from this nationalist ideology establishing a link between genetics and culture:[19] "I giapponesi erano inoltre quelli che Marco era uso definire 'razza pura' in vari sensi e direzioni: sia nella conservazione delle strutture fisiche comuni, delle abitudini culturali e delle forme in cui esse si mostravano" [The Japanese were also those whom Marco used to call "pure race" in various senses and directions: in the preservation of common physical structures, in cultural habits and in the forms in which they were shown]. By adopting Meiji's notion of "pure race," Parise fails to consider the xenophobic tension between those deemed insiders and outsiders that afflicted contemporary Japan. Beneath the proclaimed racial homogeneity, the tenuous coexistence of a variety of ethnic groups shaped by racist behaviors have prevented true social unity. Parise ignores ethnic

19   "While acknowledging the diverse origins of the Japanese, later commentators maintained that the family state was itself a reflection of the inherited qualities and capabilities of its people. These inherent and immutable national characteristics, which were the product, though not exclusively, of a shared genetic base, were also the defining feature of the *Yamato minzoku*, or Japanese race. As distinct from a race defined exclusively in narrow biological terms, the concept of *minzoku* more closely resembled that of the German *volk*, which encompassed not only blood relationships, but broader cultural concerns, including the institutional arrangements, religion, language and history of a people": Michael Weiner, 1994, *Race and Migration in Imperial Japan* (London and New York: Routledge): 19.

clashes in contemporary Japan among the *barakumin* (indigenous outcast community) and island people like the Ainu in the North and Okinawans in the South. Additionally, during the time of Parise's visit to Japan, the country's economic success brought a wave of Japanese people from Brazil. Finally, the significant presence of Koreans, Chinese and Westerners must also be considered.

What is even more relevant in this discourse is the statement of the "Japanese race" itself.

For an Italian intellectual in the 1970s, the concept of race was considered almost outdated and inappropriate as a consequence of the fall of the Fascist government and its anti-Semitic Manifesto of Race (*Manifesto della razza*, 1938). In an effort to overcome the diffusion of racist theories, as occurred in Germany and Italy during 1930s, Unesco issued in 1950 "The Race Question" in which, among many other remarks, it was suggested that the term "race" be replaced with the more ideologically neutral expression "ethnic groups." Among those involved in the debate about terminology, Claude Lévi-Strauss (1908–2009), one of the founders of ethnology, introduced an innovative way to look at race from the perspective of culture. In a public lecture delivered at Unesco in 1971 (published under the title *Race et culture* in his book *Le regard éloigné*, 1983), Lévi-Strauss considered the way culture influences the gene pool:

> Pendant tout le 19e siècle et la première moitié du 20e, on s'est demandé si la race influençait la culture et de quelles façons. Après avoir d'abord reconnu que le problème ainsi posé était insoluble, nous nous apercevons maintenant que les choses se passent dans l'autre sens: ce sont les formes de cultures qu'adoptent ici ou là les hommes, leurs façons de vivre telles qu'elles ont prévalues dans le passé ou prévalent encore dans le présent, qui déterminent, dans une très large mesure, le rythme de leur évolution biologique et son orientation. Loin qu'il faille se demander si la culture est ou non fonction de la race, nous découvrons que la race où ce que l'on entend généralement par ce terme est une fonction parmi d'autres de la culture. (Lévi-Strauss, 1983: 35–36)

> [Throughout the nineteenth and in the first half of the twentieth century, scholars wondered whether and in what way race influences culture. After establishing that the problem stated in this way cannot be solved, we now realize that the reverse situation exists: the cultural forms adopted in various places by human beings, their ways of life in the past or in the

present, determine to a very great extent the rhythm of their biological evolution and its direction. Far from having to ask whether culture is or is not a function of race, we are discovering that race – or what is generally meant by the term – is one function among others of culture.]

Rather than positing a definition of race, Lévi-Strauss restated the link between race and culture in which the latter determines biological evolution. The concept of race is diminished and replaced in its former role by the notion of culture. Yet culture still plays, in the French anthropologist's assessment, a decisive role in social relations as he establishes a relativistic idea of culture as a tool to divide and distinguish different groups:

> La richesse d'une culture, ou du déroulement d'une de ses phases, n'existe pas à titre de propriété intrinsèque: elle est fonction de la situation où se trouve l'observateur par rapport à elle, du nombre et de la diversité des intérêts qu'il y investit. En empruntant une autre image, on pourrait dire que les cultures ressemblent à des trains qui circulent plus ou moins vite, chacun sur sa voie propre et dans une direction différente. Ceux qui roulent de conserve avec le nôtre nous sont présents de la façon la plus durable; nous pouvons à loisir observer le type des wagons, la physionomie et la mimique des voyageurs à travers les vitres de nos compartiments respectifs. Mais que, sur une autre voie oblique ou parallèle, un train passe dans l'autre sens et nous n'en apercevons qu'une image confuse et vite disparue, à peine identifiable pour ce qu'elle est, réduite le plus souvent à un brouillage momentané de notre champ visuel, qui ne nous livre aucune information sur l'évènement lui-même et nous irrite seulement parce qu'il interrompt la contemplation placide du paysage servant de toile de fond à notre rêverie. Or, tout membre d'une culture en est aussi étroitement solidaire que ce voyageur idéal l'est de son train. Dès la naissance et – je l'ai dit tout à l'heure – probablement même avant, les êtres et les choses qui nous entourent montent en chacun de nous un appareil de références complexes formant système: conduites, motivations, jugements implicites que, par la suite. L'éducation vient confirmer par la vue réflexive qu'elle nous propose du devenir historique de notre civilisation. Nous nous déplaçons littéralement avec ce système de référence, et les ensembles culturels qui se sont constitués en dehors de lui ne nous sont perceptibles qu'à travers les déformations qu'il leur imprime. Il peut même nous rendre incapables de les voir. (30)

[The wealth of a culture or of the unfolding of one of its phases does not exist as an intrinsic feature, it is a function of the observer's situation in regard to that wealth, of the number or diversity of the interests he has invested in it. To employ another image, one could say that cultures are like trains moving each on its own track, as its own speed, and in its own direction. The trains rolling alongside ours are permanently present for us; through the windows of our compartments, we can observe at our leisure the various kinds of car, the faces and gestures of the passengers. But if, on an oblique or a parallel track, a train passes in the other direction, we perceive only a vague, fleeting, barely identifiable image, usually just a momentary blur in our visual field, supplying no information about the event itself and merely irritating us because it interrupts our placid contemplation of the landscape, which serves as the backdrop to our daydreaming.

Every member of a culture is as tightly bound up with it as this ideal traveler is with his own train. From birth and, as I have said, probably even before, the things and beings in our environment establish in each one of us an array of complex references forming a system – conduct, motivations, implicit judgments, – that education then confirms by means of its reflexive view of the historical development of our civilization. We literally move along with this reference system, and the cultural systems established outside it are perceptible to us only through the distortions imprinted upon them by our system. Indeed, it may even make us incapable of seeing those other systems.]

By shifting the focus from race to culture, Lévi-Strauss makes the reader aware of the difficulties inherent in the process of meeting another civilization. In fact, the differences among cultural groups are not merely defined in terms of biology, but rather in terms of what he calls a "système de référence" ("reference system"), which includes education, conduct, implicit judgments and the historical development of a determined society. As with trains that move in opposite directions, we all move along this reference system; we cannot begin to properly judge another civilization unless we are aware of this structural distance.

Parise's encounter with Japan implies a meeting with what he considers the pure Japanese race. A few years earlier Italo Calvino had given an account of his journey in the Japanese world, using Lévi-Strauss's idea of culture as the theoretical background of his representation. Between December 1976 and January 1977, Calvino published in the newspaper *Corriere della Sera* a series of articles about Mr Palomar's adventures in Japan. Some of these articles would be included in the book *Collezione di sabbia* [Collection of Sand, 1984] in the section "La forma del tempo" [The shape of the time].

In the first article, entitled "Due donne, due volti del Giappone" (1976) ["Two women, two faces of Japan"], Calvino tells a story of his train trip from Tokyo to Kyoto. At the beginning, Calvino expresses his awareness of the travel experience as an encounter between two different "reference systems" (that of the traveler and the other of the country visited), with the inevitable consequence of being exposed to a perception of a difference, a separation from his own culture, rather than experience a meeting with the other:

> Nuovo del paese, sono ancora nella fase in cui tutto quel che vedo ha un valore proprio perché non so quale valore dargli. [...] Quando tutto avrà trovato un ordine e un posto nella mia mente, comincerò a non trovare più nulla degno di nota, a non vedere più quello che vedo. Perché vedere vuol dire percepire delle differenze, e appena le differenze si uniformano nel prevedibile quotidiano lo sguardo scorre su una superficie liscia e senza appigli. (Calvino, 1995, vol. 1: 566)

> [New to the country, I am still in the phase in which all I see has value precisely because I do not know what value to attribute to it [...] When everything will have found some order and some place in my mind, I shall start to find nothing really worth noticing, to not see what I see any longer. Because seeing means perceiving differences, and as soon as differences become homogenized into a foreseeable everyday, our sight skims over the smooth surface and finds nothing to hang on to.]

Calvino then takes his place on the train and describes what is happening in the car in which he is seated: a young, cheerful woman is engaged in conversation with an old lady, whose reaction is quite indifferent as the harsh expressions on her face testify. Calvino tries to apply Western interpretative keys in an attempt to decode the meaning of the scene. Here the young lady embodies traditional Japan ("Non ha niente di occidentale, questa ragazza, è un'apparizione d'altri tempi" (566) [there isn't any Western aspect in this girl, she is an apparition from other times], while the old woman is a typical expression of the new Japan: "Nella vecchia signora, invece, quei pochi elementi occidentali, anzi americani – gli occhiali con una montatura argentea, la permanente azzurrina fresca di parrucchiere – che si sommano al costume tradizionale danno la sensazione precisa del Giappone d'oggi" (566–67) [In the elderly lady there are few Western, or rather American, elements, – the spectacles with the silver frames, the fresh azure permanent – These elements are on top of the traditional costume she is wearing and they give you a clear impression of what is Japan today].

The young girl seems to shows respect for and devotion to the older woman, by helping her eat and trying to entertain her graciously even though the woman appears indifferent to her attention:

> La giovane ora s'è seduta a fianco della signora, e parla e ride. La signora tace, arcigna, non risponde non si volta, guarda fisso davanti a sé. [...] E la vecchia? Zitta seria, dura. Non è detto che non ascolti: ma è come se stesse accanto alla radio, ricevendo una comunicazione che non implica risposta da parte sua. (570)

> [The young woman has now sat beside the lady, and talks and laughs. The lady is silent, grim, unresponsive, does not turn around, stares straight ahead [...] And the old woman? Quiet, serious, tough. This is not to say that she does not listen: but it is as if she was next to the radio, receiving a communication that does not imply an answer from her.]

Calvino's attempt to explain the irritating behavior of the old lady is based on another Western interpretative key, specifically the contrast between young and old generations and the subordinated relation of the former to the latter:

> Insomma è un'antipatica spaventosa questa vecchia! È un'egoista presuntuosa! È un mostro! [...] Così in questo momento m'infurio dentro di me contro la vecchia dama che mi pare incarni qualcosa di terribilmente ingiusto. Ma chi si crede d'essere? Ma come può pretendere di meritarsi tante attenzioni? Il mio risentimento per l'alterigia della signora cresce insieme all'ammirazione per la grazia e la letizia e la civiltà [...] che mi danno la sensazione di uno spreco imperdonabile. A guardar bene, è uno stato d'animo complesso e mescolato quello che mi travaglia in questo momento. C'è una spinta di ribellione mossa dalla solidarietà coi giovani contro l'autorità schiacciante degli anziani, coi sottoposti contro il privilegio dei signori. C'è tutto questo, certo. Ma forse c'è anche altro, un fondo d'invidia, una rabbia che viene dall'identificarmi in qualche modo, con la parte della vecchia signora, la voglia di dirle a denti stretti: "Ma

non sai, scema, che da noi in Occidente mai più sarà possibile a nessuno essere servito come sei servita tu? Non sai che in Occidente nessun vecchio sarà mai più trattato con tanta devozione da una giovane?" Ecco che solo rappresentandomi il conflitto come qualcosa che avviene dentro me stesso, posso sperare di penetrarne il segreto, di decifrarlo. Ma sarà poi così? Cosa ne so della vita di questo paese? (570–71)

[In short, this old lady is a frightening and awful thing! She is a presumptuous selfish! She is a monster! [...] So at this moment I become infuriated against the old lady who seems to me to embody something terribly unjust. But who do you think you are? But how can you claim to deserve so much attention? My resentment for the lady's haughtiness grows together with admiration for grace and gladness and civilization [...] and gives me the feeling of an unforgivable waste. Looking closely, it is a complex state of mind and is mixed with what is troubling me right now. There is a thrust of rebellion moved by solidarity with the young against the overwhelming authority of the elders, with the subordinates against the privilege of the lords. There is all this, of course. But maybe there is something else, a fund of envy, an anger that comes from identifying with some part of the old lady, the desire to tell her tight-lipped: "But don't you know, you idiot, that among us in the West it will never be possible for anyone to be served as you are served? Don't you know that in the West no old man or woman will ever be treated with so much devotion by a young girl?" Here, it is only by representing the conflict as something that happens within me that I can hope to penetrate the secret, to decipher it. But how can I be sure? What do I know about the life of this country?]

Through this apparently unimportant episode Calvino successfully conveys the distortions implied in a Western view of a culturally distant country. Through his description of the young woman Calvino offers an example of Lévi-Strauss's "system of reference," as the words he uses to describe her are taken from the traditional language of Italian poetry, familiar to Italian readers of Petrarch or Giacomo Leopardi. Calvino very keenly describes the expression of the young lady in the following way: "espressione ridente e fresca e lieve" [a joyous, fresh and delicate expression]. The transition to a poetic language, from the language of prose, is marked even by the use of the assonance of the "e" vowel and by the double diphthong (rident*e e* fresc*a e* liev*e*). Indeed, the adjectives deployed to describe the

Japanese girl turn her into "un'apparizione d'altri tempi" [an apparition of other times], as they translate her through the codified image of the most famous women of Italian poetry, from Petrarch's Laura to Leopardi's Silvia. By adopting the sameness of Italian poetic language Calvino is questioning the veracity of his interpretation through the means of a stylistic marker. In his account, the gaze of a foreigner is better positioned to perceive different aspects of a culture. However, Calvino seems to suggest that our "reference system" condemns us to transmit our viewpoint through the signifiers adopted by our language.

In the view of the narrator, relations between the Eastern and Western worlds are regulated by patterns of center–periphery or vanguard–backwardness. This is evident when the narrator explains the reason why he is so irritated: he assumes that his own society stands as a vanguard compared to Japanese society. According to this logic, the woman–girl relationship is an expression of backwardness, as the narrator assumes that future Japanese fashion will be the same as it is in the Western world today. "Ma non sai, scema, che da noi in Occidente mai più sarà possibile a nessuno essere servito come sei servita tu? Non sai che in Occidente nessun vecchio sarà mai più trattato con tanta devozione da una giovane?" [But don't you know, you idiot, that among us in the West it will never be possible for anyone to be served as you are served? Don't you know that in the West no old man or woman will ever be treated with so much devotion by a young girl?] Japan, as a referent in Calvino's discourse, is distanced and posed in a time other than the present. This "denial of coevalness" (Fabian, 1983: 31), that is, the split between the present time of the Western observer and the other time of those who are observed, implies a logic of power and dominion. According to this view, Japan (or the East in general) belongs to an earlier stage of an evolutionistic conception of time.

Yet the final questions ("Ma sarà poi così? Cosa ne so della vita di questo paese?" [But how can I be sure? What do I know about the life of this country?]) introduce a cultural gap, an empty space by which the character has the perception of a different dimension, in other words, the murky perception of the Other. These final questions correspond, in Lévi-Strauss's image of the train, with the standpoint of a passenger watching a train running in the opposite direction who can perceive only a fleeting and barely identifiable image.

Calvino's story is a narrative expression of Lévi-Strauss's claim that culture is the main element of differentiation and identification among cultural groups: each group is part of a reference system, and other systems are perceived only through the distortions imprinted on them by our own system.[20] Instead of culture, Parise still applies the category of race to depict Japanese society. For Parise, the genotypes of Japanese people are linked to their personality: their facial expressions and the shape of their eyes serve as explanations for their reportedly shy and curious personality:

> La timidezza infantile che si esprimeva soprattutto nei movimenti degli occhi era deliziosa e così anche la curiosità. [...] ma timidezza e curiosità avevano quasi sempre la meglio essendo due istinti vitali e primari anche se contrastanti: specialmente nelle donne e nei bambini questi due impulsi apparivano nello sguardo in modo inequivocabile che nessun formalismo avrebbe potuto trattenere. (Parise, 1989, Vol. II: 1079)

> [The childish shyness that was expressed above all in the movements of the eyes was delicious and so was the curiosity. [...] but shyness and curiosity were almost always predominant, as they [these two emotional states] are two vital and primary instincts even if contrasting: especially in women and children these two impulses appeared in the look in an unequivocal way that no formalism could hold back.]

This is not to claim that Parise was naïve and unaware of more sophisticated ways of addressing racial discourse. His narrative strategy claims the right for the traveler to make observations in a vacuum of preconceived notions in order to rely exclusively on the direct impression received by the eye of the beholder. The anachronistic choice of Marco (Polo) as a fictional character, intended to suggest the experience of Parise's contemporary traveler, is not so different from that of the author of *Il Milione*: in both cases there is a strict reliance on sensory experiences and immediate impressions. In a 1969 letter from Nanjing Parise says: "Gli strumenti di uno straniero che viaggia in Cina, oggi, non sono diversi da quelli di Marco Polo nel suo

---

20   Calvino was an eager reader of Lévi-Strauss's books. He also wrote a review of *Le regard éloigné* in which he expressed his enthusiasm for Lévi-Strauss's theories: "Premesso che né la biologia né l'antropologia fisica riescono a decidere cos'è una razza, mentre l'etnologo può ben dire cos'è una cultura, L.-S. rovescia i termini della questione mettendo in primo piano gli aspetti in cui fatti culturali influiscono sul patrimonio genetico: i rapporti d'allontanamento e d'isolamento tra i villaggi d'una stessa tribù, poi le fusioni secondo complicate regole matrimoniali, permettono una selezione genetica – che si riflette soprattutto nell'immunità alle epidemie – in tempi molto più veloci che quando gli scambi genetici avvengono a caso" (Calvino, 1995, vol. 2: 2068–69).

famoso viaggio. Essi sono: gli occhi per vedere, il cervello per riflettere" [We have [nowadays] the same cognitive tools as Marco Polo had: the eyes to watch and the brain to reflect] (Belpoliti and Cortellessa, 2016: 223). In a negative review of Roland Barthes' *L'Empire des signes*, Parise opposes a semiologist's approach to analyzing Japanese society, on the basis that in-depth analysis is alien to the Japanese aesthetic, which is, on the contrary, a more accessible approach privileging dazzling intuition and an instant feeling of an all-encompassing comprehension, according to the Zen concept of "satori." In fact, he writes that, "Il Giappone non si presta all'analisi ma quasi esclusivamente a una serie pressoché infinita di elettroshock, di fulminee intuizioni, quello che i giapponesi chiamano *satori*, una specie di perdita di conoscenza, e niente altro" (Parise, 1989, Vol. 2: 1547) [Japan does not lend itself to analysis but almost exclusively to a more or less endless series of electroshocks, dazzling intuitions, that are what the Japanese call *satori*, which is a kind of loss of knowledge, and nothing else]. In other words, Parise considers Zen philosophy akin to his idiosyncratic way of seeing the Asian other, while he dismisses Barthes' semiologist approach as a violation of the Japanese spirit enacted through the means of a Western (over-)analytic method (Colucci, 2016: 18–20). What is missing in Parise's account of Japan is an accounting for the presumed distance between the "Self" and the "Other," the uncertainty of the cultural distance that, in contrast, conveys a sense of anguish in Calvino's story. *L'eleganza è frigida* moves smoothly through the realm of Japanese nature. The serenity of Parise's narration is mainly due to his confidence in the accuracy of his judgments, based on his allegedly objective characterizations of the people observed. Expressions like "caratteristiche inconfondibili dei giapponesi" (1096) [unmistakable characteristics of the Japanese] are scattered throughout the book. Emphasizing race more than culture allows Parise to avoid the thorny problem of bridging a gap between his own culture and that of the country visited. The interiority of the Japanese soul is appreciated through its external appearance, without posing any questions on the neutrality of the observer's view.

On the other hand, Calvino was more concerned with the *way* of seeing rather than with the image itself, or with the use of the eyes rather than the mutual sensorial penetration of the observer and the observed subject. Parise is drawn to Japan by the Zen practice of *satori*, while Calvino chooses Japan to meditate on the ways of seeing because he is fascinated by the inside/outside dialectic, which he deems to be a central aspect of Japanese aesthetic. As Marco Belpoliti points out: "L'attenzione che Calvino dedica al Giappone non è il frutto di un esotismo, della ricerca del 'diverso,' ma è invece rivolta a un mondo che ha fatto del *vedere* l'oggetto privilegiato di una estetica che è insieme un'etica, un costume,' un modo di vivere" (Belpoliti, 1996: 248) [The attention that Calvino dedicates to Japan is not the result of an exoticism, that is, the search for the "diverse," but it is directed toward a world that has made use of the *seeing* the privileged object of an aesthetic which is, at the same token, an ethic, a "custom," a way of living]. The alternative way of seeing that Mr Palomar stumbles upon in Japan is introduced in the prose as a contrast between the Western mode of pictorial perspective and the Japanese one:

È in Occidente che i pittori del Trecento hanno risolto una volta per tutte il problema della rappresentazione degli interni nel modo che oggi ci sembra ovvio, cioè abolendo una parete e mostrando la stanza aperta come una scena teatrale. Ma un paio di secoli prima i pittori giapponesi del XII secolo avevano trovato un altro sistema, meno diretto ma più completo, d'esplorare visivamente lo spazio interno pur rispettandone la separazione dal fuori: abolivano il tetto.

[It is in the West that the painters of the fourteenth century resolved once and for all the problem of the representation of the interior in the way that today seems obvious, that is, abolishing a wall and showing the open room as a theatrical scene. But a couple of hundred years earlier the Japanese painters of the twelfth century had found another, less direct but more complete system of visually exploring the interior space while respecting its separation from the outside: they abolished the roof.]

The radically different way Japan has chosen to represent the distance between inside and outside space offers Calvino the opportunity to reflect on the fallacious nature of the way different cultures see each other. As an outsider, the eye of Mr Palomar in Japan will inevitably fail to capture the inside view of the country. Mr Palomar's meditations on "difference" inspired by his Japanese journey ("vedere vuol dire percepire delle differenze" [seeing means perceiving differences]) are a central tenet of Calvino's visual universe. They inform Marco Polo's narrative of various imaginary cities laid out for the entertainment of a melancholic Kublai Khan, in *Invisible Cities* (1972). As Beno Weiss observes, "The cities are meaningful only in relation to each other because, as in language, there are only differences" (Weiss, 1993: 151). Even *Cosmicomics* (1965) proceeds from a universe of undifferentiated and homogeneous space to a segmented grid of differences and separations. In "The Spiral," the final story in

Cosmicomics, the inside/outside meditations from which Calvino draws, Japanese aesthetics are conducive to the collapse between the barriers of "Self" and "Other." "The Spiral" stages Qfwfq as a primordial mollusk – with no eyes and no head – living a formless life on a rock. His contented existence is disrupted when he becomes sensible to the feeling of love. As a result, he develops a shell, which takes the form of a spiral, while his beloved mollusk is also developing an identical shell accordingly. Qfwfq explains that although mollusks do not have eyes, they can still perceive the spiral having colored stripes since the shell is able to create "visual images of shells" that are imprinted on the retina.

"An image therefore presupposes a retina, which in turn presupposes a complex system stemming from an encephalon. So, in producing the shell, I also produced its image" (Calvino, 1968: 150). Fast-forwarding 500 million years, the story of Qfwfq explains his miscalculation in the act of developing a form and gaining the benefit of sight. While he thinks that the creation of visual images will grant him the power of sight and the benefit of the viewer, he soon realizes that his individual identity has been objectified by the gaze of other viewers and that his internal sight has been overpowered and replaced by that of external viewers, each of them having the power to recognize and frame the self. "'The Spiral,' then, dramatizes the collapse of the barrier between internal and external dimensions by positing subjectivity as a kaleidoscopic product of the self's objectification by the non-self" (Cavallaro, 2010: 45).

The structural divisions that prevent viewers from seeing with their own eyes could not be further from what Parise's traveler believes to be the cognitive value of encountering a different race. In this sense, Parise's critical review of the *L'Empire des signes* serves as an indirect critique of Calvino's travel narratives because of its over-analytical approach to the subject matter. Parise's exotic escapade is posited as an exploration in the land of the "diverse" that culminates in replicating an outdated Western racial discourse. Calvino's approach to Japan, instead, is similar to the experience that Marco Polo narrates in visiting the city of Hypatia in *Le città invisibili*. The things he sees are anomalous to him. In Hypatia the difference concerns "not words, but things"; therefore he soon realizes that in order to make sense of Hypatia he has to free himself from the "images" that have so far presented him with the things he has sought. Confronted with the impossibility of the task, the narrator acknowledges that "there is no language without deceit" (48).

7. Conclusion: Italian Self-Abasement. A Neo-Exoticism?

In his study of French modern travel literature Charles Forsdick notices a recurrent pattern in the formation of interest in the exotic in public discourse, which is mainly the perception of an erosion of distinctiveness and a decline of cultural diversity. In other words, the decline of the exotic is a necessary premise for its reinstatement in the public discourse.

Travel literature itself profits at its best from apocalyptic perceptions of cultural entropy, as it prompts travelers to journey toward whatever culture is still perceived as diverse, although on the verge of disappearing. If the historical condition for the emerging of French *fin de siècle* exoticism was the perception of cultural leveling and homogenization, the representation of similar emotional feelings in the public domain is conducive to the formation of a new exotic imaginary. "The purported decline of diversity cannot be situated at a specific moment, but must be seen as a recurrent element constitutive of exoticism [...] itself" (Forsdick, 2005: 14). Thus, "It is always the individuality of each moment that is striking: the decline of the exotic means different things at different times, and in different contexts quite different values are being brought into question" (Forsdick, 2005: 16).

The context in which Maraini, Moravia and Parise wrote is the post-war period wherever the erosion of cultural diversity and loss of meaning shaped the travel experience. Similar paradoxically, to Lévi-Strauss's notorious travel book *Tristes tropique* (1955), in which the French anthropologist announces "La Fin des voyages" ["An end to journeying"], while at the same time exploring the last remains of the part of the world that has not yet fallen into the category of sameness. The experiences of the three writers reflect the same entropic feeling of loss of diversity, and their journey to Japan is inspired by a more or less self-conscious desire to venture into the exotic.[21] Yet the

---

21 The definition of "exoticism" that I use here eschews the pejorative connotation that the term receives in the area of post-colonial studies. For Frantz Fanon, "exoticism" is a term located within the center–periphery dynamic and describes a Western attitude to the reduction to objectification of the "Other." Bhabha, rather, "sees exoticism as essentialization, as an integral element of neocolonial representations": Charles Forsdick, 2005, *Travel in Twentieth-Century French and Francophone Cultures: The Persistence of Diversity* (Oxford; New York: Oxford University Press): 45. In using the term I rely on Charles Forsdick's discussion of the fluidity and open interpretation of the term, as well as on his invitation to update its definition, and to distinguish its use during the time of the colonial period to its most recent application. In particular Forsdick calls for a twofold process of "unthinking colonial exoticism" by focusing "first, [on] the need for

choice of Japan as a place in which to experience diversity is related less to an ethnological desire to preserve distinguished cultures and languages, and more to the historical context of post-war Italy and the frustrated attitude of an intellectual class. They all share the opinion that Italy stands in a backward position compared to Japan, as they perceive Italy as a satellite country gravitating around larger spheres of ideological, political, and spiritual influence (whether from the Vatican, the White House or the Kremlin). Japan is perceived as a country that still maintains cultural independence and is, in their views, substantially unscathed (at least temporally) from the influence of such macro powers. René de Ceccatty noticed that Moravia's infatuation with distant cultures and his inclination to travel outside Western borders betray an anxiety about the hegemonic powers of both American capitalism and Russian communism in the global context:

> Il cherche à se défaire de sa propre culture dont les principes, les idéaux, les modes de vie, les conventions, les systèmes éthiques, économiques, sociaux, politiques le hérissent, dont l'avenir, mécanisé, déshumanisé, uniformisé lui fait horreur et qu'il a vu dessiner se aussi bien aux États-Unis qu'en URSS. (De Ceccatty, 2010: 349)

> [He seeks to get rid of his own culture whose principles, ideals, lifestyles, conventions, ethical, economic, social, political systems are bothering him, whose future, mechanized, dehumanized, standardized horrifies him and that he saw outlined both in the United States and the USSR.]

As the political dream of the "Great Italy" that Mussolini sought to engender is sinking in the geopolitical context of the Cold War, the travel writings of Maraini, Moravia and Parise stand as examples of Italian post-Marxist intellectuals seeking to evade the oppressive reality of the world split into two ideological blocks. At the end of World War II when both Italy and Japan were under the sphere of US influence, Italian intellectuals critical of Italian subordination to foreign influence saw in Japan a country

---

attenuation of the term and of the process it describes; second, [on] the possibility of understanding the notion in term of reciprocity" (Forsdick, 2005: 47). In the name of Édouard Glissant's "droit à l'opacité" [right to opacity] there is a need to see exoticism as a transcultural phenomenon and as a form of resistance to Eurocentric episteme, rather than an expression of it, notwithstanding the term still retains the uneven power relation between cultures.

able to remain culturally and spiritually impermeable to the forces of globalization.²²

Nevertheless, while perceiving Japan as an exotic destination substantially "other" than Italy and the rest of the Westernized world, Maraini, Moravia and Parise managed to bring some of this exoticism back home, in the form of individual engagement with Japanese culture and society. Maraini's painstaking and unequaled effort to promote Japanese culture and language in Italy finds an echo in aesthetic responses from Moravia and Parise (and Calvino, also) to Tanizaki, Mishima and Kawabata.²³ Their rendition of a certain image of Japanese culture in Italy is certainly not authentic or objective, but I suspect that its appeal in the writings of these authors stems from it being an expression of a non-Western "aesthetic" tradition and, thus offering resistance against the pervasive ideological and moral forces dominating the Italian peninsula. If it is true that "it is easier to register the loss of traditional orders of difference than to perceive the emergence of new ones" (Clifford, 1988: 15), then we must conclude that behind the general scant resistance provided by Italian culture and society in the face of the homogenizing effect of global forces, one can still find minor but nevertheless significant attempts to contaminate and hybridize the impact of the global

---

22 For instance, Parise, in an article published in *Corriere della Sera* on October 24, 1982, indicates Japan as the only country in the world where American materialism was not hegemonic: "ci fu un ultimo viaggio, in Giappone, dove lo spirito di Salgari trionfò: unico Paese al mondo dove l'America è messa sotto i tacchi e usata come si usano appunto i tacchi, ogni cosa avendo l'aspetto e l'uso americano. L'invincibile spirito del Giappone, uguale sempre a se stesso, che dopo tanto errare fu il primo grande sospiro di sollievo. Ecco, l'essenza, lo spirito ineffabile dell'esotismo inteso non soltanto materialmente in Giappone resisteva intatto; l'acqua non era stata inquinata": Goffredo Parise, 2005, *Quando la fantasia ballava il boogie* (Milan: Adelphi): 163.
23 I have already mentioned how the journey to Japan ended up influencing Moravia's writing of *La noia*. As mediator of Japanese literature in Italy, Moravia wrote the preface to the Italian translation of Yukio Mishima, *Death in Midsummer*: *Morte di mezza estate e altri racconti* (Milan: Longanesi, 1966). He also wrote the preface to Junichiro Tanizaki's *Naomi* (translated in Italian as *L'amore di uno sciocco*) (Milan: Bompiani, 1967). Raffaele La Capria noticed how Goffredo Parise's engagement with Japanese culture was conducive to the elaboration of his major work, *Sillabari*, as series of Zen-like awakening (see La Capria, 2005, *Caro Goffredo: Dedicato a Parise*. Rome: Minimum Fax: 43). Parise's engagement with Kawabata is at the center of his final novel *L'odore del sangue* ["The smell of blood"] (published posthumously in 1997), in which the contrast between senility and youth that is staged in the *House of the Sleeping Beauties* is transported into the life of the elder protagonists Filippo and Silvia, who are involved in affairs with younger lovers.

monoculture in Italy, by virtue of interacting with the Japanese culture in translation.[24]

Works Cited

Bellah, N. Robert. 2003. *Imagining Japan: The Japanese Tradition and Its Modern Interpretation*. Berkeley, Los Angeles and London: University of California Press.
Belpoliti, Marco. 1996. *L'occhio di Calvino*. Turin: Einaudi.
—. 2010. *Settanta*. 2nd edn. Turin: Einaudi.
Belpoliti, Marco and Cortellessa, Andrea. 2016. *Goffredo Parise*. Milan: Marcos y Marcos.
Beviglia, Rosaria. 1967. "La letteratura giapponese in Italia: Parte seconda: 1950–1967." *Il Giappone*, 7: 149–61.
Calvino, Italo. 1968. *Cosmicomics*, translated by Williams Weaver. San Diego: Harcourt Brace Jovanovich.
—. 1974. *Invisible Cities*, translated by Williams Weaver. San Diego: Harcourt Brace Jovanovich.
—. 1976. "Due donne, due volti del Giappone." *Corriere della Sera*. December 5.
—. 1995. *Saggi: 1945–1985*, edited by Mario Berenghi. 2 vols. Milan: Mondadori-Meridiani.
Cavallaro, Dani. 2010. *The Mind of Calvino: A Critical Exploration of His Thought and Writings*. Jefferson, NC: McFarland.
Ciapparoni La Rocca, Teresa. 1998. "Moravia e il Giappone." *Quaderni*, 1: 63–77.
Clifford, James. 1988. *The Predicament of Culture: Twentieth-Century Ethnography, Literature and Art*. Cambridge, MA: Harvard University Press.
Colucci, Dalila. 2016. *"L'Eleganza è frigida" e "L'Empire des signes": un sogno fatto in Giappone*. Florence: Florence University Press.
De Ceccatty, René. 2010. *Alberto Moravia*. Paris: Flammarion.
De Gruchy, John W. 2003. *Orienting Arthur Waley: Japonism, Orientalism, and the Creation of Japanese Literature in English*. Honolulu: University of Hawaii Press.

---

24 In Parise's words: "A noi occidentali, lettori occidentali, oggi particolarmente afflitti da una produzione letteraria che non si dovrebbe in realtà chiamare tale, di importazione o di imitazione americana, privati ormai di una fisionomia europea che è durata fino a pochi anni fa, prima del ciclone delle cose, della *robba* da vendere, avvicinarsi a questi autori giapponesi è un po' come per gli abitanti della città sentire l'odore dell'ozono o della pioggia, della campagna e dei boschi": Goffredo Parise, 1985, "Kawabata e i segreti dell'animo femminile," *Corriere della Sera*, November 27: 3.

Fabian, Johannes. 1983. *Time and the Other: How Anthropology Makes its Object*. New York: Columbia University Press.

Forsdick, Charles. 2005. *Travel in Twentieth-Century French and Francophone Cultures: The Persistence of Diversity*. Oxford and New York: Oxford University Press.

Gentile, Emilio. 2009. *La Grande Italia: The Myth of the Nation in the Twentieth Century*, translated by Suzanne Dingee and Jennifer Pudney. Madison: University of Wisconsin Press.

Harootunian, Harry D. 1993. "America's Japan/Japan's Japan." In *Japan in the World*, edited by Masao Miyoshi and Harry D. Harootunian, 196–221. Durham and London: Duke University Press.

—. 2000. *Overcome by Modernity: History, Culture, and Community in Interwar Japan*. Princeton: Princeton University Press.

Henry, Sue and Lehmann, Jean-Pierre (eds). 1988. *Themes and Theories in Modern Japanese History: Essays in Memory of Richard Storry*. London and Atlantic Highlands, NJ: Athlone Press.

Kersten, Rikki. 1996. *Democracy in Postwar Japan: Maruyama Masao and the Search for Autonomy*. London and New York: Routledge.

La Capria, Raffaele. 2005. *Caro Goffredo: Dedicato a Parise*. Rome: Minimum Fax.

Lévi-Strauss, Claude. 1983. *Le regard éloigné*. Paris: Plon.

Maraini, Fosco. 1960. *Meeting with Japan*, translated by Eric Mosbacher. New York: Viking Press.

—. 1971. *Japan: Patterns of Continuity*. Tokyo and Palo Alto, CA: Kodansha International.

—. 1973. "Fosco Maraini." In *The Japan Experience*, edited by Ronald Bell, 3–22. New York and Tokyo: Weather Hill.

—. 1988. "Japan, the Essential Modernizer." In *Themes and Theories in Modern Japanese History: Essays in Memory of Richard Storry*, edited by Sue Henry and Jean-Pierre Lehmann, 44–63. London and Atlantic Highlands, NJ: Athlone Press.

—. 2001. *Le ore giapponesi*. Milan: Corbaccio.

Maruyama, Masao. 1988. "The Structure of 'Matsurigoto': The 'Basso Ostinato' of Japanese Political Life." In *Themes and Theories in Modern Japanese History: Essay in Memory of Richard Storry*, edited by Sue Henry and Jean-Pierre Lehmann, 27–43. London and Atlantic Highlands, NJ: Athlone Press.

Moravia, Alberto. 1960. *La noia*. Milan: Bompiani.

—. 1964. *L'uomo come fine e altri saggi*. Milan: Bompiani.

—. 1965. *Man as an End: A Defense of Humanism*, translated by Bernard Wall. New York: Farrar, Straus & Giroux.

—. 1979. *Le Roi est nu: Conversations en français avec Vania Luksic*. Paris: Editions Stock.

—. 1994. *Viaggi: Articoli 1930–1990*, edited by Enzo Siciliano. Milano: Bompiani.

—. 1999. *Boredom*, translated by Angus Davidson. New York: New York Review of Books.

Moravia, Alberto and Elkann, Alain. 2000. *Life of Moravia*, translated by William Weaver. South Royalton, VT: Steerforth Press.

Nakane, Chie. 1970. *Japanese Society*. Berkeley and Los Angeles: University of California Press.

Parise, Goffredo. 1966. *The Boss*, translated by William Weaver. New York: Alfred A. Knopf.

—. 1982. *L'eleganza è frigida*. Milan: Mondadori.

—. 1985. "Kawabata e i segreti dell'animo femminile." *Corriere della Sera*, November 27, 3.

—. 1989. *Opere*, edited by Bruno Callegher and Mauro Portello. 2 vols. Milan: Mondadori.

—. 1998. *Verba Volant: Profezie civili di un anticonformista*, edited by Silvio Perrella. Florence: libri liberal.

—. 2005. *Quando la fantasia ballava il boogie*. Milan: Adelphi.

Reischauer, Edwin O. 1977. *The Japanese*. Cambridge, MA: Belknap Press.

Richie, Donald. 2005. *The Japan Journals: 1947–2004*, edited by Leza Lowitz. Berkley, CA: Stone Bridge Press.

Samuels, Richard, J. 2003. *Machiavelli's Children: Leaders and their Legacies in Italy and Japan*. Cornell: Cornell University.

Santoro, Vito. 2009. *L'odore della vita: Studi su Goffredo Parise*. Macerata: Quodlibet.

Smith, Patrick. 1997. *Japan: A Reinterpretation*. New York: Pantheon Books.

Waley, Arthur and Shōnagon, Sei. 1929. *The Pillow Book of Sei Shōnagon*. Boston and New York: Houghton Mifflin Company.

Weiner, Michael. 1994. *Race and Migration in Imperial Japan*. London and New York: Routledge.

Weiner, Michael (ed.). 2009. *Japan's Minorities: The Illusion of Homogeneity*. London and New York: Routledge.

Weiss, Beno. 1993. *Understanding Italo Calvino*. Columbia: University of South Carolina Press.

CHAPTER FOUR

Madama Butterfly Revised

> La domanda che segue è: ma mia madre, la bella Topazia, figlia di un duca siciliano e di una selvaggia cantante cilena, era anche lei abitata dal demone del viaggio? O semplicemente seguiva mio padre, per amore? Pur non essendo una esploratrice come Fosco, la ragazza siciliana aveva nel sangue l'esperienza dell'altrove.
>
> (Dacia Maraini, *La seduzione dell'altrove*)

1. A "Belated" Ticket to Japan

In my previous chapter I conclude that Moravia's and Parise's engagement with Japanese literature in translation responds to a desire to incorporate non-Western aesthetic traditions into the Italian literary canon. Yet it is undeniable that the selection of Japanese works captures the attention of the two writers because it reflects a Westernized view of Japan, especially regarding the well-established trope of Japan as the feminine "Other." After all, what makes Tanizaki's *Naomi* (1924) an attractive story for Moravia is nothing but the fact that the woman protagonist of the novel embodies the subaltern status of Japan to the West: Naomi is "immorale perché occidentalizzata e occidentalizzata perché immorale" (Tanizaki and Moravia, 2000: ix) [She is immoral because she is Westernized and Westernized because she is immoral]. The search for literary worlds and cultural traditions beyond the Western hemisphere is a gesture of disavowal that risks going awry by falling into the discourse of the feminized Japanese body, a central trope of Western male erotic travelogs to Japan. From the outset, the language of such narratives is saturated with phallocentric connotations. This is noticeable in descriptions of Commodore Perry's description of Tokyo Bay, which rely on such expressions as the "opening" of Japan to Euro-American powers or the preference for the transitive verb "penetrate" to further allude to the promise of sexual and territorial conquest implicit in the intransitive use of the verb "opening" (Holland and Huggan, 1998: 81).[1] The feminine Orient that Pierre Loti presents to French readers is based on his interpretation of his personal experience as a French naval officer, combining travel adventures and eroticism. During one of his trips to Nagasaki, Loti posited his undisputable right to obtain a temporary wife while in Japan. Giacomo Puccini's opera *Madama Butterfly* created in the Western world the stereotype of the Japanese woman as the perfect wife whose loyalty, femininity, and readiness to obey exalts men's feeling of dominion (Littlewood, 1996: 124). In this sense there is no difference between the Japanese woman and the artistically and sexually enticing geisha, whose demure and pleasant personality makes the journey to Japan special for foreigners. But even before Giacomo Puccini debuted *Madama Butterfly*, turning the persona of Pinkerton into a new Commodore Perry and *alter ego* of Pierre Loti, the Italian audience was already familiar with the image of Japan as feminine "Other" through the lofty eroticism of Gabriele D'Annnunzio (1863–1938), as presented in his early stories. In 1884 he published a short story titled *Mandarina* in the journal *Capitan Fracassa*. The story's protagonist is the marquise Aurora Canale, whose nickname "mandarina" comes from her infatuation with Japanese art, fashion and culture. She is a Roman noblewoman but longs to live a romance in perfect Japanese style. She thus falls in love with the secretary of the Japanese embassy, the chevalier Sakumi. Her attempt to qualify as an authentic geisha by acting

---

1 Politically, the persona of the Japanese woman, her submission and her readiness to sacrifice herself correspond to the image of Japan as a subordinated civilization in comparison to the hard-male world of the West. This aspect of Japanese representation was particularly evident in Italy during the Fascist "Ventennio," where the nationalistic claim of an allegedly superior Italian civilization (as descended from Roman civilization) was the implicit premise on which feminine images of Japan were justified. In his book *Nel Giappone dei grattacieli: viaggio da Tokio a Dehli*, the Italian travel writer and colonial novelist Arnaldo Cipolla employs the metaphor of the woman to belittle the overall representation of the visited country: Arnaldo Cipolla, 1931, *Nel Giappone dei grattacieli: viaggio da Tokio a Delhi* (Turin: Paravia): 97. The methaphoric representation of Japan as a feminine country clearly serves the purpose of nationalistic propaganda: Japan appears to be a fearful nation whose violent instincts are kept repressed ("assenza di atti esteriori violenti" [absence of violent external acts]). It is a country meant to be dominated, its will exploited to make sacrifices and to bear heavy burdens ("spirito di sacrificio, resistenza al dolore" [spirit of sacrifice, resistance to pain]).

in an artistically sophisticated manner results in a grotesque caricature when the chevalier makes his sexual desire clear:

> Mandarina teneva li occhi socchiusi, come per trattenere fra le palpebre una visione fuggitiva; abbandonava il tenue fior delle membra sotto i gelsomini e i bambù della veste primaverile. E sospirò alfine, dopo un intervallo di silenzio:
> Sakumi!
> E Sakumi che le stava seduto da canto e che in quell'intervallo aveva faticosamente cercata una frase, il cavaliere Sakumi con uno sforzo di sillabazione grottesco disse alfine:
> *Je voudrais bien coucher avec vous, Madame!* (D'Annunzio, 2010: 10)

> [Mandarina kept her eyes half-closed, as if to keep a fugitive vision between her eyelids; she abandoned the soft flower of her limbs under the jasmine and the bamboo of the spring dress. And he sighed at last, after a period of silence:
> – Sakumi!
> And Sakumi, who was seated by her, and had laboriously searched for a sentence in that interval, the knight Sakumi, with a grotesque spelling effort, said in the end:
> *Je voudrais bien coucher avec vous, Madame!*]

As soon as the marquise puts herself in the shoes of an exotic geisha she cannot help but cause the chevalier's sexual turmoil.[2]

All of these images of the Japanese woman are the result of a male gaze. The dominant image of Butterfly can hardly be challenged since we rarely find male writers attempting to revise the Orientalist myth of the Japanese woman as a commodity. This is not to say, however, that such a trope has not been contested by exposing the gaps and the aberration that similar representations entail. For example, James Clifford writes:

> Cultures are not scientific "objects" (assuming such things exist, even in the natural sciences). Culture, and our views of "it," are produced historically, and are actively contested. There is no whole picture that can be

---

2   For a detailed account of the cult for the Japanese women in Italy see Anna Lisa Somma, 2016, "*Una perfetta giapponese*: la costruzione *japoisant* del Giappone e della *musmè* ne *La veste di crespo* di Matilde Serao," *Lingue, Culture, Mediazioni*, 3(2): 135–52.

"filled in," since the perception and filling of a gap lead to the awareness of other gaps. (Clifford and Marcus, 1986: 18)

Following Clifford's line of thought, feminist critics objected to Edward Said's *Orientalism* for being a monolithic account of Western encounters with the East that only considers male perspectives. They maintain that women's travel accounts question the legitimacy of the male colonialist discourse by presenting alternatives mode of representations. Clifford suggests that during the Victorian or Edwardian era women travelers were not necessarily contesting the common rules of their own societies, as their way of posing as foreigners and performing their own national identities were still modeled after a predominant male subjectivity: "Women travelers were forced to conform, masquerade, or rebel discreetly within a set of normatively male definitions and experiences" (Clifford and Marcus, 1986: 18). It is undeniable that women travelers and writers had aspirations to match their male peers, for example by embarking on long-distance journeys and having their travelogs published.

Sara Mills and others (for example, Lowe, 1991) are cognizant of the heterogeneous and contingent network of discourses existing under the generic label of Orientalism(s), to the point that they reject essentializing views predicated upon a supposedly "male-only" Orientalism, as opposed to a female alliance with the colonized in the name of a common condition of oppression. Mills makes clear that women travelers can be as Orientalist as men, especially when the two genders share the perspective that their nationality is superior to the non-Western country visited. However, she asserts that women's travel writing is more likely to escape the trap of objectifying the "Other" within a racial or gender category. According to Mills, as the woman herself is the object of a sexualized gaze, she is potentially more aware of the imperial discourse's leveling effects of reducing individuals to types. Therefore, women's travel writing may present elements more likely to "act as a critique of the colonialist enterprise since there is a stress on personal involvement" and therefore be more inclined to see "people from other countries as individuals" (Mills, 1991: 105).

The case of Italian women travelers to Japan, when discussed against the backdrop of Sara Mills' and Mary Louise Pratt's analyses of Victorian women travelogs, invites consideration related to representations of the Orient. Barbara Spackman has used the definition of "accidental Orientalists" to single out nineteenth- and early twentieth-century Italian travel writers to the Middle East as they only partially conform to the model of canonical

Orientalists (Spackman, 2017: 3–5). In fact, if Orientalist discourses share a common pan-European ideology, the *geography* of Orientalism – that is, the positions and locations of the travelers in relation to the countries visited – must be factored in as an element. In this regard, the heterogeneous and fragile Italian identity will possibly express less resistance to alternative and fluid identities encountered abroad, despite the inevitable replication of quintessentially Oriental tropes.

Finally, the examples of women's writing that I analyze in this chapter present more complex and nuanced views of Japanese women, as the travelogs mostly cover eras outside the chronology of Said's *Orientalism*. Specifically, the literature I examine relates to the second half of the twentieth century, with particular concentration on the 1980s. Compared to more popular examples of Anglo-Saxon women travel narratives, Italian women travelogs about Japan published during this period are compelling as they set up a comparison between societies in which women's status is arguably less advanced. Indeed, solidarity between women of different nationalities and ethnicities can be surprisingly strong in the case of Italian women in Japan, because a network of social and cultural similarities enables a process of gender identification. Italy and Japan are traditionally considered patriarchal societies in which women are entangled in a web of circumstances, obligations and events that make their role subaltern to that of the man. In Italy this trope features a woman who is sexually enticing but also chaste and family oriented, a maternal figure who, above all, never crosses certain lines imposed by her role as an ideal housewife. Yet this scenario was subject to change during this time period. For Japan and Italy, the 1980s represented a decade of rapid modernization and attaining prosperity. The respective economic successes of these countries implied rapid social changes in terms of traditional values and, above all, gender relations, which were reevaluated as a result of improvements in education and unprecedented material wealth. Against this backdrop, the woman's role also undertook a profound transformation in both countries, although with different results.

The fact that most travelogs about Japan penned by Italian women were published during this period is, in itself, evidence of an ongoing revision of gender roles. In Italy, the golden age for the emancipation of women was from 1968 (the year of the student movement) to 1980. These twelve years of political and cultural upheaval saw the emergence of a widespread feminist movement stirring discussion about women's rights as well as the achievement of some political victories, such as the 1978 law legalizing abortion (Willson, 2010: 149). Italian women visiting Japan encountered disruptions to traditionally gendered roles. The transitioning gender politics in Japan, as well as a strengthening economy, spurred Japanese women to pursue a more independent lifestyle, including the choice of traveling abroad. During the decades of 1980s and 1990s, "backed by the high yen and the overvalued economy, young women began traveling abroad in ever-increasing numbers, eventually surpassing by 1990, the number of young men engaging in foreign travel by a margin of 2 to 1" (Kelsky, 2001: 2). The peak of this phenomenon was the early 1990s, often referred to in Japan as *onna no jidai* ("the era of women"), followed by a backlash against gender equality throughout the subsequent decade that still persists today (Fujimura-Fanselow, 2011: 337–55).[3] Key legislation working to reduce Japan's gender gap was the 1985 Equal Employment Opportunity Law (EEOL) and the 1991 Child Care Leave Law, which established the right to unpaid child leave for either parent for up to one year following childbirth. As result of these significant policy victories, more women joined the labor force and, in general, increased their participation in social and political life outside the domestic sphere.

This chapter considers the rising post-war phenomenon of women struggling for gender equality, both in Italy and Japan, as the authors discussed in the following pages belong to this period. This is not to say that the 1970s is a unique period of improvement for women rights: in fact, comparative research focused exclusively on the Japanese and Italian cases should also consider the early years of the twentieth century as a foundation for this history. In Italy, the tendency toward excluding women from the public arena in the aftermath of the political unification was, at least partially, tempered by the surging of a feminist and suffragist movement at the start of the 1900s. Women from different social classes and political orientations took the stage: Teresa Labriola (1874–1941, the first woman to become professor in Italy's male-dominated academia) or Maria Montessori (1870–1952) among others, were part of a first wave of an Italian feminist and suffragist movement leading to the foundation of a National Committee for Women's Suffrage in 1910 (Re, 2010: 38; Willson, 2010: 24–25;

---

3   On Japanese women see also: Louise Edwards and Mina Roces (editors), 2000, *Women in Asia: Tradition, Modernity, and Globalization* (Ann Arbor: University of Michigan Press); Kumiko Fujimura-Fanselow and Atsuko Kameda (editors), 1995, *Japanese Women: New Feminist Perspectives on the Past, Present, and Future* (New York: Feminist Press at the City University of New York); Sumiko Iwao, 1993, *The Japanese Woman: Traditional Image and Changing Reality* (New York: Free Press; Toronto: Maxwell Macmillan Canada; New York: Maxwell Macmillan International); Takie Sugiyama Lebra, 1984, *Japanese Women: Constraint and Fulfillment* (Honolulu: University of Hawaii Press).

Bassnett, 1986: 98–100). Meanwhile, around the same time period in Japan, a feminist movement was on the rise in reaction to policies that limited women's political participation and marginalized their role in the public sphere. In 1911 Hiratsuka Raichō (1886–1971) founded the journal *Seitō* ["Bluestocking"], to challenge well-established conservative gender views, with a series of issues devoted to topics ranging from abortion to prostitution and drinking alcohol. The publication served also as a platform for feminist writers with alternative political views, including the socialist Yamakawa Kikue (1890–1980), who voiced the lack of support for lower-class women in the socialist movement and accused the feminist group of being elitist. Japanese women were also engaged in a suffrage movement that led to the creation of a New Women's Association (Shin Fujin Kyōkai) in 1919, even though, in the 1920s, the state progressively succeeded in channeling the feminist movement toward a subservient role in promoting the nation's, as well as the individual household's, larger interests. For instance, Ichikawa Fusae (1893–1981), although a liberal suffragist, also supported a revision of the Civil Code during the war – which established systematic gender inequality in the household and limited women's political participation – and became a staunch supporter of the state campaign for women to boost savings and reduce consumption (Faison, 2018; Bardsley, 2003; Garon, 1998).

Eventually, the decline of this first wave of Japanese and Italian feminist movements came as result of a nationalistic turn in both countries that generated the formation of new gender roles. The "New Woman" of Italian Fascism "was to embody an ideal of female self-sacrifice, whether in her role as the supreme wife and mother or as sexual object for the 'New Man,' aggrandizing male virility" (Pickering-Iazzi, 1993: xi). In Japan during the 1920s, women continued to advance their quest for social justice, by enlisting in their movement socialist organizations (such as the Red Wave Society [Sekirankai] and the Eighth Day Society [Yōkakai]), which expanded the political base of the movement to the working class. However, in the following decade, state-sponsored female organizations demanded that women back the war effort, by designing forms of public service that extended a "nurturing" role from the domestic to the public space, offering support to soldiers, wounded and sick fellow Japanese.

Finally, if 1968 was a watershed moment for the post-war feminist movement in Italy, the 1970s was a renaissance period for feminist activism in Japan as well, featuring the emergence of the *ūman ribu* (women's liberation) movement. Unlike previous calls for action, this new season of women's mobilization was more radical in scope and more transnational in its ramifications. Challenging the Japanese patriarchy was one of the main points on the political agenda, together with a focus on women's sexuality and their independence from state policies. This new form of activism – like the Italian case – was inspired by the student movements and revolutionary action of the New Left. However, activists of the *ribu* movement protested against the sexist practices of the Japanese left and the phallocentric assumptions underpinning them. The transnational scope of *Ūman ribu* is expressed by the name itself, which loosely transliterates the English term "woman lib" as an ideal reference to the larger context of the feminist movement outside of Japan. While focusing on their domestic political issues, women activists in Japan were looking at the transnational scene, ranging from the United States to Asia and Europe, as a way to build on commonalities, or at least on solidarity and dialog. Therefore, Italian women writers who visited Japan in this period were confronted with a reassessment of gender power relationships that was similar to the one they were experiencing at home. In the examples of Italian women discussed in the following pages awareness of being part of the same transnational network is certainly lacking; in fact the Italian travelers often (with the exception of Antonietta Pastore) speak from a position of Western superiority *vis-à-vis* a non-Western society. However, I argue that the *experience* of being in Japan, in close proximity to the Japanese "Other," occasionally produced the unexpected effect that they reconsidered such stereotypes by acknowledging the progress that Japanese women had made.

    The Italian writer and feminist activist Dacia Maraini (1936–) provides an ideal example of this type of new emancipated woman, not so much by virtue of her literary production (her travelogs are mainly newspaper articles and account for a minimal part of her work),[4] but rather by querying conventional gender assumptions related to her parents' travel narratives to Japan. As the daughter of Fosco Maraini and, as noted in the previous chapter, as Alberto Moravia's partner for more than twenty years, Dacia Maraini maintained an ongoing familiarity with Japan that started in her early childhood. Her first journey to the country dates back to 1938, when Dacia was only two years old as her father decided to relocate the family to Sapporo, on the island of Hokkaido, in order to pursue his research on the local Ainu population. Together they spent five years in Japan, during which time Dacia's siblings, Yuki Luisa and Antonella Kiku (who later became the writer Toni Maraini), were born. While Dacia has only fragmented memories of her childhood in Japan, she nevertheless situates her biography within

---

4   See Dacia Maraini, 2010, *La seduzione dell'altrove* (Milan: Rizzoli).

her parents' biographies by editing and publishing first her mother's journal of the first three years the family spent in Japan (*La nave per Kobe*) (2003) ["The ship for Kobe"], then her father's notes, journals and poems about his experiences abroad (*Il Gioco dell'universo: Dialoghi immaginari tra un padre e una figlia* (2007) ["The Game of the Universe. Imaginary Dialogs between a Father and a Daughter"]. In both cases the "Self" of the editor collapses the distance in regard to the author by glossing and expanding the notes of mother and father, in fact, conceiving a relational autobiography which is constructed in opposition to the traditional male narratives predicated upon the creation of an independent and autonomous self.

Taking up the notion of a relational feminist autobiography, Cinzia Sartini-Blum considers *La Nave per Kobe* a "hybrid text" that "makes creative use of conventional genres" (Sartini-Blum, 2008: 161). She encourages us to read this text as an indirect "response to one specific instance of male self-representation, the [Fosco Maraini's] autobiographical novel *Case, amori, universi* (1999) ["Houses, loves, universes"] (Sartini-Blum, 2008: 163). While the father's narrative of the family's days in Japan is individualistic and self-centered, that of Dacia/Topazia centers on the interior lives of women in terms of "the role of domestic life and affective ties" and, above all, the mother's "insights into the impact of the internment on her husband and on the couple's (deteriorating) relationship" (Sartini-Blum, 2008: 163).

Perhaps the idea of considering *La Nave per Kobe* as a rehabilitation of the familiar memories omitted from Fosco Maraini's autobiography should be revised after the publication of the above mentioned *Il gioco dell'universo* (2007) ["The game of the universe"], a book in which the daughter enacts a celebratory dialog with her father by addressing him with words such as "beloved." The subjectivity the father constructs in his notes is often criticized for being aloof and uncaring toward the rest of the family: "Vado disperatamente cercando in questi quaderni di mio padre notizie della famiglia [...] Contrariamente ai diari di mia madre, in questi quaderni di Fosco non si parla quasi mai della famiglia" (Maraini, Dacia and Fosco, 2007: 138) [I go desperately looking for my news about my family in my father's notebooks [...] Unlike my mother's diary, in these notebooks of Fosco the family is hardly mentioned]. In the conclusion Dacia makes clear that what motivated her in publishing these paternal notes was less a desire to extoll her father's memory and more to make good on a promise that she made to him.[5] A proud

---

5   In a 2007 interview Dacia Maraini explained that Fosco Maraini had initially signed a contract with Mondadori to publish his collection of notes but, then, upon his death

sense of loyalty and accountability prevails over affection and praise for her father's exceptionality: "[Sono] una lavoratrice imperterrita, che crede nella disciplina e negli impegni presi" (Maraini, Dacia and Fosco, 2007: 190) [I am an undeterred worker who believes in discipline and commitments].

Even though Dacia Maraini does not write her own Japanese travel narrative she manages to retroactively modify the gender bias often given in such accounts. By resuming the Japanese diary of her mother, while underscoring the male assumptions left undetected in her father's self-portrait ("Una volta sposati, i ruoli si sono stabilizzati nel senso più tradizionale: lui in viaggio, al lavoro, e lei a casa con le figlie," Maraini, Dacia and Fosco, 2007: 41 [Once married, the roles have stabilized in the most traditional sense: he is traveling, at work, and she is at home with his daughters]), she ultimately strives to interrogate for the reader the gender politics at stake in her family. Even if she was confined to the domestic space, her mother too had the ability and curiosity to encounter and inhabit foreign cultures:

> La domanda che segue è: ma mia madre, la bella Topazia, figlia di un duca siciliano e di una selvaggia cantante cilena, era anche lei abitata dal demone del viaggio? O semplicemente seguiva mio padre, per amore? Pur non essendo una esploratrice come Fosco, la ragazza siciliana aveva nel sangue l'esperienza dell'altrove. (Maraini Dacia, 2010: 15)

> [The following question is: but my mother, the beautiful Topazia, daughter of a Sicilian duke and a savage Chilean singer, was also inhabited by the demon of the journey? Or did she simply follow my father, out of love? Although not an explorer like Fosco, the Sicilian girl had the experience of the elsewhere in her blood.]

An important dimension of these Italian women's travelogs is how critical they are about the issue of women's rights in Japan. By looking at the Japanese model of housewife, Italian women find validations of their own lifestyle or value system (Foster and Mills, 2002: 14). They identify themselves as a positive alternative to the allegedly backward system of gender relations in Japan. It seems that by comparing their status to that of Japanese women,

---

he asked his daughter to bring the project to completion. See Luciana Sica, 2007, "'Mio padre Fosco eterno Peter Pan,'" *Il mio libro*, February 20, 2007. Available at https://ilmiolibro.kataweb.it/recensione/catalogo/6225/mio-padre-fosco-eterno-peter-pan/?refresh_ce (accessed April 20, 2018).

they demarcate their own identity as independent women. Solidarity and concern for members of their own sex conflict with chauvinistic values: by wanting Japanese women to enjoy the same privileges as they do, they affirm the superiority of Italian culture and consider their country as a template for human rights to which every culture should aspire.

We can also consider an alternative interpretation. Even though these observers generally depict Japanese women as subordinate, they occasionally notice the improvement of women's rights in Japan by focusing on elements that do not fit the traditional picture of the passive Butterfly. My readings of the accounts of Japanese women by Italian women emphasize these unconventional traits in order not only to question Western conventions but also to show how these unexpected elements "provoke recognition that other patterns of female behavior offer more freedom and opportunities than Western women enjoy" (Foster and Mills eds., 2002: 14).

Among the women's travelogs examined in this chapter, the example of Antonietta Pastore in particular demonstrates how a debunking of several stereotypes about Japanese mores results in a reconsideration of Italian upbringing and values. Subsequently, as I show, this makes her more aware of differences while helping her to overcome perceived cultural barriers. For Italian women, a consideration of gender identity represents an opportunity to communicate with the "Other" based on the common ground of a shared gender in relation to men. The core of this communication focuses on "sexual mores, marriage customs and the position of women," which are delicate points for writers struggling to carry on the battle for women's rights.

2. A Japanese Nightmare

Another Italian woman writer, Angela Terzani Staude (1939–) spent five years in Japan between 1985 and 1990. Unlike Angelina Fatta (see ch. 1), she came to Japan with her Italian husband, the well-known writer and journalist Tiziano Terzani (1938–2004), whose expertise on East Asian countries had a strong influence on his wife. She was born in Florence to German parents and studied in Munich. Terzani Staude began as an editorial writer by translating Titus Burckhardt's *L'Alchimia* (1961) and *Scienza moderna e saggezza tradizionale* (1968) into Italian. In 1987 she served as editor of the volume *Japan: The Beauty of Food*, with photographs by Reinhart Wolf. In 1972 she joined her husband on his journey around Asia as a correspondent for the famous German weekly *Der Spiegel*. Over roughly thirty years Terzani

Staude's family lived in Singapore, Beijing, Tokyo, Hong Kong, Bangkok, and Delhi, following Terzani, who was on the front lines covering epic historical events such as the end of the Vietnam War and transformations in Maoist China. Terzani Staude's experience of the Asian continent inspired the writing *Giorni cinesi* (1987) ["Chinese days"], a diary of her three years spent in China between 1980 and 1983. As a follow-up, *Giorni giapponesi* (1994) focuses on her time in Japan, about which she expresses an uneasiness and anxiety about her Japanese life:

> Se penso agli anni che ho passato in Giappone (1985–1990) assieme a mio marito Tiziano e ai nostri due figli, mi vengono in mente i coniugi Webb che nel 1932 tornarono dall'Unione Sovietica con la famosa frase: "Abbiamo visto il futuro e funziona!" Ma devo metterla al negativo. Noi, in quei cinque anni vissuti a Tokyo come famiglia, non ci siamo mai tolti di dosso l'impressione che quella vita non fosse fatta per noi. Non fosse fatta neppure per i giapponesi. Non fosse fatta per l'essere umano. Avevamo visto il futuro e non funzionava. (Terzani Staude, 1994: vii)

> [When I think of the years I spent in Japan (1985–1990) together with my husband Tiziano and our two sons, I am reminded of the Webb spouses who in 1932 returned from the Soviet Union with the famous phrase: "We have seen the future and it works!" But I have to put it to the negative. We, in those five years lived in Tokyo as a family, we never removed the impression that this life was not for us. It was not even for the Japanese. It was not made for the human being. We had seen the future and it did not work.]

Because of her husband's job as correspondent for *Der Spiegel*, Terzani Staude lived her Japanese days inside the protective cocoon of a group of Western journalists and writers, such as the American Donald Richie and the Dutch writer Karel van Wolferen. Her encounter and subsequent negative appraisal of her journey must thus be filtered through the network of Western intellectuals who were also appalled by the rising of the so-called *Jap-inc.* as a worldwide superpower.[6] Among those writers and journalists,

---

6 As Tiziano Terzani recalls: "Quando siamo arrivati in Giappone, a metà degli anni '80, la storia che affascinava il mondo era che tecnologicamente il paese era avanzatissimo rispetto a noi, no? Adesso non ci fa più paura, ma allora il Giappone era la grande minaccia economica e non era affatto escluso che nell'anno 2000 non avrebbe dominato

the influence of her husband is by far the most forceful on Terzani Staude's views. When he recalls the time spent in Japan Terzani reaches the same conclusion as his wife:

> Era triste vedere una civiltà così particolare che si suicidava, con 120 milioni di persone che ansimavano per competere economicamente con l'Occidente. I poveri giapponesi mi facevano pena, li vedevo così degradati, così disumanizzati, così soli, così poco persone. Ruoli! Questa società, di tutte quelle che poi finisco per criticare, era la più dura.
> Spingeva l'uomo verso comportamenti standard dal momento in cui si alzava fino a che, vomitando, buttava di nuovo la testa sul guanciale. (Terzani, 2006: 263)

[It was sad to see such a unique civilization commit suicide, with 120 million people panting to compete economically with the West. The poor Japanese made me feel sorry, I saw them so degraded, so dehumanized, so alone, so little humans. Roles! This society, of all those that I end up criticizing, was the hardest. It pushed the man toward standard behaviors from the moment he got up until he threw his head back on the pillow, while vomiting.]

The consequence of this negative impact of the new country was that Terzani went through a difficult period of depression, which must be taken into account when considering Terzani Staude's point of view:

> Avevo tempo e silenzio: qualcosa di così necessario, di così naturale, ma ormai diventato un lusso che solo pochissimi riescono a permettersi. Per questo dilaga la depressione!
> A me era cominciata in Giappone. La vita era una continua corsa piena, di doveri. Ogni rapporto era difficile, contorto. Non avevo – o credevo di non avere – mai un momento in cui tirare il fiato; mai un attimo in cui non mi sentissi in colpa per qualcos'altro che avrei dovuto fare. Mi alzavo la mattina e mi pareva di avere sulle spalle il fardello del mondo; c'erano giorni in cui il solo vedere il pacco dei quotidiani sotto la porta di casa mi faceva venire il groppo in gola.

il mondo": Tiziano Terzani, 2006, *La fine è il mio inizio*, edited by Folco Terzani (Milano: Longanesi): 56.

Ovviamente il Giappone in sé, con la sua società tutta in una camicia di forza, con la sua gente sempre a recitare una parte e mai naturale, era opprimente. (Terzani, 2011: vol. 2, 302–03)

[I had time and silence: something so necessary, so natural, but now they have become a luxury that only very few can afford. This is why depression is rampant!

It had started in Japan. Life was a continuous full run, of duties. Every relationship was difficult, twisted. I never had – I thought – a moment to breathe; never a moment when I did not feel guilty about everything else I should have done. I got up in the morning and it seemed to me that I had the burden of the world on my shoulders; there were days when just seeing the parcel of newspapers under the door gave me a lump in my throat.

Obviously, Japan itself was oppressive, with its society all in a straitjacket, with its people always playing a part and never natural.]

Her husband's influence on Terzani Staude's views is remarkable not only for his ideas, but also because it determined the network of people with whom she came into contact with during her days in Japan. Even the local people that she encountered were not met by chance but were Japanese journalists and intellectuals who had experience in dealing with Europeans and Americans. This was the case with Otomo, a journalist charged with accompanying Terzani and his wife on his journey. Terzani Staude had the opportunity to meet Japanese women intellectuals with Westernized educations and values, such as the feminist activist Shidzué Ishimoto, whose autobiography *Facing Two Ways: The Story of my Life* (1935) brought her international recognition.[7] The core of Ishimoto's ideas was not "made in Japan" but originated in the American wave of the feminist movement that she experienced during her several journeys to the United States.

---

7   At the time of the encounter with the Terzanis Ishimoto was a popular speaker and advocate of women's rights. In an interview with the Italian journalist she stated: "I giapponesi non hanno coscienza. Dietro l'Occidente industrializzato c'è almeno il cristianesimo, per cui anche le persone non religiose sanno cos'è bene e cos'è male; cosa è giusto e cosa ingiusto. Ai giapponesi, che non possiedono testi sacri, questo criterio manca. L'uomo onesto cerca di rimanere fedele a se stesso e si dice: 'Manterrò la fede nell'imperatore e nella bandiera giapponese!' E lo dice per quanto questi ideali si siano rivelati falsi: altri valori cui rifarsi non mancano": Angela Terzani Staude, 1994, *Giorni giapponesi* (Milan: Longanesi): 180.

Among her favorite acquaintances there was Steven Platzer from the University of Chicago, whose major effort consisted in making the public aware of the alleged threat represented by Japanese ambitions to rule the world:

> Steven Platzer, il suo [Tiziano Terzani] nuovo amico e alleato, un iamatologo americano della Chicago University incontrato un giorno per caso davanti al palazzo imperiale e diventato da allora un frequentatore abituale della nostra casa, sostiene che i suoi ideologi sono i filosofi della scuola di Kyoto degli anni '30, influenzati dal pensiero della destra tedesca: gli ideologi della "giapponesità." I politici di oggi, dice, continuano a orientarsi su quel modello di sviluppo nato negli anni '30. Per fortuna dei giapponesi, è un modello estremamente efficace che ha permesso al paese di diventare una potenza economica vincente. Il fine di questo "sistema giapponese" sarebbe la dominazione del mondo. Il suo prezzo, il controllo totale del cittadino. (Terzani Staude, 1994: 174)

[Steven Platzer – Tiziano Terzani's new friend and ally, an American iamatologist from Chicago University, whom we met one day by chance in front of the imperial palace and has since become a regular visitor to our home – claims that today's Japan ideologists are the Kyoto school philosophers of the 1930s, influenced by the thought of the German right: the ideologists of "Japaneseness." Today's politicians, he says, continue to orient themselves on that model of development born in the 1930s. Fortunately for the Japanese, it is an extremely effective model that has enabled the country to become a winning economic power. The end of this "Japanese system" would be the domination of the world. Its price consists in the total control of the citizen.]

Platzer would go on to be the English translator of *Educational Thought and Ideology in Modern Japan* (1988) by Teruhisa Horio, a Japanese professor at the University of Tokyo, who is also a leading activist against the Japanese Ministry of Education's sponsored ideology that is predominant in the nation's public schools.

Finally, another relevant figure in Terzani's environment is the Dutch journalist, writer, and professor Karel van Wolferen (1941–), who lived in Japan for thirty years. At the end of this period he published the book *The Enigma of Japanese Power* (1989), an articulate investigation into the system of censorship and repression that lies behind Japanese economic achievements.

The list of illustrious scholars and keystone books that are quoted in Terzani Staude's diary is even longer, but those mentioned here are enough to accentuate the common ground on which they stand: they all represent a critical voice regarding the paradigm of "Japan as Number One" (to quote Ezra Vogel's essay), that is, they oppose the large movement of cultural and political consensus in support of Japan's rise as a superpower (the so-called "Japanese Phoenix") from the debris of World War II. Terzani Staude's diary is embedded in this movement of "historical revisionism" that came to the fore at the end of the Cold War in terms of an international reassessment of geopolitical forces at the end of the Communist threat. It is an international movement that is mainly American, and French to a lesser degree, and that has no relevance in the Italian intellectual context; for this reason Staude's references are, above all, in English. Such a critical voice was hardly popular during the 1980s, but drew more favorable attention a few years later when the Japanese economic bubble burst and the revisionists' theses gained momentum. In Patrick Smith's words:

> At the brink of the Cold War's end the Chrysanthemum Club [by which Smith means those intellectuals who, during the Cold War, were uncritical apologists of Japan] was openly challenged for the first time in many years. It was the challenge of journalists and scholars known as the revisionists. They were (and remain) a loose group; on many questions they are far from universal agreement. None of them especially likes the revisionist label (as members of the Chrysanthemum Club did not like theirs). But they are legitimately bound by a simple assumption: The paradigm is false; the West should reassess the way it looks at Japan. [...]
>
> Revisionism arrived like fresh air in a windowless room. It was an act of creative destruction in that it began the work of dismantling the post-war paradigm. It bore no ideological load, no Cold War imperative, so that it made the prospect of clear sight at last realistic. (Smith, 1997: 154, 157)

Like these revisionists, Terzani Staude warns Italian readers about the fallaciousness of the Japanese paradigm:

> I giapponesi sono sempre stati bravissimi nell'imporre al mondo un'immagine pubblicitaria del loro paese e hanno sempre avuto i loro "protagonisti." Personaggi come D.T. Suzuki, il divulgatore dello zen

come espressione di un misticismo eminentemente giapponese, e Inazo Nitobe, che progagò l'idea che il Giappone fosse una civiltà così misteriosa e raffinata da non poter essere capita da nessuno, hanno dato enormi contributi nel quadro di questa opera di propaganda e disinformazione.

Oggi, fondazioni giapponesi e gruppi di pressione come la lobby giapponese a Washington, la più grande fra le lobby americane, portano efficientemente avanti il lavoro di quei personaggi del passato. L'utilità del loro operato è stata eloquentemente espressa da un filosofo di Kyoto studiato dal Platzer che disse: "Controlleremo il mondo quando controlleremo quel che il mondo pensa del Giappone." (Terzani Staude, 1994: 221-22)

[The Japanese have always been very good at imposing an advertising image of their country to the world and have always had their "protagonists." Personalities like D.T. Suzuki, the popularizer of Zen as an expression of an eminently Japanese mysticism, and Inazo Nitobe, who conceived the idea that Japan was such a mysterious and refined civilization that it could not be understood by anyone, made enormous contributions in the context of this activity of propaganda and disinformation.

Today, Japanese foundations and pressure groups like the Japanese lobby in Washington, the largest of the American lobbies, efficiently carry on the work of those characters from the past. The usefulness of their work was eloquently expressed by a Kyoto philosopher studied by Platzer who said: "We will control the world when we will control what the world thinks of Japan."]

Since Terzani Staude's goal is to debunk a well-established trope about Japan, she offers a revised image of the Japanese woman. While she notes the subjugation of the wife to the husband and the mother-in-law, she also emphasizes an ongoing change in gender relations. "Butterflies," whose former goal was to please their husbands at all costs, were now gaining slightly more authority and independence despite appearances:

Le donne, obbligate a consumarsi servendo la suocera e gli anziani, lo hanno fatto docilmente per secoli. "Non sarai felice, ma diventerai forte," diceva la madre alla figlia che si sposava, avvolgendole la testa con un panno bianco, il giorno del matrimonio, in modo da nascondere le sue "corna," la sua volontà. Nel corso di centinaia d'anni di questa scuola, la donna si è liberata dalla indipendenza sentimentale del suo sposo.

La sua dipendenza oggi è puramente finanziaria; questa certo è ancora grande perché il Giappone non permette alle donne di emanciparsi e di lavorare. Mi pare però che la donna cominci a raccogliere le proprie forze, freddamente, spietatamente se si vuole, e che gli uomini, ingaggiati nella guerra economica e meno liberi di pensare, d'informarsi, di sbizzarrirsi, comincino a rendersi conto che le donne, che fanno tante belle moine e che parlano la loro lingua "mite," in verità recitano una parte: e sempre più controvoglia. (Terzani Staude, 1994: 52)

[Women, obliged to consume themselves by serving their mother-in-law and the elderly, have done it meekly for centuries. "You will not be happy, but you will become strong," said the mother to the daughter who was getting married, wrapping her head with a white cloth on the wedding day, so as to hide her "horns," her will. Over the course of hundreds of years of this school, the woman has freed herself from the sentimental independence of her husband. Her dependence today is purely financial; which is still relevant because Japan does not allow women to emancipate themselves and work. It seems to me, however, that the woman begins to gather her strength, coldly, ruthlessly, if you want, and that men, engaged in the economic war and less free to think, to inquire, to indulge, begin to realize that women are very affected and that they speak their "mild" language, in truth they play a part: and they do it more and more unwillingly.]

Terzani Staude concludes that Japanese women have mastered the role of playing "Madama Butterfly" as soon as their husbands arrive home or when couples have to make public appearances. The women of the 1980s still shoulder the burden of marriage duties; nevertheless, according to Terzani Staude, they are increasingly comfortable with the life they live since they can make the best of a situation in which they disguise their identities in order to gain room for freedom and independence. This is what Terzani Staude determines by listening to the story of Ayako, her husband's secretary, an educated girl who lived in the United States for a few years before returning home and settling down with a Japanese husband:

"Una volta sposate, noi giapponesi partiamo dal presupposto che il matrimonio deve durare fino alla morte," mi spiega Ayako nel suo modo piacevole e diretto. "Escludiamo la possibilità del divorzio e accettiamo il marito com'è. Tutt'al più cerchiamo, per amore dei figli, di stringere un po' d'amicizia con lui. Voi vi rifiutate di vivere con un uomo che non amate e ci commiserate perché i nostri mariti non sono mai a casa. Noi invece diciamo: 'Il marito ideale è sano e sempre fuori' [...] perché così siamo libere di fare quel che vogliamo. Io sono contenta così. Non so però cosa sia meglio" (Terzani Staude, 1994: 85)

["Once married, we Japanese people assume that marriage must last until death," Ayako explains to me in her pleasant and direct way. "We exclude the possibility of divorce and accept the husband as he is. At the most we try, for the sake of our children, to develop some sort of friendship with him. You [Western women] refuse to live with a man you do not love and commiserate us because our husbands are never at home. We instead say: 'The ideal husband is healthy and always out' [...] because we are free to do what we want. In this way I'm happy. But I do not know what is better"]

The traditional image of the Japanese family in which the man holds absolute authority and the woman is unconditionally loyal and faithful is only a façade; what is really happening is a sort of performance in which each actor respects the other's role. This is what Ayako and the journalist Otomo explain to the Terzanis:

Tiziano s'informa con Ayako sui costumi delle giapponesi.
    "Di che cosa si meraviglia tuo marito?" mi ha poi chiesto lei. "È di moda andare a letto con gli sconosciuti. Da voi no?" "No. Da noi le ragazze vanno a letto con il loro ragazzo." "Sono all'antica! Da noi vanno a letto con chiunque." Otomo dice che le ragazzine preferiscono gli uomini anziani per il semplice fatto che le pagano. Anche le donne sposate cominciano a tenersi un qualche uomo o a frequentare club dove si affittano gli accompagnatori. Otomo questo lo chiama "divorzio interiore" e sostiene che le giapponesi lo preferiscono a quello reale. La moralità non è coinvolta. Il sesso per la donna giapponese è come farsi la doccia, è qualcosa che fa bene alla pelle. (Terzani Staude, 1994: 130)

[Terzani inquires with Ayako about the customs of the Japanese. "What is your husband wondering about?" She asked me. "It's fashionable to go to bed with strangers. Isn't it the same in your country?" "No. In our country girls go to bed with their boyfriend." "They are old-fashioned! We go to bed with anyone." Otomo says that young girls prefer older men for the simple fact that they pay them. Even married women begin to hold on to some man or to go to clubs where they are rented out. Otomo calls this an "inner divorce" and claims that the Japanese prefer it to the real one. Morality is not involved. Sex for the Japanese woman is like taking a shower, it's something that is good for the skin.]

From these examples, which show a lack of lasting moral concerns, disenchantment about any feelings of love, or any sincere behavior, Terzani Staude begins to reflect on her own identity, comparing it with these distant models. By using the Japanese as an alternative example, she draws an image of the 1980s Italian woman – as we can assume by observing her and her husband's reactions to this alternative model – believing in domestic love; they still engage in mutually faithful relationships and do not hesitate to reveal their true feelings, either positive or negative. It is interesting to note that Terzani Staude does not dismiss the alternative as hypocritical and corrupt; on the contrary, she detects positive aspects. On the one hand, she observes that the Japanese woman appears quite satisfied with the life she is living. On the other, despite the supposedly higher level of freedom, the Italian woman feels more anguish and restlessness:

Le donne come categoria non mi hanno mai interessato, né mi interessa in teoria il problema della loro emancipazione, ma le donne giapponesi nella loro disciplinata rassegnazione del tutto priva di aggressività mi ispirano una grande simpatia. In loro non si manifestano mai la rabbia, lo scontento, la frustrazione, il nervosismo che possono rendere le donne occidentali così spiacevoli e come divorate da una quotidiana delusione. (50)

[I have never been interested in women as a category, nor am I interested in the problem of their emancipation in theory, but Japanese women in their disciplined resignation totally devoid of aggression inspire me with great sympathy. They never show the anger, the discontent, the frustration, the nervousness that can make Western women so unpleasant and as devoured by a daily disappointment.]

This observation is similar to that of the American writer Jane Condon. In her book *A Half Step Behind: Japanese Women in the '80s* (1985), she describes the serenity of the Japanese woman's life as opposed to the Western model: American women in Japan are not accustomed to being jostled in the elevator or to having their opinions only begrudgingly listened to. The number one complaint of American women living in Japan is that they are not taken seriously.

But Japanese women have never been first off the elevator. They are accustomed to deferring to men and keeping their opinions to themselves. In one survey of women in six countries, Japanese women topped the list in believing in separate roles for women and men (71 percent); putting one's husband and family first (72 percent); and affirming that housework is the woman's responsibility (89 percent). Another survey revealed that most Japanese men and women were content with their lives, and at 80 percent, compared to 74 percent, women scored even higher than men. The majority of Japanese women are, in short, satisfied with their lot in life. They speak of a web of circumstances, obligations and events that have made their role what it is. Although some talk as if they were indeed caught in a web, others see societal restrictions as a warm and protective cocoon (295).

Terzani Staude, of course, does not go so far as to reassess the image of the Japanese woman of the 1980s, or to use this model to criticize her fellow Italians. Nevertheless, she notices significant shifts within a supposedly immobile Japanese society and observes that women in Japan seem more comfortable with gender roles than Italian women, who, in her view, show more uncertainty and uneasiness.

But this image of the Japanese woman falls short of being representative of Japanese society, insofar as Terzani Staude's encounter with the visited country is obviously limited. Most of the local women mentioned in the diary are highly educated, Westernized people, some of whom have lived in the United States or Europe; they strongly criticize their own society and gender roles in light of Western values. In general, most of the Japanese people that Terzani Staude is in contact with hardly identify themselves with the society to which they belong and they implicitly offer a confirmation of her critical perspective of their lives. For instance, Otomo's criticism of women's identity in Japan is the result of a point of view that is alien to his own society. The person speaking is a Japanese man, but his ideas are equivalent to those of an outsider:

> "Cosa ne pensi delle ragazze giapponesi? Non le trovi ipocrite?" mi ha chiesto Otomo l'altra sera. "In Giappone gli uomini sembrano forti ma in realtà sono deboli; le donne sembrano vittime ma in realtà sono forti e spietate. Da noi la donna gioca il ruolo della madre, tipico in se stesso del matriarcato. È lei che prende tutte le decisioni, è lei che perdona. Con questo tiene in ostaggio il marito." (Terzani Staude, 1994: 53)

["What do you think of Japanese girls? Don't you find them hypocritical?" Otomo asked me the other night. "In Japan, men seem strong but in reality they are weak; women seem victims but in reality they are strong and ruthless. Here the woman plays the role of the mother, which is the typical role of a matriarchal society. It is she who makes all the decisions, it is she who forgives. With this she holds her husband hostage."]

Unlike Otomo, Terzani Staude finds these hints of an oncoming revolution in gender roles attractive; nevertheless, having her own voice (in the diary) supported by alleged representatives of the other world is ultimately satisfying to her.[8]

3. Attempts at Comprehension

Of a completely different sort is the experience of Antonietta Pastore (1946–), a Turin-born writer who spent sixteen years in Japan between 1977 and 1993. While she was studying pedagogy in France under the supervision of Jean Piaget, she met a Japanese man who would eventually become her husband. Together they decided to move to Japan and start a new life.[9] While her husband experienced major problems in developing a career after many years spent abroad, Pastore served as a teacher of French and Italian at the Osaka University of Foreign Studies. During these years Pastore was able to overcome the linguistic barriers by learning to speak and read Japanese, which opened up the opportunity to become one of the most appreciated Italian translators of Japanese novels by the likes of Abe, Ikezawa, Inoue and Murakami. In 2004 she published a book titled *Nel Giappone delle*

---

8   For a similar highly dismissive view of Japan see Renata Pisu, 2000, *Alle radici del sole. I mille volti del Giappone: incontri, luoghi, riti e follie* (Milan: Sperling & Kupfer). She reaches the same conclusion about Japan as a society projected toward an ugly future: "Sarà per questo che il Giappone prefigura, perché già li vive, i nostri futuri incubi" (162).
9   As she states in her account: "Prima di stabilirmi in questo paese ho vissuto a Parigi con mio marito, che è giapponese; insieme a lui conducevo un'esistenza precaria ma spensierata tra studio, lavoro saltuario, letture, frequentazione assidue di cinema *d'art et d'essai*, musei e gallerie. Dopo sette anni però quella vita non ci soddisfaceva più, e il malumore costante dei parigini cominciava a pesarci. Così abbiamo concepito l'idea di trasferirci in Giappone, paese che mi aveva conquistato, durante un primo breve soggiorno, per la cortesia della popolazione e la raffinatezza della cultura": Antonietta Pastore, 2010, *Leggero il passo sui tatami* (Turin: Einaudi): 3–4.

donne ["Women in Japan"], in which she described the condition of the Japanese woman and her place in society by telling the stories of her personal encounters.[10] In 2010 she wrote an autobiographical novel on her Japanese experience, *Leggero il passo sui tatami* ["Light step on the tatami mats"], and, in 2016, a second biographical novel based on the life of a Japanese relative who was an *hibakusha* (an Hiroshima survivor).

The case of Antonietta Pastore is remarkable for many reasons. First, it breaks the traditional narrative that features Japanese women marrying Western men in order to escape the oppressive and backward Japanese husband. According to this narrative, the Western man (usually an American) is the symbol of the liberal and progressive Western society, while the Japanese man represents the feudal and traditional Japan, which has eluded the course of progress. Pastore's experiences reenact a female version of the Western encounter with Japan, querying the traditional narrative by staging an arrival in the East Asian country, a love story with a Japanese man that ends up with her decision to divorce him and eventually to return to her native country. This is a transgressive narrative, not only because it rejects both the patriarchal codes of Western societies and traditional skepticism in Japan for interracial marriage: in fact, it is also a dismissal of the Orientalist plot that reads the exotic love story in Japan, and the subsequent end of it, as an act of metaphorical conquest and submission of the Oriental "Other" by the superior Western visitor. On the contrary, the episode of the divorce is not located at the end of the story, as an abrupt farewell, but is rather a watershed moment that enables the protagonist to experience a deeper understanding and integration with the country visited. In *Leggero il passo sui tatami*, Pastore's decision to divorce her husband (in 1985) serves as the turning point of her story, after which she is able to start a new life, for eight more years, as an independent Italian woman in a country in which marriage is considered an obvious, natural step in a person's life. Unlike other women writers, Pastore does not conceive of her journey in Japan as transitional: even after the divorce, she chooses to stay in the foreign country, trying to build a future and a career that does not include a return home in the short term.

To my knowledge, Pastore is the only Italian woman writer who integrates into Japanese society to the point of marrying a Japanese man and living with him and her parents-in-law for many years. Unlike Terzani Staude, whose resistance to the visited country keeps her at a distance, Pastore has

---

10   In *Nel Giappone delle donne* (2004) Pastore underlines the unequal condition of the Japanese woman, and describes the social constraints and obligations implied in her role.

the existential need to fill the gap between her culture and that of her new relatives. From an initial feeling of displacement and alienation, Pastore is able to gain more confidence and familiarity with her second country day after day. Paradoxically, crucial to the end of the relationship seems to be the fact that Pastore does not accept any judgment of Western superiority at face value, while her husband seems to have embraced an internationalist attitude that brought him to live abroad in order to avoid the dire working situation of the *sarariman* (who must cope with the unbearable stress of the heavy working schedule). Instead, Pastore eschews an initial perception of the lower status accorded to Japanese women in comparison to Western women, thanks to her lasting friendship with Misako, her ex-mother-in-law, with whom mutual understanding and affinity take precedence over cultural differences.

At first this internationalist group helps Pastore strike a balance[11] between her Italian roots and her will to become more familiar with native people:

> Di recente è aumentato il numero dei giapponesi che mio marito ed io frequentiamo, mentre è diminuito quello degli occidentali. Abbiamo stretto amicizia con un gruppo di ex sessantottini che hanno a loro tempo rifiutato di farsi irregimentare nel meccanismo delle grandi ditte private, e si barcamenano svolgendo lavori free lance più o meno creativi nel mondo dello spettacolo e dei mass media. Sono persone alternative che hanno portato nella mia vita una ventata di aria fresca. (Pastore, 2010: 79)

---

11   In other parts of *Leggero il passo sui tatami* Pastore expresses her dissatisfaction about living in the community of foreigners and her desire to be more involved with the natives: "Gli occidentali che frequento sono persone colte e stimolanti, venute a stabilirsi in Giappone per interesse verso questa civiltà. La maggior parte di loro studia con impegno un'arte tradizionale ed è sposata o convive con dei giapponesi, che sono per l'appunto quei pochi con cui sono riuscita a stringere rapporti di amicizia. In compagnia di queste coppie miste mi sento a mio agio e passo ore piacevoli, ciononostante non sono del tutto soddisfatta: mi sento a metà fra l'integrazione nella popolazione locale e l'isolamento in uno di quei circoli composti da occidentali venuti in Giappone per conto di ditte private, poco interessati alla cultura del paese e arroccati nelle usanze dei loro luoghi d'origine. Mi disturba la sensazione di non capire i meccanismi profondi che regolano la società in cui vivo, di non saperne cogliere l'essenza vera. Ho come il sospetto, o piuttosto l'intuizione, che molte cose mi sfuggano. Soprattutto quando un evento inatteso crea uno squarcio nella mia visione superficiale della realtà, rivelando per un attimo aspetti sorprendenti dell'ambiente che mi circonda, in apparenza omogeneo e rassicurante" (53).

[Recently, the number of Japanese people that my husband and I hang out with has increased, while that of Westerners has diminished. We have a close friendship with a group of former 1968-inspired activists, who have refused to be regimented in the mechanism of large private companies, and they get by carrying out more or less creative freelance jobs in the world of entertainment and the mass media. They are alternative people who have brought a breath of fresh air into my life.]

Eventually, the process of integrating as an Italian woman in an Asian country leads to divorcing her Japanese husband, who is paying the price of being isolated from a society that does not easily readmit nationals who left the country looking for a better life:

È proprio adesso, poco dopo il trasloco, che comincio ad avvertire in mio marito i primi segni di distacco nei miei confronti. Sento crescere in lui, che non riesce a esprimere la sua intelligenza e il suo talento artistico in un lavoro che lo soddisfi, una progressiva amarezza. Amarezza che io non posso condividere, perché in questo momento della mia vita mi sento piena di energia e tesa verso le nuove possibilità che mi si offrono, verso le cose che vado scoprendo, verso il futuro. Questa discrepanza inevitabilmente mina il nostro rapporto, l'unione simbiotica che ci ha legati per tanti anni si allenta, aspettative e interessi diversi ci allontanano l'uno dall'altra. È una constatazione dolorosa che per molto tempo cerchiamo entrambi di ignorare, continuando a vivere insieme con reciproco rispetto, ma consapevoli in fondo al cuore che la distanza fra noi va aumentando. Mio marito si ripiega gradualmente sulla sua disillusione, mostrando verso di me una crescente freddezza e legandosi sempre più al gruppo di ex sessantottini; mentre io, che dopo un primo momento di entusiasmo ho cominciato a percepire nel loro desiderio di marginalità una componente di ipocrisia, a poco a poco me ne distacco per frequentare persone meno platealmente alternative, ma più coerenti con le idee progressiste che professano. (Pastore, 2010: 87–88)

[It is now, shortly after the move, that I begin to sense in my husband the first signs of detachment from me. I perceive emerging in him a growing bitterness, since he cannot express his intelligence and his artistic talent in a job that satisfies him. A sense of bitterness that I cannot share, because in this moment of my life I feel full of energy and I am projected towards the new possibilities offered to me, towards the things I am discovering, towards the future. This discrepancy inevitably undermines our relationship, the symbiotic union that has bound us for so many years is loosened, different expectations and interests move us away from each other. It is a painful fact that for a long time we both try to ignore, continuing to live together with mutual respect, but aware at the bottom of our hearts that the distance between us is increasing. My husband gradually turns back on his disillusionment, showing towards me a growing coldness and binding more and more to the group of former 1968-inspired activists; while I, who after a first moment of enthusiasm began to perceive in their desire to live at the margins of society a certain dose of hypocrisy, I gradually detach myself to go to people who are less blatantly alternative, but more coherent with the progressive ideas that they profess.]

Despite her willingness to overcome the cultural and linguistic barriers preventing her full integration in Japanese society, Pastore at a certain point must cope with the daunting task of incorporating a foreign identity into the national identity, and the result is far from perfect. Pastore is aware of the limits of her deeds; nevertheless, her openness to and appreciation of her second homeland is by no mean jeopardized:

Mi rassegno ad ammettere che per quanto io cerchi di comprendere la società giapponese e di adattarmi alle sue usanze, oltre una certa soglia non posso arrivare. Giungo a questa conclusione serenamente, senza amarezza, perché se è vero che mi scontro a volte con differenze culturali insormontabili, so anche che le virtù dei giapponesi mi hanno aiutata a crescere, e che la loro umanità, tenuta di solito sotto il livello di visibilità ma sempre pronta a manifestarsi concretamente quando se ne presenti il bisogno, mi ha sostenuta nei momenti difficili.

E poi non tutte le differenze culturali sono inconciliabili, molte le ho assimilate, al punto da trovare normali comportamenti che dieci anni fa mi apparivano esotici: mi viene spontaneo togliermi le scarpe quando entro in casa, adoro dormire in un futon, quando leggo un libro voltando le pagine da sinistra a destra non ho più l'impressione di sfogliarlo al contrario. E soprattutto mi piace vivere sui tatami, su queste stuoie fresche a gradevoli al tatto, che rendono intimo lo spazio e leggero il tatto. (Pastore, 2010: 136)

[I resign myself to admitting that as much as I try to understand Japanese society and adapt to its customs, I cannot pass beyond a certain threshold.

I come to this conclusion serenely, without bitterness, because if it is true that sometimes I encounter insurmountable cultural differences, I also know that the virtues of the Japanese have helped me to grow, and that their humanity, usually held below the level of visibility but always ready to manifest itself concretely when the need arises, sustained me in difficult moments.

And then not all the cultural differences are irreconcilable, I have assimilated many of them to the point of finding normal behaviors that appeared exotic to me ten years ago: I spontaneously take off my shoes when I enter the house, I love sleeping in a futon, when I read a book turning the pages from left to right, I no longer have the impression of leafing it backwards. And above all I like to live on the tatami, on these fresh mats that are pleasant to the touch, that make the space intimate and the touch light.]

The rhetorical strategy of the book is here revealed in the effort of avoiding giving the unbridgeable differences in detail, while being very specific in listing the "translatable" aspects of her experience, such as her appreciation for the futon and the tatami mats. Her decision to return home is not a drastic and obvious step in her life, but rather a thoughtful resolution after having pondered reasons for staying or leaving. The passing of the years and the progressive immersion in the culture are conducive to a more comfortable stay in Japan; however, the prospect of growing older in a foreign land and thus making her journey in Japan a definitive and lifetime choice, makes Pastore suddenly feel nostalgic for her motherland, to the extent of concretely setting out a plan to return home:

Dopo quattordici anni che abito in Giappone, proprio quando potrei vivere serena in questo paese, comincio ad avvertire una certa irrequietezza. Il fatto è che sento in maniera sempre più acuta la mancanza della mia famiglia d'origine e provo una nostalgia crescente del mio paese, dei suoi paesaggi, della bellezza delle sue città, di certe sue atmosfere. Ogni volta che vi passo una vacanza, poi, quando sono sull'aereo per tornare a Osaka, trovandomi di colpo in un ambiente prevalentemente giapponese, non posso fare a meno di chiedermi "Cosa ci faccio qui?" Eppure ho simpatia per questa gente, ne condivido tante abitudini e in parte anche la mentalità, ma tra queste persone che tornano a casa provo un senso di estraneità che non avverto quando sono in Giappone. Forse perché vengo percepita da loro come una turista, una straniera, nonostante stia tornando a casa anch'io. O perché nel mio inconscio "tornare a casa" significa andare in direzione contraria, da Oriente verso Occidente. (Pastore, 2010: 152)

[After fourteen years that I've been living in Japan, just when I could live quietly in this country, I begin to feel a certain restlessness. The fact is that I feel more and more acutely the lack of my family of origin and I feel a growing nostalgia for my country, its landscapes, the beauty of its cities, its certain atmospheres. Every time I spend a holiday there, then, when I'm on the plane to go back to Osaka, suddenly finding myself in a predominantly Japanese environment, I cannot help but ask myself, "What am I doing here?" And yet I have sympathy for these people, I share many habits and partly also the mentality, but among these people who return home I feel a sense of strangeness that I do not feel when I'm in Japan. Maybe because I'm perceived by them as a tourist, a foreigner, even though I'm coming home too. Or because in my unconscious "going home" means going in the opposite direction, from East to West.]

4. A Gendered Perspective

In this narrative featuring a foreigner in Japan who overcomes the initial displacement and discovers affinity with the locals, the gender perspective is a crucial aspect. During these fourteen years Pastore had the benefit of being a peer to other Japanese women as she shared the nationality and status of "Japanese wife." This experience came with highs and lows, despite an initial deep attraction to the refinement and elegance of female mannerisms:

E poi la grazia delle donne, la soavità dei loro gesti: invidio l'eleganza con cui sbucciano un frutto, il garbo con cui scartano una caramella, ammiro la loro capacità di infondere sollecitudine nel semplice gesto di porgere un bicchier d'acqua [...]
   In confronto ai modi delicati delle giapponesi, giudico bruschi i miei, temo che la mia spontaneità venga presa per sfacciataggine, e al fine di adeguarmi ai canoni di femminilità vigenti cerco di contenere la mia gestualità e renderla più aggraziata. Il problema è che la donna giapponese è per me un modello solo dal punto di vista estetico, non da quello socioculturale, così finisco col fare una gran confusione e rischio di perdere il senso della mia identità. (Pastore, 2010: 13–14)

[And then the grace of women, the sweetness of their gestures: I envy the elegance with which they peel a fruit, the grace with which they discard a candy, I admire their ability to instill solicitude in the simple gesture of offering a glass of water [...]

In comparison to the delicate ways of the Japanese, I judge my manners brusque, I fear that my spontaneity is taken for brazenness, and in order to adapt to the existing canons of femininity I try to contain my gestures and make them more graceful. The problem is that the Japanese woman is for me a model only from the aesthetic point of view, not from the socio-cultural one, so I end up making a great confusion and risk of losing the sense of my identity.]

In the narrative evolution of her fictional self, Pastore's initial observation portrays the newly arrived foreigner in Japan as a late follower of the *fin de siècle* aesthetic of *japonisme*, who admires the Japanese woman only for her aestheticism. The sense of her identity is constantly at odds with her role as a "Japanese" wife,[12] which offers the opportunity to assert her perceived privileged status as a Western woman. In fact, she is adamant in disrupting the conventional gender rules within the household space, by being outspoken about her expected rights. While the Japanese woman conceals her influence over the husband, the Italian cannot help but express her sense of independence and dignity:

La mia indignazione è tanto più forte davanti a comportamenti che mi coinvolgono personalmente: non sopporto che un uomo dia per scontato che io gli ceda il passo sulla soglia di una porta, e mi dà fastidio che venga servito prima di me a tavola. Quando qualcuno mi chiede cos'ho preparato di buono per cena "al mio signor marito," mi tolgo la soddisfazione di rispondere che dal momento che torno a casa dal lavoro alle dieci di sera, mi aspetto che la cena la prepari lui, per tutti e due. Cosa che peraltro non ha mai costituito un problema nella mia vita matrimoniale.

---

12 In *Nel Giappone delle donne*, Pastore emphasizes the sense of inhibition that a Western woman has to overcome: "La donna occidentale percepisce subito quanto il proprio modo di 'stare al mondo' sia diverso da quello di una giapponese, quanto il proprio atteggiamento sia più appariscente, più ingombrante, al punto che finisce spesso col limitare, consciamente o no, la propria spontaneità. Per sentirsi in armonia con l'ambiente, per non stonare troppo [...] Nel mio caso, tutte queste motivazioni insieme hanno a lungo esercitato un'azione inibitoria sulla mia gestualità": Antonietta Pastore, 2004, *Nel Giappone delle donne* (Turin: Einaudi): vi.

Quanto all'atteggiamento di deferenza delle donne nei confronti degli uomini, mi esaspera al punto che giudico la loro decantata grazia una forma di affettazione, e trovo i loro movimenti, più che eleganti, legati. E a volte scopro dietro la loro apparenza delicata una mentalità strettamente pragmatica. (Pastore, 2010: 36–37)

[My indignation is much stronger in the face of behaviors that involve me personally: I cannot stand that a man takes for granted that I give way on the threshold of a door, and it bothers me that he is served before me at the table. When someone asks me what I have prepared for dinner "to my Mr. husband," I am proud to answer that since I come home from work at ten o'clock at night, I expect him to prepare dinner for the two of us. Which, however, has never been a problem in my married life. As for the attitude of deference of women towards men, it exasperates me to the point that I judge their vaunted grace a form of affectation, and I find their movements, more than elegant, tight. And sometimes I find a strictly pragmatic mentality behind their delicate appearance.]

As Terzani Staude noted the pragmatic attitude of the new Japanese women, so too does Pastore have to revise her initial fascination for female refinement and turn to a more materialistic criterion to explain their behavior. Such a pragmatic approach to life, apparently at odds with their outward demeanor, is particularly at play when women are engaged in their choice of their significant other. Nothing is more wrong than thinking that Japanese women of the 1980s would perpetuate Puccini's image of a woman giving herself up for a ruthless naval officer. Pastore is literally bewildered when telling the story of one of her students who readily breaks up with her boyfriend in order to meet someone better able to offer a wealthy life:

Yoko, che non ha l'avvenenza di Junko, vuole sì convolare a nozze, ma non con il suo attuale *bōy furendo*, nel quale non riscontra le qualità a suo avviso necessarie per costituire un buon partito: il ragazzo è troppo giovane, non guadagna abbastanza per provvedere ai bisogni e ai capricci della futura moglie, né si intravedono per lui possibilità di carriera [...]

Che le sorelle Yoshida non fossero delle anime romantiche l'avevo già intuito, ma la disinvoltura con la quale sono pronte ad accantonare i loro rispettivi ragazzi per stringere legami economicamente più vantaggiosi mi è del tutto incomprensibile. (38–39)

[Yoko, who is not as attractive as Junko, wants to get married, but not with her current *bōy furendo*, in which she does not find the qualities she believes are necessary to make a good party: the boy is too young, he does not earn enough to provide for the needs and the whims of the future wife, nor is there any chance of career for him [...]

I had already guessed that the Yoshida sisters were not romantic souls, but the ease with which they are ready to set aside their respective boyfriends to secure more economically advantageous relationships is completely incomprehensible to me.]

The issue of pragmatism in the choice of husband and in the general conduct of life is what shapes consensus among Italian women in Japan regarding their perspectives of Japanese women.

Marcella Croce (1949–) is another Italian writer who reached a similar conclusion. Croce was born in Palermo; after earning a PhD in Italian at the University of Madison Wisconsin, she taught Italian at the University of Isfahan (Iran) and Kyoto on behalf of the Italian Ministry of Foreign Affairs between 2005 and 2006. Her experiences on the Asian continent drew her attention to the issue of women's rights and identity in these countries. As a result, in 2002 Croce published the book *Oltre il chador – Iran in bianco e nero* ["Beyond the chador – Iran in black and white"] and, in 2009, *L'anima nascosta del Giappone* ["The hidden Japanese soul"] in which she gives the account of her experience in Kyoto. At the turn of the twenty-first century Croce stresses the same attitude toward marriage that Terzani Staude and Pastore detected in Japan during the 1980s:

"Massimo dieci anni": con questa dura sentenza Yoko, Yumi, e molte altre donne giapponesi mi hanno definito la durata media di un matrimonio, dopo di che di norma si passa non a un divorzio, ma a una semplice convivenza dove sull'altare della reciproca convenienza si celebra quello che i sociologhi chiamano "scambio di servizi." [...] A Yoko e Yumi, mie coetanee, appariva invece stranissimo che mio marito e io, dopo ben trent'anni di matrimonio, avessimo ancora effettivamente voglia di stare insieme. (33–34)

["No more than ten years": with this harsh sentence Yoko, Yumi, and many other Japanese women have described to me the average duration of a marriage, after which they normally pass not to a divorce, but to a simple cohabitation where on the altar of a reciprocal convenience is celebrated what sociologists call "exchange of services." [...] To Yoko and Yumi, my peers, it seemed rather strange that my husband and I, after thirty years of marriage, still really wanted to be together.]

Although Italian women praise their long-lasting and love-based relationships, when faced with the disenchanted alternative model they have to admit that Japanese wives enjoy more freedom and independence compared with an allegedly superior Italian example. Croce recognizes that Japanese women experience a great deal of time away from their husbands, focusing on a variety of different activities:

Le mogli spesso non lavorano, si occupano dei figli se sono piccoli, altrimenti, con una libertà di movimento impensabile nella coppia media italiana, si incontrano con le amiche, vanno a cena fuori, viaggiano per conto loro, anche perché il marito di norma consegna loro l'intero ammontare del suo sudatissimo stipendio. (Croce, 2010: 33–34)

[The wives often do not work, instead they take care of the children if they are small, otherwise, with a freedom of movement unthinkable in the average Italian couple, meet with friends, go out to dinner, travel on their own, also because the husband normally delivers to them the full amount of his very hard-earned salary.]

Despite the striking contrast that Croce notes, her observation is quite recent and must be situated in the context of Italian women gaining more financial independence and freedom in general. The traditional role of the mother as housekeeper was being replaced by a more complex figure of a woman who is somehow able to split her daily time between family and work. During the 1980s this process was just beginning, as Pastore, by looking back at the disparity between her own society and the other at the time of her journey, observes:

Possibile che in un paese in cui la parità tra i sessi, da quel che avevo letto o sentito, era ancora lontana, le donne godessero già di una libertà che in Europa iniziavamo appena ad assaporare? Durante i sedici anni che ho trascorso in seguito in Giappone, dal '77 al '93, ho avuto modo di constatare quanto fosse giusta quella mia prima impressione: le donne giapponesi hanno un'ampia facoltà di muoversi autonomamente, di ritrovarsi con le amiche in caffè e ristoranti, andare al cinema e a teatro, spostarsi e viaggiare senza essere accompagnate da un uomo. (Pastore, 2004: v–vi)

[Is it possible that in a country where gender equality, from what I had read or heard, was still far away, women already enjoyed a freedom that we were just beginning to enjoy in Europe? During the sixteen years I spent in Japan, from '77 to '93, I was able to see how right my first impression was: Japanese women have a wide freedom to move independently, to meet up with friends in cafés and restaurants, going to the cinema and theater, getting around and traveling without being accompanied by a man.]

Indeed, Pastore must tackle a striking contradiction between what she knows about women in Japan and the reality she is experiencing:

Una contraddizione incomincia allora a delinearsi. Come coniugare efficienza e decisione, spontaneità e naturalezza, con quella cappa di inibizioni che continua a contenere, a ricoprire come una seconda pelle il corpo di queste donne? Come conciliare l'evidente autorevolezza della madre di famiglia, il suo libero potere d'acquisto, con l'atteggiamento sottomesso, addirittura servile, della donna nei confronti dell'uomo?
 Perché il sistema sociale che per secoli ha represso la donna non ha condizionato tutta la sua sfera d'azione, salvaguardando per lei sorprendenti zone di autonomia e un'innegabile libertà di movimento? (Pastore, 2004: xii)

[A contradiction then begins to take shape. How to combine efficiency and decision, spontaneity and naturalness, with that set of inhibitions that continues to contain and to cover the body of these women, like a second skin? How to reconcile the evident authority of the mother of the family, her free purchasing power, with the submissive, even servile woman's attitude towards a man? Why the social system that for centuries has repressed the woman has not conditioned her whole sphere of action, safeguarding for her surprising areas of autonomy and an undeniable freedom of movement?]

Beyond the unacceptable image of the obedient housewife, the Italian woman finds in her Japanese counterpart a dimension of freedom and independence that is not part of the conception of the female role during the

1980s in Italy. On the one hand the role of the father as absolute authority of the family, the image of the *pater familias*, has definitely dissolved. But on the other, the mother's role has become increasingly central to the Italian family: "the new 'supermother' who, juggling the many balls of family responsibilities and employment, was determined to prove that she could cope" (Willson, 2010: 181). Splitting her daily schedule between work and family duties, the new Italian woman longs for time to focus on herself, as in the apparently more constrained life of the Japanese woman.

Both Pastore and Croce feel uneasy with the quietness and compliance of her Japanese counterpart. They are also astonished by the extreme flexibility and pragmatism of the typical Japanese couple. From their Italian female perspective it is not easy to come to terms with the idea that the vows of marriage will not last. In a country with a solid Catholic tradition, it is not common for someone to accept alternative models of union. However, Croce – by pointing to the fact that in Italy married couples are encountering difficulties in their relationships regardless of the low divorce rate – raises the problem of an unresolved conflict in the Italian family where the ongoing process of secularization has undermined the Catholic model of the union without offering any reliable alternative. As a result, while Italy has the lowest divorce rate in Europe, according to a 2007 statistical survey it also has one of the lowest marriage rates in the European Union. The pragmatic attitude of Japanese women, especially when the time comes to choose their significant other, generates surprise and displacement in the three Italian writers. Their restlessness and dissatisfaction speak of an unclear gender role, which is still far from being equal despite the astonishing progress made over the last twenty years. At first, they cannot tolerate the passivity of the Japanese woman, but, when they are able to see beyond appearances, the writers discover a space of freedom and independence that is still missing in their own lives.

5. A Transnational Solidarity

The relationship with Misako represents the narrative core of Pastore's last book *Mia amata Yuriko* ["My beloved Yuriko"]. In this novel the Italian protagonist takes an interest in her former husband's aunt, who was a Hiroshima survivor (she died in 1990 of leukemia) and an independent woman who chose not to remarry after her early divorce. Pastore admires Yuriko for her courage in withstanding the prejudice directed at single women and expresses empathy with and solidarity for her as a victim of discrimination. In fact, Pastore eventually discovers that Yuriko chose to walk away from her marriage because her in-laws were pressuring her husband to abandon his wife, for fear that the radiation of the atomic blast could contaminate the rest of the family. Yuriko belonged to the group of so-called *hibakusha* (Hiroshima or Nagasaki survivors) who live their lives at the margin of the Japanese society. Pastore learned the entire story of her former relative Yuriko in 1999, during one of her visits to her ex mother-in-law, Misako. However, she decided to write about it only in 2011 when she realized that the Fukushima accident, causing a nuclear reactor to release radioactive material, had the effect of reviving old discriminations against individuals affected by the fallout. Therefore, her semi-fictional novel is not only a rebuke of Oriental travel narratives, it is also a transnational gesture of solidarity toward women who are currently experiencing discrimination.

Mia amata Yuriko is constructed as a novel within a novel, since Pastore gradually apprehended Yuriko's story through her occasional conversations with Misako. In the other story/plot, the Italian protagonist reveals her difficulties in adjusting her life to the inevitable cultural differences and her struggle to be accepted as a foreign wife. The intercultural negotiation is ultimately successful thanks only to the human relationship that Pastore is able to establish and consolidate throughout the years with her mother-in-law. In fact, the origin of her decision to leave Europe for Japan was not her husband's nostalgia for his native country, but rather discovering the humanity of her in-laws, especially compared to her own rigid family upbringing in Italy.

> In quella casa di legno dalle porte di carta e i pavimenti in tatami, mi sentivo accolta con una benevolenza incondizionata. Non avevo timore di dire o fare la cosa sbagliata, né bisogno di conquistare di continuo l'approvazione dei miei suoceri. Una condizione del tutto nuova per me che da ragazza, a casa dei miei genitori, avevo sempre dovuto dimostrare di meritare il loro amore – peraltro profondissimo – ed ero vissuta nell'ansia perenne di incappare nel loro malcontento. Nella famiglia di mio marito, questa tensione si era sciolta come neve al sole. (Pastore, 2016: 39–40)

> [In that wooden house with paper doors and tatami floors, I felt welcomed with unconditional benevolence. I was not afraid to say or do the wrong thing, nor needed to constantly win the approval of my in-laws. A completely new condition for me as a girl, at my parents' house I had

always had to show that I deserves their love – however profound – and I lived in constant anxiety to run into their discontent. In my husband's family, this tension had melted like snow in the sun.]

Thus Pastore's final novel reverts the traditional Orientalist narrative by considering as "home" the Asian country of destination, while rejecting as cold and aloof the native place of the Western traveler. However, during a visit to her relatives by marriage living in the island of Etajima in 1982, Pastore is caught up in a delicate situation in which she must walk a fine line between observing the societal norms of respect toward the elders while standing up for her identity and values. At a certain point during the meal, one of her husband's uncles revealed that the only reason he could accept the marriage of his nephew to a foreigner was because Italy and Japan were once allied during the Second World War, thus inviting Pastore to share the same nationalistic nostalgia. Feeling that her fundamental beliefs were being tested, Pastore does not hesitate to respond that she was educated to recognize the positive values of struggle against fascism, and to embrace the cause of pacifism. This episode strengthened her relationship with the rest of her in-laws, who approvingly supported her irreverent response and voiced their own critique of fascism. This episode serves as a turning point of her narrative aimed at constructing a transnational identity that is able to critically evaluate and reposition itself as result of a continuous cross-cultural exchange: "Quel soggiorno a Etajima aveva segnato una piccola svolta nel mio percorso di adattamento alla società giapponese. Il confronto con un uomo aggressivo e prevaricatore mi aveva aiutata a rendermi conto che per desiderio di essere beneaccetta stavo perdendo la mia identità" (Pastore, 2016: 101) [That family visit in Etajima had marked a small turning point in my path to adaptation to Japanese society. The confrontation with an aggressive and authoritarian man had helped me to realize that I was losing my identity for the sake of being well accepted]. After having rejected her European life for a more fulfilling life in Japan, Pastore is now confronted with her mixed cultural belonging and a quest for loyalty. It is an unsettling moment that provokes an inquiry into difference, not a regressive movement toward reclaiming her "authentic" national identity. In fact, the awkward exchange with the uncle at a family gathering did not expose her to the sense of estrangement and alienation that a foreigner normally experiences when caught up in situations in which a radical cultural diversity emerges. On the contrary, Pastore decides to respond to the very familiar issue of the anti-fascist struggle, which is a legacy of an historical, political and cultural entanglement between Japan and Italy. Instead of entrenching herself in a statement of national allegiance, Pastore indicates that anti-fascist sentiment is a cause that connects her Italian heritage with her new Japanese family.

In this story of cultural integration and mutual comprehension the national boundaries and differences inscribed within the categories of gender, class and ethnicity are not elided, yet neither do they hinder the mechanism of cohesion and human affinity. In presenting the case of Pastore, I am not arguing that only women writers can revisit well-established sexual tropes about the Japanese woman, but that it is inevitable that gender solidarity among women coming from male-dominated societies is a powerful way to avoid seeing the "Other" as an alien, but rather as a recognizable identity with whom one can enter a cross-cultural conversation. Above all, the militant aspect of Pastore's most recent book, written to uphold the case of Japanese women victims of the Fukushima disaster, calls for a deeper understanding of the relations between mobility, feminist perspective and cosmopolitanism. This sense of loyalty within a group opens up the possibility of a global community where cultural differences are not suspended but a sense of empathy toward the "Other" travels across national boundaries.[13]

Pastore's experience in Japan is a suitable example of the type of cosmopolitan subject that Thomas Bender describes as "engaged but always slightly uncomfortable, even at home" (Bender, 2017: 119). Reverting a widespread notion of the cosmopolitan travelers as globetrotters who travel smoothly and easily across nations and cultures, these alternative cosmopolitans feel the impact of diversity and, as result, proffer a new perception of the self at the end of a self-reflective inquiry into the foreign culture. Pastore's biographical writings describe the new understanding of oneself and of the "Other" through human interactions, showing that empathy among strangers is possible provided that individuals are willing to travel outside their comfort zones.

---

13 On the feminist movement from the transnational perspective see Alys Eve Weinbaum... et al. (editors), 2008, *The Modern Girl around the World: Consumption, Modernity, and Globalization* (Durham: Duke University Press); Robin Morgan (editor), 1984, *Sisterhood is Global: The International Women's Movement Anthology* (Garden City, NY: Anchor Press/Doubleday).

6. A Revised Stereotype

In conclusion, all these Italian women writers compare the situation of women's rights in Japan with the ideal of gender roles created by the Western feminist movement of the 1970s. As a result, Japanese society is considered conservative and unequal, regardless of the acknowledgment of a significant improvement in gender relations since the end of World War II. However, a more accurate observation of women's lifestyle in Japan allows these writers to detect certain privileges and advantages that are not part of the supposedly more progressive level of women's lives in Italy. The discovery that feminist struggles for a more gender-equal society are not a unique Western feature can be unsettling, since it goes against chauvinistic perceptions of Japan, a country stagnating in its own traditional gender inequalities. The portrait of the new modern Butterfly spotlights the restless Italian woman in the midst of a struggle for her own new, stable identity.

In addition to this enhanced self-awareness for the Italian woman traveler, this chapter showed that international solidarity among women is an aspiration, and therefore cannot be taken for granted. While they noticed that the Japanese woman did not completely fit the stereotype they had in mind, Italian women traveling to Japan missed the opportunity to connect the historical process of emancipation at home with a similar movement that was taking place abroad. The cross-gender comparison that dominates these narratives created a false sense of equality, with the result of hiding other differences, especially those caused by the power of ethnicity and race. However, the contrast between the experiences of Angela Terzani Staude (living in Japan but within the group of Western journalists and writers) and Antonietta Pastore (who developed strong bonds with locals) proved that a concrete, non-rhetorical sense of empathy among women fighting for a common cause is possible (but not inevitable) when there is willingness to reach out the "Other" across the liminal space of the "translation zone," and in fact results in an enriching relationship through difference.

Works Cited

Bardsley, Jan. 2003. "Seitō and the Resurgence of Writing by Women." In *The Columbia Companion to Modern East Asian Literature*, edited by Kirk Denton, Bruce Fulton, and Sharalyn Orbaugh, 93–98. New York: Columbia University Press.

Bassnett, Susan. 1986. *Feminist Experiences: the Women's Movement in Four Cultures*. London: Allen & Unwin.
Bender, Thomas. 2017. "The Cosmopolitan Experience and its Uses." In *Cosmopolitanisms*, edited by Bruce Robbins and Paulo Lemos Horta; with an afterword by Kwame Anthony Appiah, 116–26. New York: New York University Press.
Cipolla, Arnaldo. 1931. *Nel Giappone dei grattacieli: viaggio da Tokio a Delhi*. Turin: Paravia.
Clifford, James. 1997. *Routes: Travel and Translation in the Late Twentieth Century*. Cambridge, MA: Harvard University Press.
Clifford, James and Marcus, George E. 1986. *Writing Culture: The Poetics and Politics of Ethnography*. Berkeley: University of California Press.
Condon, Jane. 1985. *A Half Step Behind. Japanese Women of the '80s*. New York: Dodd-Mead.
Croce, Marcella. 2009. *L'anima nascosta del Giappone*. Milan: Marietti.
D'Annunzio, Gabriele. 2010. *Novelle sparse*. Rome: Bel-Ami Edizioni.
Faison, Elyssa. 2018. "Women's Rights as Proletarian Rights: Yamakawa Kikue, Suffrage, and the 'Dawn of Liberation.'" In *Rethinking Japanese Feminisms*, edited by Julia C. Bullock, Ayako Kano and James Welker, 15–33. Honolulu: University of Hawaii Press.
Foster, Shirley and Mills, Sara (eds). 2002. *An Anthology of Women's Travel Writing*. Manchester and New York: Manchester University Press.
Fujimura-Fanselow, Kumiko (ed.). 2011. *Transforming Japan: How Feminism and Diversity are making a Difference*. New York: City University of New York Press.
Garon, Sheldon. 1998. "Fashioning a Culture of diligence and thrift: savings and frugality campaigns in Japan, 1900–1931." In *Japan's Competing Modernities: Issues in Culture and Democracy, 1900–1930*, edited by Sharon A. Minichiello, 312–34. Honolulu: University of Hawaii Press.
Holland, Patrick and Huggan, Graham. 1998. *Tourists with Typewriters: Critical Reflections on Contemporary Travel Writing*. Ann Arbor: University of Michigan Press.
Kelsky, Karen. 2001. *Women on the Verge: Japanese Women, Western Dreams*. Durham, NC: Duke University Press.
Littlewood, Ian. 1996. *The Idea of Japan: Western Images, Western Myths*. Chicago: Ivan R. Dee.
Lowe, Lisa. 1991. *Critical Terrains: French and British Orientalisms*. Ithaca: Cornell University Press.
Maraini, Dacia. 2010. *La seduzione dell'altrove*. Milan: Rizzoli.
Maraini, Dacia and Fosco. 2007. *Il gioco dell'universo*. Milan: Mondadori.
Mills, Sara. 1991. *Discourses of Difference: An Analysis of Women's Travel Writing and Colonialism*. London and New York: Routledge.

Pastore, Antonietta. 2004. *Nel Giappone delle donne*. Turin: Einaudi.
—. 2010. *Leggero il passo sui tatami*. Turin: Einaudi.
—. 2016. *Mia amata Yuriko*. Turin: Einaudi.
Pickering-Iazzi, Robin. 1993. *Unspeakable Women: Selected Short Stories Written by Italian Women during Fascism*. New York: Feminist Press at the City University of New York.
Pisu, Renata. 2000. *Alle radici del sole. I mille volti del Giappone: incontri, luoghi, riti e follie*. Milan: Sperling & Kupfer.
Re, Lucia. 2010. "Italians and the Invention of Race: The Poetics and Politics of Difference in the Struggle over Libya, 1890–1913." *California Italian Studies*, 1(1): 1–58.
Robbins, Bruce and Horta, Paulo Lemos. 2017. *Cosmopolitanisms*. Afterword by Kwame Anthony Appiah. New York: New York University Press.
Sartini-Blum, Cinzia. 2008. *Rewriting the Journey in Contemporary Italian Literature*. Toronto: University of Toronto Press.
Smith, Patrick. 1997. *Japan: A Reinterpretation*. New York: Pantheon Books.
Spackman, Barbara. 2017. *Accidental Orientalists: Modern Italian Travelers in Ottoman Lands*. Liverpool: Liverpool University Press.
Tanizaki, Junichiro and Moravia, Alberto. 2000. *L'amore di uno sciocco*, translated by Carlo De Dominicis. Milan: Bompiani.
Terzani Staude, Angela. 1994. *Giorni giapponesi*. Milan: Longanesi.
Terzani, Tiziano. 2011. *Tutte le opere*, edited by Àlen Loreti. 2 vols. Milan: Mondadori.
—. 2006. *La fine è il mio inizio*, edited by Folco Terzani. Milan: Longanesi.
Willson, Perry. 2010. *Women in Twentieth-Century Italy*. New York: Palgrave Macmillan.

Postscript

This story began in Florence by observing the discontinuity between Fosco Maraini's *Biblioteca orientale* and the Renaissance *palazzo* in which the library is hosted (see Introduction p. 1). Yet the Asian library was only one in a long line of attempts that were made to intervene in the city's cultural map by adding an alien Eastern component. Long before, the ambitious project of expanding the cultural references of Florence, and by extension of Italy, outside the Mediterranean region and beyond the limits of Western humanism had already loomed large in the minds of the political architects of the newly unified Italian Kingdom. For example, a visit today to the *Museo Nazionale di Antropologia e Etnologia* in Florence still reveals the majestic collection for a planned, but never opened, *Museo Asiatico*. Florence did, however, become the most important Orientalist center of unified Italy, by gathering top scholars of Asian Studies around the *Istituto di Studi Superiori Pratici e di Perfezionamento* [Institute for Higher Practical and Specialization Studies] founded in 1859.[1] The first classes in Chinese and Japanese language opened in 1864 when Antelmo Severini (1828–1909) left Paris – where he studied Chinese under the supervision of Stanislas Aignan Julien and Japanese under Léon de Rosny – to join the Institute. His role as chair of *Lingue dell'Estremo Oriente* [Languages of the Far East] represented the beginning of Chinese and Japanese studies in Italy.[2]

---

1 Michele Amari was the Professor of Arabic language and literature; Giuseppe Baldelli and Angelo De Gubernatis taught Sanskrit and Fausto Lasinio covered the Indo-European languages.
2 The appointment of Antelmo Severini as Professor of Chinese and Japanese literature at the *Istituto* is the result of a scheme that the Italian government pursued in order to fill the gap of Asian knowledge with France, England and Russia. Severini was able to study Chinese and Japanese in Paris thanks to a generous scholarship that Minister of Education Terenzio Mamiani granted him.

Severini faced the challenge of teaching Japanese without any prior knowledge among Italians in the field. He provided the first textbook of Japanese conversation, translating the French original curated by Léon de Rosny in 1866[3] (the same year of the first treaty of friendship and trade between Italy and Japan[4]). He also translated for the Italian public the 1821 novel by Ryūtei Tanehiko (1783–1842) *Ukiyo-gata rokumai byōbu*, which appeared under the title of *Uomini e paraventi* (1872) and became the first Italian translation of a Japanese book.

Even more important was his translation of the tenth-century folklore tale, *Taketori monogatari*, under the title *La fiaba del nonno Tagliabambù* (1881), because it was the first European translation of such a story, thus demonstrating the Italian translator's decision to act independently of the French and English translation markets.

Following the example of Florence, other institutions devoted to the study of the languages of the Far East appeared in other major Italian cities. In contrast with the rising wave of *japonisme* that Italian artists and intellectuals imported from France, these cultural centers were less interested in an aesthetic appreciation of Japan, or in an imaginary Japan of samurais and geishas, and were instead focused on the study of the history, the language and the culture of this perceived new nation entering the world stage together with Italy. In Venice, the *Regia Scuola Superiore di Commercio* [Royal High School of Commerce] opened the first classes in Japanese in 1873 and became the first school to provide teachers who were native speakers. Indeed, the idea of making Venice a cultural hub for East

---

3 Léon de Rosny, 1866, *Guida della conversazione giapponese preceduta da una introduzione alla pronuncia in uso a Yedo: ridotta ad uso degli Italiani da Antelmo Severini* (Florence: Ermanno Loescher).
4 On the experience of the first Italian ship arriving on the Japanese shore with a delegate of the Italian government on board see Enrico Giglioli Hillyer, 1866, *Viaggio intorno al globo della R. pirocorvetta italiana Magenta* (Milan: V. Maisner). The commander of the Italian pirocorvette Magenta, Vittorio Arminjon, left a diary of his journey: Vittorio Arminjon, 1869, *Il Giappone e il viaggio della Corvetta Magenta nel 1866* (Genova: Co' Tipi del R.I. dei sordo-muti). Arminjon's journal sometimes takes a chauvinistic tone and the author often remarks the superiority of the Catholic religion compared to the religious practice that he came across while in Japan. For instance: in order to regenerate Japan, Arminjon says, it is necessary to "distruggere la piaga dello scintoismo e togliere quell'abisso che regna fra noi e la famiglia pagana. Questo potrà farlo solo la propagazione del vangelo e della filosofia Cristiana" (14).

Asian studies was the project of Count Fè d'Ostiani, who was appointed minister plenipotentiary for China and Japan in 1870.

The inaugural year of Japanese classes in Venice coincided with the arrival of the Iwakura mission in Italy. The Japanese delegation, led by Prince Iwakura Tomomi, traveled first to the United States and Britain in 1872 and, the year after, visited Italy among other European countries. The impression that these visitors retained of Italy was not exclusively exotic or geared toward its rich historical heritage: in fact, they also "experienced the feeling that they were visiting a new country, united as recently as 1861, with problems some of which resembled their own" (Nish, 1998: 5). Indeed, the collaboration between the two countries deepened after this visit and, between 1875 and 1876, the Japanese government hired several Italian experts in key strategic fields. In Tokyo, Edoardo Chiossone was recruited to manage the state-run printing works. A few months later the architect Giovanni Vincenzo Cappelletti, the sculptor Vincenzo Ragusa and the painter Antonio Fontanesi were hired in the same city as teachers at the Kōbubijutsu gakkō [School of Fine Art]. The partnership had a military dimension as well, with Major Pompeo Grillo traveling to Osaka to help with the construction of cannons, later deployed during the Sino-Japanese war.[5]

In Naples, the Chinese had already been regularly taught since the foundation in 1732 of the *Collegio de' Cinesi* [the Chinese College], which is considered the first Sinology School to be opened in Europe. Father Matteo Ripa (1682–1746) founded the school upon his return from a fourteen-year mission in China with the intention of providing a Catholic education to Asian visitors. After the Italian unification, the *Collegio* became part of the state's education system and in 1868 was renamed *Reale Collegio Asiatico* [Royal Asian College]. In 1903, Giulio Gattinoni – the author of the 1890 *Grammatica giapponese nella lingua parlata* – offered the first classes in Japanese language, beginning a tradition that was later continued by Pietro Silvio Rivetta and Shimoi Harukichi (see chapter 2). This group of scholars in Naples contributed greatly to the popularity of Japanese studies in Italy, by supporting an intense publication agenda (for instance, the journals *La Diana*, or *Sakura* [*il ciliegio*] and the book series "Rami fioriti di *Sakura*"), that would introduce the Italian public to authors unknown until then, such as Futabatei Shimei, Mori Ōgai, Ichiyō Higuchi and Yosano Akiko.[6]

---

5   See Gaetano D'Angelo, 1904, *Impressioni militari di un viaggio al Giappone* (Livorno: S. Belforte & Co.).
6   For more information on the impact of these and other editorial initiatives conceived

The foundation of these institutions in the years following the Italian unification points in the direction of a lesser known historical trajectory that modern Italy had been pursuing since its foundation. While the colonial enterprise was moving the geopolitical interests of the country toward the African continent, a parallel *non-violent* movement of diplomatic, cultural and commercial exchanges took place with Japan, reaching its peak during the period of the Axis alliance. Of course, as in the case of the African campaigns, the pursuit of interests in the Far East was another way for Italy to catch up with the other European powers that already had established long-standing ties with Japan. In the case of Italy, however, the lack of colonial interests in the Pacific region, as well as a set of historical similarities, oriented this relation of power on a far more equal basis. In fact, the perception that Japan was succeeding in reversing the unequal balance with other Western powers (especially after the Russo-Japanese war) fostered the feeling of Japanophilia among Italians, who were also struggling to pursue parity with other dominant nations. The Axis alliance represented for Italy the culmination of this gradual process of converging with the East Asian country, by combining Japanophilia with nationalism.

The end of Fascism and the post-war period of Pax Americana abruptly interrupted these historical ties. The removal of the material evidence of this alliance could represent an especially symbolic gesture of disavowal of the past: during the period of the Allied Occupation (1946–52), for instance, American troops removed the Roman column that Mussolini had donated in 1928 to the provincial town of Aizu Wakamatsu, as a gift of friendship between Italian and Japanese people (Hofmann, 2015: 32–37). The erasure of this chapter of history was so effective that the notion of these two countries as international partners seems almost counterintuitive today. The perception of cultural distance between Italy and Japan only increased during the Cold War and, in fact, Italian travelogs of this period reinstated neo-exotic perspectives that posed the two countries at the opposite ends of a comparative spectrum. Nevertheless, as this book has argued, a positive overarching approach toward Japan resisted historical change: from Italian unification to the present day, "searching for Japan" remains an ideal point of reference for Italians to reflect on the place of Italy in the world.

---

in Naples and spread in the rest of the country see Teresa Ciapparoni La Rocca, 1997, "Japanese Studies in Italy: A Century of Literary Translations," *Rivista degli Studi Orientali*, 71(1/4): 257–62.

Works Cited

Arminjon, Vittorio. 1869. *Il Giappone e il viaggio della Corvetta Magenta nel 1866*. Genova: Co' Tipi del R.I. dei sordo-muti.

Hofmann, Reto. 2015. *The Fascist Effect: Japan and Italy, 1915–1952*. Ithaca, NY: Cornell University Press.

Nish, Ian (ed.). 1998. *The Iwakura Mission in America and Europe: A New Assessment*. Richmond, Surrey: Japan Library.

Index

Abe, Kōbō 214
Abu-Lughod, Janet L. 3n
Agamben, Giorgio 66, 82
Ainu people 40, 176
Akinari, Ueda 114
Akutagawa Ryūnosuke 8n
Albertini, Luigi 53
alienation 91, 154–55, 159, 170, 216, 228
Alighieri, Dante 47, 51–52, 106, 108–09, 128
Allen, Laura W. 72n
Alliata, Topazia 141, 193, 201–02
Allied occupation of Japan at the end of World War 130–32, 236
Aloisi, Pompeo 129
Amari, Michele 233n
Anderson, Benedict 9
Angelelli, Claudia V. 82
Anti-Comintern Pact 25, 29, 111
Appelius, Mario 86, 112–14, 133, 135
Appiah, Kwame Anthony 14n, 28, 33–34, 48, 59–60, 62, 82, 231
Apter, Emily 55, 82
Aravamudan, Srinivas 28
Arminjon, Vittorio 22, 33, 234n, 237
Auriti, Giacinto 114

Bachelet, Vittorio 165
Bacon, Alice Mabel 70, 78
Baer, Brian J. 82
Baker, Mona 68–69, 82
Baldelli, Giuseppe 233n
Banchoff, Thomas 33
Barakumin (indigenous outcast community) 176

Bardsley, Jan 199, 230
Barthes, Roland 6, 33, 122, 135, 184
Bartoli, Domenico 150n
Barzini, Ludina 116n, 135
Barzini, Luigi Jr. 82
Barzini, Luigi Sr. 4, 11, 27–28, 37, 53–69, 82, 85, 116–17, 135
Bassnett, Susan 10–11n, 33, 49–51, 82, 199, 231
Beck, Ulrich 4n, 13n, 33
Belasco, David 57
Bell, Ronald 191
Bellah, N. Robert 30, 139, 141, 148, 150, 190
Belpoliti, Marco 165, 184, 190
Bender, Thomas 229, 231
Benedict, Ruth F. 152
Ben-Ghiat, Ruth 96n, 103, 135
Benvenuti, Giuliana 89n, 135
Berenghi, Mario 163n, 190
Berenson, Bernard 1n
Berlinguer, Enrico 172
Bernaerts, Lars 62n
Berque, Augustin 13, 33
Beviglia, Rosaria 114n, 152, 190
Bhabha, Homi K. 9, 33, 187n
Bielsa, Esperanza 83
Bird, Isabella L. 40
Bishop, Elizabeth 1
Blaagaard, Bolette 13n
Bloomsbury Group 157–58
Bobbio, Norberto 67n, 82
Bonavia, Hilda 83
Bongie, Chris 6–8, 33
Boone, Joseph Allen 100n

Boscaro, Adriana 8n
Brah, Avtar 3n
Braidotti, Rosi 13n
Breckenridge, Carol A. 14n, 34
Bucknell, Margaret 39
Bucknell, William 39
Bullock, Julia C. 231
Burckhardt, Jacob 1n
Burckhardt, Titus 203
Burdett, Charles 86, 97n, 135, 136
bushido (way of the warrior) 109–10, 116
Buthelezi, Mbongiseni 83–84

Cabral, Francisco 18
Calamanca, Daniela 123n
Callegher, Bruno 192
Calvino, Italo 30–31, 163n, 165n, 173, 178–87, 189–90
Camerini, Mario 96n
Cappelletti, Giovanni Vincenzo 23, 71, 235
Carletti, Antonio 19
Carletti, Francesco 19–20
Casanova, José 19, 33
Casati Law 79
Cavallaro, Dani 186, 190
Ceretti Borsini, Olga 9
Cheah, Pheng 14n
Chiossone, Edoardo 23, 235 *see also* Edoardo Chiossone Museum of Oriental Art
Chow, Rey 15–16, 33
Christianity and the West 69, 74n, 142, 149, 150, 160, 162, 167
Christianity in Japan 18–21, 115, 148
Churchill, Winston 120n
Ciapparoni La Rocca, Teresa 152, 190, 236n
Cipolla, Arnaldo 29, 86–88, 104–11, 133, 135, 194n, 231
Clark, Steve 40, 82
Clifford, James 3, 28, 33, 41, 52, 82, 99n, 189–90, 195–96, 231
Cochrane, Lydia G. 67n, 82
coeval exoticism 7–8
Cohen, Robin 14n
Cold War 26, 31, 138, 166, 200, 208, 236
Colla, Elisabetta 20n

Colucci, Dalila 184, 190
Comisso, Giovanni 29, 86, 88–89, 92–102, 133, 135
Condon, Jane 212, 231
Conference on Modernity in Hakone, Japan 144–45
Consiglio Nazionale delle Donne Italiane 73
continuity and change 30 *see also* Conference on Modernity in Hakone, Japan; modernization; tradition and change
Corradini, Enrico 67n, 69, 82
Cortellessa, Andrea 184, 190
cosmopolitanism 13–17, 28, 30–31, 48, 51–52, 59, 62, 64, 66, 133, 229 *see also* discrepant cosmopolitanism; patriotic cosmopolitanism
Craig, Gordon 128
Croce, Benedetto 108
Croce, Marcella 223–24, 226, 231
Cronin, Ciaran 4n, 33
Cronin, Michael 10, 46, 55, 82, 91, 135
Culler, Jonathan 46, 82
Cultural translation 10, 47–48, 125–26
Cumings, Bruce 6, 33
Cuomo, Daniela 57n, 82

Dainotto, Roberto M. 4n, 33
Damiani, Rolando 93n, 97n, 135
Damrosch, David 83–84
D'Angelo, Gaetano 235
D'Annunzio, Gabriele 25, 41, 97, 108, 194–95, 231
Davidson, Angus 192
D'Azeglio, Massimo (Massimo Taparelli, Marquess of Azeglio) 23
De Aldisio, Eugenio 119n
De Bary, William Theodore 21, 33
De Ceccatty, René 151n, 154, 156, 188, 190, 202
De Goncourt, Edmond (Edmond Louis Antoine Huot de Goncourt) 24
De Gruchy, John W. 158, 190
De Gubernatis, Angelo 233n
De Laude, Silvia 34

Del Re, Arundel 14, 29, 87, 108, 127–33, 135
Del Re, Harriott Joan 128
De' Medici, Ferdinando (Grand Duke of Tuscany) 19
De Michele, Francesco 70
Denton, Kirk 230
De Rosny, Léon 233–34
Dingee, Suzanne 148n, 191
Diogenes 16
discrepant cosmopolitanism 52
Dissanayake, Wimal 9, 35
Doak, Kevin 21, 33
Dollimore, Jonathan 98n, 136
Dos Passos, John Roderigo 151
Duncan, Derek 97–98, 99n, 100n, 136

East–West relationships 8, 23, 75, 130–33, 137 *see also* Japan and the West
economic miracle, Japanese and Italian 26, 30, 139, 141, 152, 155, 166, 171
Edo period 20, 115
Edoardo Chiossone Museum of Oriental Art 24
Edwards, Louise 198n
Elkann, Alain 151, 162, 192
Eurocentric 13, 17, 31, 49
Ewick, Patricia 69, 82
exoticism 6, 43–47, 49, 53, 73, 189 *see* coeval exoticism; neo-exoticism

Fabian, Johannes 182, 191
Faison, Elyssa 199, 231
Fanon, Frantz 37, 187n
Farge, William J. 21, 33
Fascism 25–26, 30, 85–135, 194n *see also* Fascist virility
Fascist delegation in Japan 122–23 *see also* *Sogno delle Hawaii*
Fascist virility 97, 100–02, 133
Fatta, Angelina 70, 73–74, 203 *see also* Villaurea, Marchesa di
Fè d'Ostiani, Count Alessandro 235
Ferraris, Clemente 29, 103–04, 136
Fiume, occupation 25, 97
Fontanesi, Antonio 22, 71, 235
Forsdick, Charles 44, 46, 82, 187–88n, 191

Foscolo, Ugo 108–09
Foster, Shirley 70, 83, 202–03, 231
Foucault, Michel 101n
Fraccaroli, Arnaldo 87–88
Frediani, Federica 70, 83
Fujimura-Fanselow, Kumiko 198, 231
Fukazawa, Shichirō 8
Fukushima nuclear fallout 15–16, 227, 229
Fulton, Bruce 230

Gandhi, Mohandas Karamchand 89
García Márquez, Gabriel 11n
Garibaldi, Giuseppe 80
Garon, Sheldon 199, 231
Gasco, Alfonso (console) 107
Gattinoni, Giulio 235
Geertz, Clifford J. 38, 83
Gentile, Emilio 30, 65n, 148n, 151n, 191
Gentile, Giovanni 108
Gibson, Gloria 68
Gide, André 98
Giglioli, Enrico Hillyer 234n
Glick Schiller, Nina 14n
Glissant, Édouard 188n
Gluck, Carol 33
Gnecchi-Soldo, Organtino 19
Goldoni, Carlo O. 162
Gozzano, Guido 89n
Grasso, Silvana 97n
Gregory XIII (Pope) 115
Grewal, Inderpal 3n, 34
Griffis, William Elliot 119
Grillo, Pompeo 235
Grossberg, Lawrence 33

Habermas, Jürgen 13n
Hakuseki, Arai 20–21
Hanafin, Patrick 13n
Harootunian, Harry 33, 150n, 191
Harris, Peter 34
Hasegawa, Kizu 9
Hayashi, Fumiko 8n
Hearn, Lafcadio 152
Heidegger, Martin 162
Held, David 13n
Henning, Joseph M. 119n
Henry, Sue 145n, 191

Henshall, Kenneth 75, 83
Hester, Nathalie 20, 34
Hibakusha (Hiroshima or Nagasaki survivors) 31, 215, 227
Hideyoshi, Toyotomi 19
Higuchi, Ichiyō 8n, 235
Hinsch, Bret 100n, 136
Hirohito (emperor of Japan) 85
Hiroshima, atomic bomb 15, 151, 215, 226–27
Hitler, Adolf 118
Hofmann, Reto 26n, 107, 110n, 136, 236–37
Hogan, Patrick Colm 62n
Hokenson, Walsh J. 44n, 83
Hokusai 44
Holland, Patrick 194, 231
Horio, Teruhisa 207
Huggan, Graham 194, 231
Hughes, Christopher W. 83

Iacobelli, Pedro 16n
Ibuse, Masuji 8n
Ichikawa, Fusae 199
Ikezawa, Natsuki 214
Illica, Luigi 57–58
Inghilleri, Moira 66–67, 83
Inoue, Yasushi 8, 214
Irving, Andrew 14n, 34
Ishii, Motoaki 24n
Ishimoto, Shidzué 206
Italian colonialism in Africa 7, 65, 97, 102
Italian Japanophilia 5, 18, 27, 64–65, 236
Italian nationalism 24, 42–43, 53, 236 *see also* nationalism
Italian orientalism 3, 5
Italian Republic 30
Italian Social Republic (Republic of Salò) 120, 128
Italian travel writing 2
Italian unification 22
Italian women writers in Japan 31, 74
Itaria No Tomo No Kai 113
Iwakura mission 235
Iwao, Sumiko 198n

Japan and the West 142, 156 *see also* East–West relationships
Japanese colonialism 107
Japanese ethics 6, 29, 143, 148–49, 165
Japanese Society in Wellington 15
Japanese women 126–27, 144, 147, 152n, 197–230
Japanese women's rights movements 147
japonisme 23–24, 28, 44, 48, 56–57, 221, 234
Jesuit mission in the Far East 18–21
Julien, Stanislas Aignan 233

Kabbani, Rana 58n
Kahn, Herman 148n
Kakuzō, Okakura 65n
Kameda, Atsuko 198n
Kano, Ayako 231
Kant, Immanuel 13
Kawabata, Yasunari 8, 152, 163, 189
Keene, Donald 65n, 83
Keevak, Michael 62n, 83
Kelsky, Karen 198, 231
Kemal, Vlora Alessandro 119n, 120
Kennan, George 119
Kersten, Rikki 138, 145, 191
Kikue, Yamakawa 199
Knapp, Arthur May 119
Knightley, Phillip 53–54, 83
Kowner, Rotem 119n
Kristeva, Julia 137
Kuehn, Julia 82

Labriola, Teresa 198
La Capria, Raffaele 189n, 191
La Diana (journal) 25, 235
La difesa della razza (journal) 118–20
La donna (journal) 73
Lasinio, Fausto 233n
Latin/Mediterranean race 118 *see also* race
Laurence, Patricia 100n
Leary, Danton 16n
Lefevere, André 49, 51
Lehmann, Jean-Pierre 145n, 191
Lemos Horta, Paulo 14, 34, 231–32

Leopardi, Giacomo 181–82
Lévi-Strauss, Claude 6, 176–78, 181–83, 187, 191
Littlewood, Ian 194, 231
London, Jack 54
Loomis, Arthur K. 132
Loreti, Ålen 232
Loti, Pierre 12n, 24, 38, 44–45, 47–48, 63, 77, 81, 194
Lowe, Lisa 196, 231
Lowitz, Leza 152n, 192
Luksic, Vania 191

McCarthy, Mary 1n
Magellan, Ferdinand 11n
Magenta (Pirocorvette) 22
Mamiani, Terenzio 233n
Manifesto degli intellettuali fascisti 116
Manifesto della razza 118, 176
Maraini, Dacia 74, 126–27, 193, 200–02, 231
Maraini, Fosco 1, 2, 6, 12, 17, 21n, 30, 140–52, 166, 169, 187–89, 191, 201–02, 233
Maraini, Toni (Antonella Kiku) 200
Maraini, Yuki Luisa 200
Marcus, George E. 99n, 196, 231
Marinetti, Filippo Tommaso 24
Marsden, William 34
Maruyama, Masao 30, 137, 139, 145, 190
Mascagni, Pietro 57
Meiji era 2, 5, 22–23, 40, 70, 75, 81, 108n, 126, 134n, 144, 149, 175
Melas, Natalie 83–84
Micca, Pietro 47
Michelangelo di Lodovico Buonarroti 128
Mignolo, Walter D. 14n, 34
Mills, Sara 196, 202–03, 231
Minichiello, Sharon A. 231
Mishima, Yukio 8n, 139, 151–52, 172n, 189
Miyake, Toshio 5, 33
Miyoshi, Masao 33, 191
modernization 30, 145, 153 *see also* continuity and change; tradition and change
Monro, Harold 128

Montessori, Maria 198
Moran, Joseph F. 19n
Morante, Elsa 152n
Morasso, Mario 65, 68–69, 83
Moravia, Alberto 6–8, 30, 89n, 140, 151–62, 169–70, 187–89, 191–93, 200, 232
Moro, Aldo 165
Morrison, George Ernest 54
Mosbacher, Eric 191
Mosse, George L. 102–03n
Mostra d'arte giapponese (Roma Aprile-maggio 1930) 133–34
Murakami Haruki 214
Mussolini, Benito 12n, 25, 29–30, 42, 84–85, 87, 98, 102–03, 109–13, 115, 120, 123, 128, 134n, 136, 141, 148, 167, 188, 236

Nakane, Chie 30, 139, 145–48, 192
Naldini, Nico 93n, 135
Namiki, Mieko 141
Napoleon 2
nationalism 60–61, 88 *see also* Italian nationalism
Nelson, Cary 33
neo-exoticism 7, 31, 187, 236
Nietzsche, Friedrich 68
Nish, Ian 235, 237
Nitobe, Inazo 209
Novelli, Maria Roberta 8n
Nugent, Donald M. 131, 132n

Ōgai, Mori 235
Ogura, Tadao 72n
Okinawans 176
O'Malley, John W. 19n
Orbaugh, Sharalyn 230
Oriani, Alfredo 56, 65, 83
Orient (as a metaphor) 2, 10n, 43, 89n, 97–99, 100n, 101, 194, 196 *see also* porno-tropics literature
Oriental Society of Australia 15
Orientalism 2–4, 10, 13, 43, 45, 47–48, 86, 100, 124, 133, 158, 195–97, 228
Otamà, Kiyohara 71 *see also* Ragusa, Eleonora; Tama, Kiyohara

Pacific War 113–14, 120, 122
Papini, Giovanni 108
Pardo, Guido 57
Parise, Goffredo 6, 12n, 30–31, 140, 162–73, 175–76, 178, 183–84, 187–90, 192–93
Pascoli, Giovanni 24
Pasolini, Pier Paolo 8–9, 34
Pastore, Antonietta 12, 15–17, 27, 31, 200, 202, 214–30, 232
Pastorelli, Timo 105–06, 108
Patriarca, Silvana 97n
patriotic cosmopolitanism 63
patriotism (Italian and Japanese) 18, 25, 60–62, 65, 69, 87, 108n, 167, 172
Patti, Ercole 29, 86, 88–93, 96–98, 101–02, 116–17, 133, 136
Pearl Harbor (raid) 112, 114n, 122
Pecorini, Daniele 4, 7, 12n, 17, 27–28, 37–40, 42–53, 83
Pecorini-Manzoni (family) 39, 45
Pellegrino, Angelo 87–88, 89n, 136
Perrella, Silvio 192
Perry, Matthew Calbraith (Commodore) 21, 193–94
Petrarch, Francesco 181–82
Piaget, Jean 214
Pica, Vittorio 24
Pickering-Iazzi, Robin 199, 232
Pieri, Piero 83
Pigafetta, Antonio 11n
Pisanty, Valentina 119, 136
Pisu, Renata 214n, 232
Platzer, Steven 207, 209
Podoksik, Efraim 1n
Poggi, Christine 24n
Polezzi, Loredana 10, 34, 41, 48, 83
Polo, Marco 18, 34, 183
porno-tropics literature 97 *see also* Orient
Portello, Mauro 192
Porter, Denis 10n, 34
postcolonial 9
Pound, Ezra 128
Pratt, Mary Louise 3, 34, 41, 55, 196
Puccini, Giacomo 24, 38, 57–58, 74, 194, 222

Pudney, Jennifer 148n, 191
Pulce, Graziella 96

Raban, Jonathan 32, 34
Rabinow, Paul 101n
race (Aryan and Japanese) 41, 118–20, 174–76 *see also* Latin/Mediterranean race
race and culture 31, 173, 175, 177
Ragusa, Eleonora 71 *see also* Otamà, Kiyohara; Tama, Kiyohara
Ragusa, Vincenzo 23, 71, 235
Raichō, Hiratsuka 199
Rainey, Lawrence 24n
Ramadan, Tariq 14n, 34
Re, Lucia 198, 232
reception zone 3, 56, 65
Regia Scuola Superiore di Commercio, Venice 234–35
Regio Istituto Orientale, Naples 25, 123, 235
Reina, Luisa 70n, 73, 83
Reischauer, Edwin O. 139, 145, 150, 192
relational orientalism 5, 127
reporter 53, 54, 57, 66–67, 88–89, 101, 104, 151 *see also* war correspondent
Ricca Suga, Atsuko 8n
Ricci, Matteo 100n
Richie, Donald 152, 192, 204
Ricorda, Ricciarda 70, 83
Rintarô, Takeda 114
Ripa, Matteo 235
Rivetta, Pietro Silvio (Toddi) 12, 29, 87, 114, 123–27, 133, 136, 235
Robbins, Bruce 14, 28, 34, 51, 83, 231–32
Roces, Mina 198n
Roman empire legacy 26, 30, 43, 61, 194n
Roosevelt, Franklin Delano 120n
Roosevelt, Theodore Jr. 64
Ross, Andrew C. 19n
Russell, David 42n, 50n
Russo-Japanese war 12, 27–28, 37–70
Ryokuu, Saitō 163
Ryûnosuke, Akutagawa 114

Said, Edward 2, 4n, 34, 81, 84, 89n, 136
Sakura (journal) 235

Salgari, Emilio 189n
Salsa, Tommaso 97n
Salvemini, Gaetano 26, 138
Samuels, Richard J. 22–23, 26–27, 34, 138, 192
Samurai 66
Santoro, Vito 163n, 192
Sartini-Blum, Cinzia 74n, 83, 201, 232
Sartre, Jean-Paul Charles A. 162
Schiller, Nina Glick 34
Schwab, Gabriele 99, 136
Schwartz, Benjamin 145
Scipione, Borghese (Prince Luigi Marcantonio Francesco Rodolfo Scipione Borghese) 53
Scuola di Arti Orientali 71
Seidensticker, Edward G. 9
Seitō ("Bluestocking") (journal) 77, 199, 230
Serao, Matilde 195n
Severini, Antelmo 57n, 233–34
Shikibu, Murasaki 127
Shimei, Futabatei 235
Shimoi, Harukichi 25–26n, 34, 235
Shōnagon, Sei 127, 157, 192
Sica, Luciana 202n
Siciliano, Enzo 192
Sidotti, Giovanni Battista 20–21
Silbey, Susan S. 69, 82
Silone, Ignazio 151n
Simmel, Georg 1, 34
Siti, Walter 34
Smethurst, Paul 82
Smith, Patrick 166, 192, 208, 232
Società Amici del Giappone 113
Sogno delle Hawaii (Fascist propaganda booklet) 120–21, 136
Somers, Margaret R. 68
Somma, Anna Lisa 195
Spackman, Barbara 2n, 34, 101n, 103n, 110, 136, 196–97, 232
Spadaro, Maria Antonietta 71n, 84
Spender, Harold Stephen 151–52
Steinbeck, John Ernst Jr. 151
Stopes, Marie Charlotte C. 70
Stutler, Ross 21n, 34
Sugiyama, Lebra Takie 198n

Sullivan, Edmund J. 35
Susmel, Duilio 136
Susmel, Edoardo 136
Suter, Rebecca 19, 34
Suzuki, Daisetsu Teitarō 208–09
Sweeney, Michael 54, 69n, 84
Sweet, David LeHardy 3n, 35

Taiheiyō Gakai (Pacific Society) 71
Takahashi, Shinnosuke 16n
Tama, Kiyohara 71 *see also* Otamà, Kiyohara known as (清原お玉) or O'Tama Chiovara; Ragusa, Eleonora
Tamburello, Adolfo 82
Tanehiko, Ryūtei 57n, 234
Tanizaki, Jun'ichirō 8–9n, 152, 163, 189, 193, 232
Tarling, Nicholas 57, 84
Taylor, Charles 12n, 34
territorial either/or theory of identity 4, 86
Terzani, Folco 232
Terzani Staude, Angela 12n, 203–15, 222–23, 230, 232
Terzani, Tiziano 203–05, 207, 211, 232
Teti, Mario 8n
Thompson, Carl 32, 35
Thubron, Colin 34
Tiedemann, Arthur 33
Tōjō, Hideki 112
Tokugawa Shogunate 22
Tomasi di Lampedusa, Giuseppe 80
Tomomi, Iwakura Prince 235
Tosti, Armando 119
tradition and change 76, 137–39 *see also* continuity and change; modernization
translation zone 55–56, 65, 230
transnational 9, 13, 131, 133
transnational communities 4, 27
travel and translation 11, 41, 45, 47–48, 51 *see also* translation zone
travel writing 10, 32
Treichler, Paula A. 33
Tripartite Pact (Axis alliance) 15, 26, 86–87, 112, 118, 122, 127, 236

Troise, Alberto 57
Tsuboi, Sakae 114
Tucci, Giuseppe 114

Ueda, Tatsunosuke 132n
Ūman ribu (women's liberation movement in Japan) 199–200
Ungaretti, Giuseppe 25
Unione femminile nazionale 73
Universal Exposition of London 24

Valignano, Alessandro 18–19, 115
Van Wolferen, Karel 204, 207
Venuti, Lawrence 48, 51, 55, 84
Vergani, Orio 87–88
Vertovec, Steven 14n
Villaurea, Baronessa di 28, 37–38, 70–81, 84 *see also* Fatta, Angelina
Vita femminile (journal)
Vogel, Ezra 166, 208
Voltaire 13

Waley, Arthur 157–58, 192
Wall, Bernard 191
war correspondent 53, 57, 63–70
Ward, Robert E. 145
Weaver, Williams 190, 192
Webb, Beatrice 6
Webb, Sidney and Beatrice 204
Weiner, Michael 175n, 192

Weiss, Beno 185, 192
Welker, James 231
Wells, Herbert George 6, 35
western hegemony 2, 105
Wilde, Oscar 98
Willson, Perry 73, 80, 84, 197–99, 226, 232
Wilson, Angus, Frank Johnstone 151–52
Wilson, Rob 9, 35
Wittman, Laura 24n
Wolf, Reinhart 203
Women's Educational School 78–79
Wright, Thomas 34

Yamato (journal) 114
Years of Lead 165
Yeats, William Butler 128
yellow peril 4, 28, 38, 42, 49, 53, 62, 102, 119
Yosano Akiko (also known as Shō Hō) 25, 235
Yosano Tekkan (also known as Yosano Hiroshi) 25
Yoshida, Fujio 72
Yoshida, Hiroshi 71
Yoshida, Kasaburō 71
Yosirō, Andō 114n, 135
Yukichi, Fukuzawa 23

Zander, Patrick G. 103n
Zuroski Jenkins, Eugenia 13n